# Finding Your Own
# Philosophy of Life

# FINDING YOUR OWN PHILOSOPHY OF LIFE

BURTON PORTER

Algora Publishing
New York

Library of Congress Cataloging-in-Publication Data —

Names: Porter, Burton F., author.
Title: Finding your own philosophy of life / Burton Porter.
Description: New York: Algora Publishing, 2016.
Identifiers: LCCN 2016034072 (print) | LCCN 2016034269 (ebook) | ISBN
    9781628942255 (soft cover: alk. paper) | ISBN 9781628942262 (hard cover:
    alk. paper) | ISBN 9781628942279 (pdf)
Subjects: LCSH: Life. | Philosophy. | Religion. | Theology. | Conduct of life.
Classification: LCC BD431 .P635 2016 (print) | LCC BD431 (ebook) | DDC
    128—dc23
LC record available at https://lccn.loc.gov/2016034072

Printed in the United States

# Table of Contents

# Preface

In this book you will confront what you think and why you think so, the basic philosophy behind your choices and actions. You will be challenged to think clearly and deeply about the ideas you cherish. The ultimate purpose is for you to find a personal direction for your life, one that is informed by the thoughts of philosophers for over 2500 years.

We will consider how to develop a clear mind, what is the nature of human nature, how to trust what we think we know, and whether there is a God who governs our existence. We will examine whether we are wholly conditioned by society or make free decisions; if art is a matter of taste or if there's good taste and bad taste; and if we have a spiritual center hidden within our physical body. We will also examine whether moral values are invented or discovered, what a just war and a fair distribution of wealth might be, and whether life ends at the grave or continues in an eternal heaven or hell.

The book will challenge you to judge the various answers to these questions that have been proposed by profound thinkers, and in the light of these, to find your own philosophy of life. Your answers will be personally satisfying but must also be defensible, based on good reasons. You must have the courage to face an inconvenient truth rather than accepting the comforting lie. Your conclusions will change, of course, as you experience new situations, but you can become conscious of your present assumptions and be rationally equipped to address the fundamental question of how best to live your life. You can only hit the mark if you know the target.

# Chapter 1. Thinking Straight

We all can think, but not equally well. If we want to arrive at a solid conclusion, we should think as clearly as possible. A child might believe that a crowing rooster makes the sun rise, or that birds flying south bring on winter, but adults know better. The sun would rise even if there were no roosters, and winter would arrive even if we caught all those birds.

Suppose we were wondering about Unidentified Flying Objects, flying saucers in the Southwest. (For some reason, aliens prefer the Southwest to the Northeast, particularly Roswell, New Mexico. In fact, a roadway there has been officially named "Extraterrestrial Highway.") In the mid-20th century especially, people reported seeing strange objects in the sky, moving at unearthly speeds and turning at impossibly sharp angles. Most of these objects were disc shaped, some looked like triangles, chevrons, boomerangs, spheres, or even had the shape of horses or jellyfish. They could be coming from blue holes in the Caribbean, which served as portals to another dimension. Some people described being beamed up to a mother ship and having their body openings probed by translucent beings. Their interpretation was that extraterrestrial creatures with extraordinary intelligence were scrutinizing our species, preparing for imminent colonization. After all, the Nazca lines in Peru were clearly landing strips for alien spacecraft...

How should we address the truth value of these U.F.O. reports?

We should, of course, first establish the reliability of the witnesses. They could be perpetrating an elaborate hoax, making fools of the public. Fake photos have been taken of pie tins, hubcaps, and lids of garbage cans tossed into the air, and scale is hard to determine. They could also be extremely gullible, not trying to trick others but deceiving themselves. One psychologist named C. G. Jung claims that the shape of the flying saucer, the ellipse, is an ideal form, and people imagine superior beings in elliptical spacecraft who can help us solve our problems. To Jung, this is wishful thinking. What's more, if these witnesses are psychotic, then they are certainly unreliable. They could be experiencing hallucinations or delusions, thinking for example, that they're being controlled by other minds, even demonic creatures. If the person further claims his heart or stomach is missing, as some psychotics do, then we can conclude they are unhinged. Visions are hard to separate from hallucinations and are akin to out-of-body experiences reported both by mystics and schizophrenics.

But what if several people saw the same object, and it is an uncanny or remarkable one? Then we might consider the possibility of mass hysteria. When H.G. Wells' drama "War of the Worlds" was broadcast in America in 1938, many people assumed it was a real invasion: they smelled poison gas and saw explosions in the sky.

In Portugal in 1917 up to 100,000 people saw the sun spin, emit various colored lights, and dip toward the earth. Since thousands witnessed the event, should we believe it? Not necessarily. The scientific explanation is that these were optical effects of dancing light caused by prolonged staring at the sun. The mass delusion was due to human perception, its weaknesses and projections. If all alcoholics see insects, snakes, or rats during their withdrawal, we should not assume they saw real insects, snakes, or rats. The answer lies in delirium tremens or "the horrors." They were in an abnormal, physiological state.

The general rule is that if we hear hoof beats, we should think horse before we think zebra. That is, we should assume the most probable explanation before we accept the unlikely or outlandish one. This rule is called Ockham's Razor, and it states that if we have the option of an adequate, ordinary explanation, we should not choose a bizarre, extraordinary one instead.

But what natural explanation can there be for flying saucers? Various possibilities have been suggested: sun flares, experimental rockets, the light glinting off a plane, pieces of a satellite entering the atmosphere, the aurora borealis, weather balloons, birds, meteors, clouds, searchlights, flares, kites, and so forth. We should also include drones that are becoming a more frequent sight in the sky. In addition, the Southwest is particularly prone to dust devils, small whirlwinds of debris forming into different shapes, and to mirages caused by the shimmering heat rising from the desert floor. Any of these options would be more plausible than space ships, piloted by little green men, buzzing our planet.

As one philosopher, David Hume, put it, our love of wonder can eclipse our common sense. Or as one astrophysicist said, flying saucers are as real as rainbows — optical effects that we regard as substantial, with, of course, a pot of gold at the end.

But why does everyone report the same disc shape? Doesn't that add credibility to the reports that come from different people from different points on the earth? No, because a disc is the standard shape fixed in the public consciousness. For the same reason we know that aliens have large, bald heads, huge eyes, and thin arms and legs.

In the case of flying saucers we should also consider that, given the laws of time and space, and the outer limit of speed, the chances are extremely remote that aliens will ever travel here; the distances, calculated in light years, are simply too great, even allowing for anti-matter fuel, or hydrogen or nuclear fusion. Astronomers tell us the odds are heavily in favor of there being intelligent life on other planets orbiting other stars — planets with conditions even more favorable than ours, super earths. In fact, the question is not whether there is intelligent life on other planets, but whether there is intelligent life on earth. But these life forms are subject to the same physical laws that we are. Lightning itself cannot go faster than the speed of light (even if it didn't zigzag). One day we may receive a radio signal from outer space; in fact, arrays of telescopes are searching for such signals today. But we can hardly expect a visit from space creatures.

Voyager I will reach the first planet outside our solar system in 40,000 years, traveling at 42,000 mph. Some of the planets within our solar system may have microorganisms, but no higher life forms. A robotic spacecraft recently flew by Pluto, a dwarf planet 3 billion miles from earth, which took nearly a decade to arrive traveling at 31,000 mph. The closest star system to our sun, Alpha Centauri, is 4.22 light years away, a light year being the distance traveled by a ray of light in one year traveling at 186,281 miles per second. If the planets orbiting Alpha Centauri have civilizations, it is extremely unlikely we will ever meet its citizens.

Some people fear the coming of extraterrestrials who must have weapons of immense power and would be intent on destroying our civilization. Others, such as followers of Jung, welcome the thought of superior creatures coming to earth, descending like gods for our salvation. But the chances are infinitesimally small of our ever meeting aliens face to face. In the realm of faith, we may believe in resurrections where mortals ascend to heaven, or in avatars where gods descend to earth, but if we follow science we should not expect a close encounter of any kind.

This example of flying saucers is meant to show that we have to think things through and not jump to conclusions, especially satisfying ones. Wearing a hat does not cause baldness, rather bald men tend to wear hats, and a flapping flag does not make the wind blow. Arizona has a large population of people with respiratory illnesses, but that does not mean the climate is bad; people with respiratory illnesses often move to Arizona.

Disproving the reality of flying saucers or ancient aliens, Sasquatch, the Loch Ness monster, or the uncanny Bermuda triangle is relatively easy. (No more ships have been lost in the Bermuda Triangle than in shipping lanes in other parts of the ocean) at least we know how to go about settling the question. The same is true of a variety of other issues. If we wonder about the composition of salt, a chemistry book will tell us it is made up of sodium and chloride (NaCl); we can even conduct an experiment in the laboratory to prove it. If we wonder about the voting patterns of Latinos, we can take a sociological survey and find that the Latino population is heavily Democratic. And if we wonder about the causes of the Revolutionary War, historians have a standard list of factors: the Boston Massacre, the Quartering Act, the Townshend Act, and, in general, taxation without representation.

But how do we go about evaluating a philosophic claim? How do we know whether we are closer to organisms or mechanisms; whether feelings, thoughts, and dreams are real; whether people have an inborn sense of right and wrong; or whether life has any intrinsic meaning? How do we determine if the universe is a mindless cluster of elementary particles, or a purposeful whole, designed by a benevolent God?

## "What Is Truth?" retorted Pilate

A traditional approach to solving such issues is to use the "standard of reasonableness." According to this standard we must first make sure that we are being consistent and *not contradicting ourselves,* for then our position becomes absurd. We are talking nonsense if we make a statement and deny it at the same time; it is not possible to have our cake and eat it too. As Aristotle put it, "We cannot say of something that it is and is not." That makes no sense.

For example, if we talk about a black whiteness, a rough smoothness, or the whispering silence, that conveys no meaningful information. Although the terms are paired, they are mutually exclusive. In the same way, we cannot say someone is second best or the second winner, or that we have an original copy or heard a concert live on tape. In this context we also wonder about the Buddhist koan of one hand clapping. Is it a paradox expressing a higher truth, or is it just nonsense? Can we picture a square circle?

Obviously, self-contradictions should be avoided, however we can join things that seem to contradict each other but both are true in different respects. A pin drop is both soft and loud, that is, soft to a person and loud to a gnat; it is only contradictory to say the pin drop is be both soft and loud in the same way at the same time to the same perceiver. Charles Dickens begins *A Tale of Two Cities* by writing, "It was the best of times, it was the worst of times." He is talking about different aspects of the same period.

In the same way, an "oxymoron" is only an apparent contradiction, often used for comic effect. The popular examples are 'jumbo shrimp,' 'pretty ugly,' and 'military intelligence.' Here we can make sense of what is said; we understand the irony. Other oxymorons include 'young Republican,' 'male compassion,' 'pop culture,' 'safe tan,' 'build down,' 'genuine imitation,' 'airline cuisine,' and 'Circle Line.' There is also 'Southern efficiency and Northern charm.' Although incongruous words are being put together, the phrases are meaningful. They sometimes provoke thought as in Shakespeare's "parting is such sweet sorrow," and the phrase "silent scream," which makes us think of Munch's painting.

Aside from genuine, verbal self-contradictions, we should also avoid illogical statements that clash with each other, generating friction. If we say "All generalizations are false," we are then generalizing, so our statement itself is false. And if we say "There's an exception to every rule," then that rule must have an exception, in which case some rules don't have exceptions.[1]

There are other logical self-contradictions: that we can never actually know anything; that it's really true that everything is relative; and that whatever we say is absurd. Should we avoid clichés like the plague, or give up on altruism because it just doesn't pay? Similarly, we cannot say that we'd kill for the Nobel Peace Prize, that we'd give our left arm to be ambidextrous, or that we wouldn't be paranoid if people didn't pick on us all the time. (If you tell a man who is paranoid that people are not out to get him, he will think "Now you've joined them too!") And we contradict ourselves in the very utterance if we say "Don't ever start a sentence with a negative," or "Ending a sentence with a preposition is something we should not put up with."

More significantly, Sigmund Freud claimed that all reasoning is rationalization for what we want to believe, but if that is so, then Freud's claim is a rationalization for what he wants to believe. Ironically, Freud built a rational system while opposing rationality. B. F. Skinner maintained that whatever we do or say is conditioned by prior factors, in which case he did not freely decided that his ideas are true; he is only conditioned to believe them. In the same way, A. J. Ayer, a philosopher who was part of the logical positivist school, asserted that the only meaningful propositions are those that can be scientifically verified, which implies that the principle itself is meaningless. In a similar way, we cannot claim we should believe in God

---

[1] Bertrand Russell and A, N. Whitehead have proposed a theory of types which claims a class statement cannot be a member of its own class, but their resolution of the conflict has been seriously questioned.

because the Bible says he is real, and the Bible is the holy word of God. That is circular reasoning. Solipsism is the view that I alone exist, and a solipsist once said that he was a solipsist and he wished everyone else were. A wit named Oscar Levant once wrote a book called "Memoirs of an Amnesiac."

Besides contradictions in logic, we sometimes find ourselves in psychological tangles. These are called double-binds where ideas are at odds with one another and put us in a quandary. For example, our parents want us to emulate them but at the same time to be our own person. If we copy our parents' beliefs, behavior, or ideals, we feel as though we have not achieved independence, whereas if we disagree, we feel as though we have betrayed them. The children of immigrants feel this conflict very strongly, and experience guilt whether they follow their family traditions or assimilate into American culture

Hell-fire and brimstone preachers can also induce a double-bind if they tell us we must banish all thoughts of lust. If the preacher says, "Lust, lust, don't think of lust," then that is all we can think about. We have to keep in mind what we must put out of our mind. It is like a judge instructing a jury to ignore an attorney's remark. Things heard can't be unheard, any more than something said can be unsaid — which is what the attorney counted on. Similarly, there is a mean game you can play with children. You can tell them there is a treasure hidden in the garden, but they can only find it if they don't think of a white rabbit. When they return empty-handed you can say, "I'll bet you thought of a white rabbit." They can't deny it, because they had to remember the thing they needed to forget.

Another form of self-contradiction to be avoided is proverbs that are opposed to each other. Many people tend to trust in old sayings, adages or "old saws" that contain the wisdom of the ages, but sometimes these proverbs are mutually exclusive. For instance, "Too many cooks spoil the broth," but "Many hands make light work;" "Absence makes the heart grow fonder," but "Out of sight, out of mind;" "If it's not broken, don't fix it," but "A stitch in time saves nine" (do not defer maintenance). "You can't teach an old dog new tricks," but "It's never too late to learn"; "Everything comes to he who waits" but "Nothing ventured, nothing gained"; "Strike while the iron is hot," and "He who hesitates is lost," but "Decide in haste, repent at leisure." The list can be extended, but the lesson is obvious: You can find a proverb to support almost any position, which means that proverbs are not proof; they only add the appearance of weight to an argument.

Sometimes, of course, apparent contradictions in proverbs can be reconciled. One French writer said, "Absence diminishes mediocre passions and increases great ones, as the wind extinguishes candles and fans fires."

Self-contradictions in words, clashing statements, and inconsistent proverbs are often easy to detect, but a more subtle form of contradiction occurs in a more general form. People can maintain two or more broad theories that can't co-exist logically, but they are often unaware of the double-think.

For example, part of our national mythology is the belief that if we are hard-working, honest, and able, then we will succeed. Anyone who plays by the rules is bound to win the game; cheaters always lose and winners never cheat. In particular, if we get high grades at school, work diligently at our job, take advantage of opportunities, and treat people fairly, we are certain to get ahead. This is the land of opportunity and justice prevails. Almost all of our stories in books, plays, TV, and films reinforce this belief. They are morality tales in which sincerity and perseverance are repaid, and the lazy, dishonest villain gets what he deserves in the end. The lesson taught is that virtue will be rewarded, vice punished; character will triumph.

But at the same time we are told that nice guys finish last, that you have to be hard-nosed to succeed and leave your school-boy scruples behind. In the competitive struggle you can't afford much conscience or you will become a casualty or victim. Having high virtue is fine in church but not in the marketplace. Those at the top did not get there by being kind and thoughtful but by being willing to trample on people who get in their way. The sympathetic, sensitive, and caring are the losers, consoling themselves that they have clean hands.

We might believe the first or the second to be true, but we cannot believe both simultaneously. Does the cream rise to the top, or is it the scum? Does the world operate by wealth and power or is there a system of moral justice?

Another example is with regard to freedom. Liberty is taken as a fundamental value in our society, and we believe people are free to make of themselves whatever they choose to be. The future is open-ended, there for the taking by anyone ambitious enough to take it, and people are only held back by a lack of initiative. We fight wars for freedom, and consider our liberty an inalienable right.

However, we also consult horoscopes, psychics, and fortune tellers to find out what the future will bring, thereby indicating that we assume we have a fixed destiny. On this view, the book of fate is already written, and we are simply acting out our part. Whether we will be, sick or well, married or single is already determined, as is the day of our death. Whether we will be born at all was also preordained, although most of us think we simply had to be. Additionally, many people believe that a divine providence directs human life, and that fatalism is not compatible with free choice. According to religion, every hair of our head is numbered, and no sparrow will ever fall without our Father's consent. It is all in the lap of the gods.

Obviously, we cannot have it both ways. Either we are free, or we are forced to do what we do. If we are the masters of our fate and the captains of our soul, then we are agents of change with the power to shape our lives, but if the future is known then it is unchangeable and as fixed as the past. (Even God cannot change history, although some claim that historians can.) Shakespeare expressed this idea in *Romeo and Juliet*, a drama of star-crossed lovers, although he contradicts himself in *Julius Caesar*: "The fault, dear Brutus, lies not in our stars but in ourselves, that we are underlings."

Shakespeare did not have a point of view, and that works well in literature; but in thinking philosophically we should try to be consistent. Either we shape our own lives, or whatever we do is inevitable.

## Relevant Facts and Plausible Interpretations

Avoiding self-contradictions is a major part of thinking straight, but the standard of reasonableness contains other rules. We must also *take into account the relevant facts.*

For example, in thinking our way through the causes of crime we have to consider the effects of poverty, broken homes, poor education, run-down neighborhoods, drugs and alcohol, lack of opportunity, parental neglect, peer influence, and greater amounts of dopamine than serotonin in the criminal's body. We also cannot ignore the fact that about 45% of the prison population is black even though only 13% of the nation is black, and over 10% of African-American men are incarcerated.

Having confronted these facts, we then must see the implications to society, the possible causes and the remedies. Is the answer tougher sentencing laws to send a message to the perpetrators and potential criminals? (In one film W.C. Fields was about to be hanged and as his last words he said, "This will certainly teach me a lesson.") Do the statistics indicate a failure on the part of society, and are we blaming the victim? Are street crimes and drug dealing more visible than white collar crime, and therefore detected more often and punished more severely? Do the facts show selective enforcement of the law; profiling blacks as more likely to be criminals, and do the courts-and-prison system exhibit systematic racism? If you look for crime in the ghetto, you're going to find it. Does it show that blacks generally have poorer lawyers — public defenders who tend to be young and inexperienced, and are blacks therefore more likely to be convicted?

Whatever decision we reach on the causes of crime, it will be an informed decision because we have considered the essential facts. If we omit any of these considerations, our conclusion will be unreliable.

Or in judging the morality of homosexuality, we must consider its relation to AIDS. According to the Center For Disease Control, homosexual contact is responsible for two thirds of HIV cases — the virus that causes AIDS. Although there are other sources such as sharing needles, HIV affects gay men more than any other group, principally because of anal sex. Worldwide, 78 million people have been infected with HIV, and 39 million have died. AIDS is ranked as a major, global epidemic.

Knowing these facts should inform the debate about the rights or wrongs of gay sex. We could conclude that, since it is a significant risk to public health, it should be prohibited. People cannot be permitted to engage in actions that endanger human life and health. Or we could conclude that if homosexuals practice safe sex, as all people should, then there is little danger. Using a condom significantly reduces the chance of HIV transmission. Besides, in the modern antiviral (ARV) era, the death rate is continuing to drop and AIDS patients are living longer.

Again, the facts must be taken into consideration. Otherwise, we will decide in terms of our bias, reaching the conclusion we want to believe.

Another example would be redistributing wealth using the progressive income tax, a stringent capital gains tax, or other means, we should first know the extent of the inequality. The wealthiest 1% own 40% of the nation's wealth, while the bottom 80% own 7%; the richest 1% possess more wealth than the bottom 90%. One startling statistic is that the average worker needs to work more than a month to earn what the CEO makes in one hour.

But perhaps the rich have earned what they own, so the wealth gap is not unfair. Did the rich earn their wealth, and do the poor deserve their poverty? Whatever decision we reach, we must take the relevant facts into account.

To take another example, in deciding on toxic emissions we should know that it is directly linked to global warming. Because of pollution from carbon and other gases, we are experiencing extreme weather conditions — heat waves, droughts, and floods as well as blizzards, torrential rains, and wild fires from lightning strikes. Glaciers and polar ice caps are melting and ocean levels are rising; numerous species are endangered by the rising temperatures. Such climate change may get worse, or perhaps we will adjust to it, develop new technologies, or find advantages in the higher temperatures. In time, Maine may have coconut trees, and land in Vermont could become waterfront property. The consensus of climate scientists is that the planet is warming due to human activity.

Of course, sometimes we do not know when a fact is relevant. For instance, adultery is often taken as grounds for divorce. But a marriage can be sound even though adultery has taken place, and a marriage could be beyond repair even though no adultery has occurred. The real question is whether the marriage can be saved, or whether the couple would be happier apart than they were together. In any case, the issue is usually not adultery but infidelity, the breaking of trust, and that goes to the heart of the relationship.

A third rule is to find *the best interpretation of experience*. We do not want just any explanation of events but the most likely or plausible one. In the case of flying saucers, we saw that it was far-fetched to interpret the sightings as alien spaceships.

Suppose someone says that for deer to cross at deer crossings is a sign of intelligence; maybe it even shows they can read. A better interpretation is that we erect signs at places where deer often cross the road. In Amsterdam, the more storks there are, the more babies there are. Does this mean that mother was right: storks bring babies? Probably not. The more babies there are, the more houses are built with chimneys on which storks can roost. So babies bring storks; storks do not bring babies. And the Pilgrims left Plymouth, England, and landed exactly on Plymouth Rock. Is this uncanny? They did not have sophisticated navigation equipment or a global positioning system. Obviously, the place where they landed was named Plymouth Rock.

In the Middle Ages comets, meteor showers, rainbows, and eclipses were interpreted as divine signs. Comets in particular were "harlot stars doing the work of the devil," and they "portend revolutions of kingdoms, pestilence, winds, or heat." The vapor is "the thick smoke of human sins, rising every day, every hour, every moment, full of stench and horror, before the face of God, and becoming gradually so thick as to form a comet." By contrast, rainbows were considered blessings, symbols of God's promise not to send another Flood; they were bridges of light leading to heaven. The worst omens, of course, were eclipses when darkness fell upon the earth during the day, and people feared that God might withhold the light forever. They were evidence of divine displeasure. When a disk of blackness appeared with a white line around its edge, it resembled the eye of God glaring down on the earth in anger.

We now know that comets are astronomical objects composed of common elements of hydrogen, carbon, nitrogen, and oxygen, that circle the sun in an erratic, elliptical pattern. Rainbows are a spectrum of light that appears when sunlight shines through rain; the drops refract the light into variegated colors. And eclipses are the obscuring of the sun by the intervention of the moon.

We cannot blame people at the time for coming up with "just-so" stories, and perhaps a God is behind these phenomena in some way, but the religious accounts appear fanciful in the light of present knowledge. Demons are on a par with gremlins as explanations for what happens. The modern interpretation of events seems much more convincing.

We should also get our facts straight. Martin Luther King did not nail 95 theses to the door of All Saints' Church in Wittenberg, and Groucho Marx did not write *The Communist Manifesto*.

## Avoiding the Pitfalls

In addition to the standard of reasonableness, there are other rules of thought that we should follow and, more significantly, mistakes we should avoid. Once we know the snares and traps, we can step around them.

One such error is called the *post hoc* fallacy, or in its complete form, *post hoc ergo propter hoc*: after this, therefore caused by this. Here we make the mistake of thinking that because one event preceded another, that the first event must have caused the second. But temporal sequences are not always causal connections, any more than correlations are causes. We have already seen this fallacy in the naive assumption of a child that the sun rose because the rooster crowed.

Very often "post hoc" thinking is the basis for superstition: bad luck will follow because a black cat crossed our path, especially since it walked away rather than toward us; a death occurred in the family because we put a hat or shoes on the bed; and an acorn in the window will keep lightning away (the proof being that people who do this are never struck by lightning). If you blow out the candles on your birthday cake, you will get your wish; a bee in the house means a visitor will arrive (and visitors do arrive, eventually); and the Apollo 13 mission to the moon failed because of the number it was given. Thirteen is unlucky, we think, as evidenced by the fact that Jack the Ripper, Charles Manson, and Jeffrey Dahmer all had names with thirteen letters. But that seems irrelevant. A pattern is seen where there is only a coincidence.

The overall mistake is to confuse something subsequent with something consequent, that is, to take a series of events as cause and effect. Politicians do this all the time, taking credit for good things that happened during their administration as if it was because of their administration. Or a recent example is the dispute over immunizations and autism. The number of vaccines children receive is increasing, and the number of cases of autism is also on the rise; therefore, vaccinations must cause autism. The injection came first, the autism second, so there must be a causal link. But this is like saying that if a man dies after being given last rites, the last rites were responsible for his death. Does marriage make people happier, or is it that happier people tend to marry?

Obviously, some happenings are causally linked, and in these cases the order cannot be reversed. We cannot bleed and then get cut because the cut is responsible for the bleeding. We say "ready, aim, fire," not "fire, aim, ready," and the gun goes off because we pulled the trigger. But in other cases, one thing happens after another, not on account of another. Your wish did not come true because you rubbed that lucky charm.

If an athlete wins a game after wearing his favorite hat, he may be tempted to wear that hat again the next time he plays. You never know, and why not cover all bets? But if he thinks about it he will realize that the hat had no power to influence the outcome of the game; it is not a lucky hat. And maybe a student got a good grade on an exam using a red pen, but the high grade is not due to the pen. It had more to do with his studying. And it does not help to use the same pen on the exam as we did in studying for it; the answers are not in the pen.

A second common mistake is called *excluded middle*, derived from formal logic, but we do not have to master formal logic in order to understand it.

Suppose someone says that money is green, and leaves are green, therefore money grows on trees. This is obvious nonsense, but why exactly? Because leaves are not the only things that are green, so from the fact that money is green we cannot infer it is the same as leaves and grows on trees. A more serious error of this kind occurs when we think "All terrorists are Muslims; Abdul is a Muslim; therefore Abdul is a terrorist." We are not told that all Muslims are terrorists, only that all terrorists are Muslims.

Sometimes the fallacy of undistributed middle is obvious, at other times more hidden. If someone says, "All dogs have four legs; my cat has four legs, therefore my cat is really a dog," we can see the flaw in the thinking. But if a woman says, "The rich are smart, my husband is smart, therefore he is rich," the mistake is more subtle. Her husband may be rich, but not necessarily because he is smart. Inheritance, connections, and luck can account for wealth. In the same category is the argument, "The president supports universal health care; socialists want universal health care; therefore, the president is a socialist." If we think about it, we realize that not everyone who wants universal health care is a socialist. Some non-socialists feel that health care is a human right and should not be provided for profit.

These are all examples of what is broadly called "non sequiturs"; they do not follow. It stands to reason that we are much more likely to reach the truth if we avoid mistakes in thinking.

Of course, we can reach the right answer without following the rules of thought. We could say, for instance, that Einstein is a great scientist because he can swim. The conclusion may be correct, but not for that reason. Because of such accidents, one commentator states that men are more rational but women are more often right. Sometimes we stumble across the truth by chance, not by logic.

But overall, reasoning seems more reliable than chance, if it is done correctly, and if it is done badly, that is not the fault of reason. We cannot blame the instrument for the way in which it is used. Traveling is broadening but not for everyone, any more than reading a good book is always enlightening; it depends on the person. The German philosopher Arthur Schopenhauer once said, "If when a book and a head come into collision, and a hollow sound results, it isn't always the book." But if the premises are true, and the structure is valid, then the conclusion can be trusted.

Certainly in deciding philosophic questions, we should use reason and think carefully. And we must respect contrary opinions, insofar as they are rational. If someone presents a sound argument, supported by logic and facts, then we should accept it, whether we like it or not. In the discussion on climate change, some people choose their science in terms of their politics. But we cannot go against reason just because reason goes against us. Otherwise, it would be like playing chess, and when our opponent says "check," we kick over the chessboard.

# Chapter 2. Human Nature: Are We Beastlier Than Any Beast?

Can we ever know our own nature? According to the Heisenberg principle, observation itself affects what is observed, which raises questions as to whether we can ever know anything, much less our own nature. But more specifically, how can the 'I' achieve self-understanding when the 'I' is part of what must be understood? Isn't it like trying to shine a flashlight on its own beam of light, or turning on a lamp to see the nature of darkness?

Almost every figure in intellectual history has had a crack at defining human nature. Are we the creature that is self-conscious, who wants to know, laughs, learns from his mistakes, relishes beauty, gets bored, seeks God, or is never satisfied? Are we the only bipedal creature, who consistently walks on two legs? Mark Twain called man "the only animal that blushes, or needs to." Are we the only tool-using or tool-making animal? No, a chimpanzee will select a stick, sharpen the end, and insert it into a termite's nest; when the termites grip onto the stick to defend against an intruder, the chimpanzee will withdraw the stick and eat the termites. We are hardly the only creatures who are aggressive or who practice mass violence; nature is red in tooth and claw, sometimes because of organized, mass attacks. Neither are we unique in forming societies or a political organization; animals arrange themselves into hierarchies, pecking orders, and begging circles. We aren't unique in having an opposable thumb and forefinger since giant pandas, possums, some frogs, and Old World monkeys have that same characteristic.

Are we the only creature that eats when he isn't hungry, drinks when he isn't thirsty, and makes love all year round? More darkly, are we unique in committing suicide? Group hysteria seems to be behind the "lemming rush," not an urge for self-destruction.

The basic question is what differentiates us from beasts, renders us closer to angels or to machines. In what way are we different from animals, with characteristics that are singular? Sometimes we say that we are animals, after all, but then tell each other not to act like an animal; and a robot with artificial intelligence is hard to separate from a human being — especially if the robot is made to look like a person.

## Historical Notions of Human Nature

In tracing the notion of human nature in philosophy, we must begin with the ancient Greeks, specifically with Plato in the fourth century BCE. In the *Republic* Plato lays out his theory that the soul, the mind, or what might even be called the self is divided into three parts. One element is rationality that enables us to understand what is real as opposed to what is apparent, and allows intelligent decisions to be made on how to live; it is the thinking part of ourselves. A second element, the spirit or spiritedness, is the will that initiates action but also submits to reason. Rational reflection is a passive activity; it is our spirit that stimulates us to action. The final element is appetite, our physical desires for food, drink, and sex, as well as shelter, friendship, and reproducing the species.

These three parts must work in harmony, each performing its proper role but under the governance of reason. In another dialogue, the *Phaedrus*, Plato compares the rational element to a charioteer whose vehicle is driven by two horses, one that initiates movement (spirit), the other, powerful and difficult to rein in (appetite) — is a different model. Plato saw a correspondence between the parts of the person and the parts of the state. They carry out the same functions and must be kept in equilibrium. In his utopia, the rational people are put in charge of the government; they are the rulers or guardians of the state. Those who are most spirited should be in the military because they thrive on action, excitement, and adventure; they are the most courageous. And those in whom the appetites dominate ought to be workers — the merchants, weavers, farmers, traders, and so forth. Their main purpose is to materially support the economy, and the wealth they acquire is used to satisfy their physical desires.

Each person can be classified as belonging mainly to one of these three categories because of their predominant traits, and different aptitudes suit people for different jobs. As Plato put it, we are made principally of gold (guardians), silver (soldiers), or bronze (workers). People are happiest when they do what they do best, and society benefits most when people give what they are best able to give. Therefore, people should not be free to choose their occupations in society; their roles should be assigned. If a spirited type declares that he wants to be a ruler (which would be a military dictatorship), we must tell him, "I'm sorry, you just aren't fit for it." Neither do we want governance by the wealthy, because the ability to make money does not necessarily translate to skill in governance (that would be a plutocracy). Only the brightest and best should rule the nation, an intellectual aristocracy of intelligent and generous rulers. Ideally, we want kings to be philosophers, and philosophers to be kings.

The state is only the individual writ large, and by analogy, justice has the same character in both. In the just person the three parts are integrated and balanced; in the unjust person they are disparate and warring. Society is the same, and in both cases, reason should be in charge. That is what distinguishes human beings from all other forms of life.

Aristotle is another well known Greek philosopher, a pupil of Plato's who became at least as celebrated and influential as his teacher. His writings are wide ranging, with speculations on the nature of reality, aesthetic judgment, reliable means of knowing, logical reasoning, ideals in living, and so forth. Aristotle is the principal philosopher of the Catholic Church, having been "baptized" retroactively by St. Thomas Aquinas.

Aristotle wondered about human nature as well, asking how people differ from other living things. What are the distinguishing features that separate humans from plants and animals? In his vocabulary, he asked what is our special "function."

From his study of biology, Aristotle concluded that everything has a function, which is termed a "teleological" world view. An apple tree's function is to bear apples, and an excellent apple tree grows large, juicy apples, of proper shape and color. The heart pumps blood, the stomach digests food, and our skeletal structure protects our organs, holds us upright. An axe is meant to chop, and a fine axe chops well, a well built house keeps us warm and dry, a good spear flies true, a good plow cuts a straight furrow, and a good lyre makes sweet music. What, then, is the function of human beings?

We are not unusual in consuming nourishment and growing because plants do that, and sensation and feeling is the type of life we share with animals. What, then, makes us different and constitutes our essence? Aristotle thinks it is our ability to reason — a conclusion reminiscent of Plato. The Greeks in general, emerging from barbarism, wanted to separate themselves from lower forms of life, and they celebrated the mind as our primary distinction.

We know today that many animals can reason, although what constitutes genuine intelligence and cognitive ability is hotly debated. Whales and dolphins, the great apes, parrots, elephants, dogs, crows, otters, and so forth all exhibit problem solving skills. Dolphins communicate with clicks and whistles, cockatoos can pick almost any lock, dogs can learn 165 commands, and crows drop stones in a water vessel to raise the level for drinking. The great apes seem the brightest. Chimpanzees hunt with sharpened sticks, and primates have been taught to communicate using American Sign Language; they have conversations with their trainers. The bonobos, or pygmy chimpanzees, may be our closest ancestor, and they are self-aware, use flake technology, and can learn 3000 words.

Animals do reason but maybe not the same way we do, not having the same complexity in their cerebral cortex. They may learn sign language but they cannot grasp grammar, and they seem unable to think abstractly. Even chimpanzees cannot do differential equations or send a rocket into outer space. When a seagull drops a shellfish onto a rock to crack it open, that may be tool-using, but it isn't the same as designing a computer with integrated circuits or composing a piano concerto. We may not even be on a continuum with animals but unique, operating on a different qualitative level. Our higher brain functions may be distinctive to our species. Quantitative changes can lead to qualitative differences, as when water becomes steam or ice.

Aristotle affirms reason, believing that our mental capacity makes us exceptional, and he gives reason two roles: chiefly, to engage in philosophic reflection, but more practically, to make the right choices. We should follow the rationally balanced path of moderation in all things, choosing the middle way between excess and deficiency, neither too much nor too little of anything. The "golden mean" is the ideal.

(Of course, uniqueness is a tricky concept. Being unique may not confer importance; no two snowflakes are alike, but that does not make each one important. And if each one of us is unique, then being unique is not unique.)

## The Depravity of Man

After the Greeks, the question of human nature was taken up by Christian theologians in the Middle Ages, relying on the Bible and particularly the writings of St. Paul. According to Christian teachings, the first humans, Adam and Eve, were created in God's likeness, and were loving, generous, and compassionate. Genesis (1:27) reads "So God created man in his own image, in the image of God he created him, male and female he created them." The Lord "formed man from the dust of the ground, and breathed into his nostrils the breath of life; and the man became a living being." The Lord God then gave man the Garden of Eden as his home, an earthly paradise of pleasant fruit trees and a river of fresh water.

The only rule was that they not eat "of the tree of the knowledge of good and evil...for in the day that you eat of it you shall die." But Satan in the form of a snake persuaded Eve to taste the forbidden fruit, and she in turn tempted Adam to rebel against God's commandment. For their disobedience they were expelled from Eden, and forced to work, experience pain, and endure the pangs of death.

This "Fall" not only affected them but tainted all subsequent generations. Evil was embedded in the human soul, and from that point on everyone was born corrupt. It was St. Augustine who said that "original sin" entered the world, and every baby has an inherently depraved nature. All human life possesses free will and can choose between good and bad, but we have a propensity toward wickedness. Adam's Fall felled us all. Only faith in Christ can cleanse us, so that we regain the paradise that was lost. In order to be purified we must be washed in the blood of the lamb.

This vision of humanity has strongly affected Western culture. It teaches that we are not innately decent and kind but selfish creatures from the moment of birth, acting only for our own advantage. Grace and charity have been replaced with the seven deadly sins of greed, anger, sloth, pride, lust, envy, and gluttony.

A number of modern philosophers agree that human beings are decadent, with an inherently malicious disposition. The British philosopher Thomas Hobbes in the 17th century is usually mentioned as the prime representative of this point of view. In his major work, *The Leviathan*, Hobbes focuses on the "state of nature," what human beings were before they formed themselves into organized societies. Because we have no records of pre-history, he conducts a thought experiment to determine what we must have been in a primitive state.

According to his speculations, humanity lived a life that was "solitary, poor, nasty, brutish, and short." Everyone was at everyone else's throat, competing for power and domination, for the largest share of the earth's goods. Selfishness ruled the day, a continual warfare, "bellum omnium contra omnes," a war of all against all. Humans were "without a common power to keep them all in awe." There were no laws, institutions, or police, no governing force to mediate conflicts, but only individuals battling for their own advantage and for their very lives. "In such conditions," writes Hobbes,

> [T]here is no place for Industry, because the fruit thereof is uncertain...
> and consequently no Culture of the Earth, no Navigation, nor use of
> commodities that may be imported by Sea; no commodious Building,
> no Instruments of moving or removing,...no Knowledge of the face of

the Earth, no account of Time, no Arts, no Letters, no Science, and which is worst of all, continual Fear and danger of violent death.

People soon realized that these circumstances were far from ideal. Power decided disputes, not justice. And since all humans are equal in faculties of body and mind, no one ultimately benefitted from the chaos.

> In order to have greater stability, people joined together in a "social contract," based on a natural precept: "that a man be willing, when others are so too, as far forth as for peace and defence of himself he shall think it necessary, to lay down this right to all things; and be contented with so much liberty against other men as he would allow other men against himself.

In this way civil society was formed, for mutual benefit. Individuals surrendered some of their freedoms for the sake of mutual security, and they owe allegiance to government for keeping the peace.

*The Lord of the Flies* by William Golding re-states this view in literary form. Without government, privileged schoolboys quickly degenerate into savages. Here civilization is depicted as a thin overlay beneath which there is naked aggression and the drive for dominance.

Oddly enough, Sigmund Freud in the 19th century affirmed this low view of human nature in his psychoanalytic theory. Of the three energy systems that make up the psyche, the "Id" is the driving force, and it consists of dynamic, up-surging desires for personal satisfactions. Reason, to Freud, only acts to justify our emotional impulses. We always give noble reasons for our actions, but they are never the real reasons; they are only rationalizations for pleasure or aggression. A surgeon, for example, attacks people with a knife, but he does so in an operating room, with a scalpel, and with a medical degree. The same action on the street could mean a long prison sentence, but the surgeon is rewarded with wealth and status because he has the validation of society. The boxer too assaults people, trying to give his opponent a concussion, but he fights under a license, in a social sport, to cheering fans.

To Freud, we always act under the "pleasure principle" (Eros) as well as the forces of destruction (Thanatos), and all of civilization is built on the displacement of those drives. Girls ride horses as a substitute for sexuality, and artists paint pictures of nudes in place of having sex; football is thinly disguised warfare, as are battles for dominance in the corporate boardroom (and between couples). The constant energy that impels us is never extinguished, only diverted into respectable directions. Unconsciously, we are "a cauldron full of seething excitations," and we always find an outlet that will bring us pleasure rather than pain.

Freud is largely in disrepute in psychology today because there is little empirical proof for his theories, including his notions of the Oedipus conflict, penis envy, and castration anxiety. His findings are regarded as too intuitive and anecdotal, lacking in hard, experimental data. He also treated repressed Viennese women of the late 19th century, then extrapolated his findings to all women. What's more, once his patients knew his theory, they began dreaming in Freudian symbols, which contaminated the evidence. In psychotherapy one third of the patients get better, one third get worse, and one third stay the same; identical statistics apply to those who do not go into therapy. Today Freudianism seems almost obsolete, a "faith-based" doctrine.

However, in some quarters Freud is being resurrected. Psychoanalysis as well as cognitive behavior therapy is partnering with neuroscience. Brain-imaging studies have revealed changes in the brain as a result of therapy. That is, there appear to be physical consequences to "the talking cure," to dredging our deep-seated feelings to the level of consciousness. The mind does seem to affect the brain. A shift occurs in various cells, leading to changes in behavior.

Freud, of course, opposed religion while accepting the idea of original sin, which he translated as the Id. To Freud, religion is an "infantile neurosis," an emotional disorder that occurs in children who cannot accept their father's defects. They have to project a heavenly father who is perfect in every respect, an omnipotent being who can protect them from all harm, someone who knows everything and can be absolutely trusted for guidance. "The face that looks down on us from heaven is the face that looks down on us in the cradle," Freud writes. If we admit we are weak, sinful children and ask for forgiveness from our father in heaven, then he will grant us the highest expression of his love, eternal life, but if we disobey him, we will be punished in hell for eternity.

The healthy personality has no need of a supernatural father, having come to terms with the limitations of their earthly one, not needing to be twice-born but to grow up. Balanced individuals adopt a realistic view of their parent's strengths and weaknesses, accepting the world for what it is and not needing support from the supernatural. Only the infantile personality clings to religion in order to cope with life, and with death.

To Freud, all religious phenomena can be explained away psychologically. If someone has an out-of-body experience that is an instance of schizophrenia; if a mystic goes into a trance, that is a catatonic state; and if a believer hears a heavenly choir, that is a psychotic episode of hearing voices. Differently put, if we talk to God, that is prayer, but if he talks to us, that is psychosis — and timing has a great deal to do with the success of prayers. Depending on the society, people who experience such things are either canonized as saints or institutionalized as emotionally disturbed.

In any event, Freud maintains we are governed by our Id desires and he depreciates the rationality and benevolence of human beings. Galileo proved we are not the center of creation, that the earth revolves around the sun, not vice versa; and Darwin established that we are not a singular creation but descendants of primates. All three, Freud, Galileo, and Darwin reduced man's status, so that we have a much humbler view today of our place in the universe.

## Basic Decency and Goodness

This negative perspective on human nature, presented by Christianity, Hobbes, and Freud, was opposed by various thinkers who took a much sunnier view. Primary among these was the 18th century, French philosopher Jean Jacques Rousseau. He was an inconsistent thinker because he wanted to do justice to the varied aspects of human experience; "a foolish consistency is the hobgoblin of little minds." But His views on human nature, as presented in the *Discourse on Inequality*, were fairly consistent. They did not contradict Hobbes but re-interpreted selfishness as the basis of our generosity.

In keeping with custom of the day, his starting point was the state of nature — to his mind, an idyllic time. As primitives, human beings were roaming, rootless creatures, having some loose associations but no strong relationships. Purity and innocence prevailed, without knowledge or language or moral judgments, "before men knew how to sin." Love and family were absent, and there was no morality or private property. People were neither rational in the Greek sense nor depraved as in Christian model, and they were not brutal as Hobbes claimed. Man was wholly guiltless and dignified, naturally aristocratic.

To Rousseau rationality was not present at the start; moral sentiments moved people, and these feelings created the early beginnings of justice. Specifically, there was *amour de soi*, which translates to love of oneself, but that does not mean self-centeredness; which leads to false values of honor and vanity. Rather, he meant self-respect, self-pride, and self-preservation. We do not need to make others look small so that we can feel big.

The other major sentiment is *pitié*, which translates to sympathy and compassion for our fellow man. More properly, it stands for empathy for other people's pain. "When the strength of an expansive soul makes me identify with my fellow, and I feel that I am, so to speak, in him, it is in order not to suffer that I do not want him to suffer. I am interested in him for love of myself... Love of men derived from love of self is the principle of human justice."

This is not genuine altruism but a type of selfishness, helping others not for their sake but for our own. Nevertheless, it seems a version of the golden rule: Do unto others as you would have them do unto you; love others as you love yourself.

To Rousseau, it is civilization that has degraded human beings, preventing their natural sentiments from flourishing. In society people live in mutual fear and distrust, estranged from one another in an attitude of hatred and "the most horrible state of war."

This contrasts with simple, good hearted indigenous peoples, which Rousseau identifies with the "noble savage." This myth strongly influenced Romantic writers such as Wordsworth, Keats, Byron, Thoreau, and Cooper who painted sentimental portraits of the country life.

Are savages noble, or are they just savage; are brutes, brutal? Voltaire once remarked that Rousseau was so convincing, he almost got down on all fours. But even Rousseau qualified his belief in the superiority of natural man, extolling the virtues of social organization. By joining civilization,

> [man's] faculties are so stimulated and developed, his ideas so extended, his feelings so ennobled, and his whole soul so uplifted...that he would be bound to bless continually the happy moment which took him from [the natural state] forever, and instead of a stupid and unimaginative animal, made him an intelligent being and a man.

The noble savage ideal has gripped people's imaginations, and it forms part of the current American mentality. We are told that nature is good, that country folk are the salt of the earth, uncorrupted by modern, industrialized, urban society. Life in cities is frenetic, characterized by crime and pollution, overcrowding, poverty, dirt, cut-throat competition. People live in glass and steel boxes far removed from the natural environment, and they compensate by keeping pets, raising plants indoors, and traveling to the beach or countryside on weekends. They become addicted to comfort and luxury, separated from what is essential.

In comparison, country life is wholesome, the work is honest, the air is pure, and neighbors help one another. Most Americans live in cities, but the myth still resonates that rural life is better, with space and silence, and everyone is healthier. Here, there is clean living because people's natural decency is allowed to flourish. We should escape to the country whenever we can for hiking, rock climbing, camping, and generally clean living.

This positive view of nature is expressed in the environmental movement which wants to protect all living things. We are stewards, managers, custodians of the land rather than having "dominion" over it. Even predatory animals such as wolves or alligators must be protected because they contribute to the balance of nature; in the same spirit, we should value trees, oceans, and mountains. The welfare of animals ought to be respected, and that respect should be extended to every manifestation of nature. The natural world, which is our home, should be carefully guarded, for our well being as well as for its own sake.

In the 21st century we are conscious of the fragility of the environment, including species that are endangered. We want humane treatment of animals on factory farms, at the slaughterhouse, and as domestic pets. We have condemned bull fighting and cock fighting, although that is because it brought pleasure to the spectators rather than pain to the animal. What's more, we worry about the morality of hunting, of caging creatures in zoos, habitats, and water parks, and of training animals to do tricks in circuses; tigers do not jump through flaming hoops naturally. There is also a large vegetarian movement, opposed to using animals for food, and vegans reject animal products such as milk and eggs, even though the animal is not harmed. Both groups lobby for a ban on animal experimentation, even to save human lives (much less for cosmetics). Many naturalists oppose the use of animals for clothing, including material of wool, fur, and leather; wearing an animal seems barbaric, especially when synthetic fabrics are readily available.

But is nature the model for human life, displaying kindness rather than cruelty? Certainly eating natural foods seems better than the processed kind with chemical additives, preservatives, and pesticides, but medicine may be different. If we have cancer, we want chemotherapy or radiation treatment. We would not want to cure a ruptured appendix with herbs; here, we want the skills of a modern surgeon. We may have a romantic longing for a primitive life, but we would bring with us inoculations, antibiotics, and the full arsenal of pharmaceuticals.

And not every organism on the planet is benevolent. Some animals are vicious, particularly the carnivores that tear their prey to shreds and attack us if we are in the wrong place at the wrong time. Neither do we value all viruses and bacteria because some cause hepatitis, polio, multiple sclerosis, and so forth. No one mounts the barricades to save the scorpion or the Ebola virus. And would it really destroy the balance of nature if there were no rattlesnakes or black widow spiders, no crocodiles, piranhas, or moray eels? Nature would establish a new balance through time, as it has in the past. 98% of all species that have lived are now extinct, but there is still a balance.

Championing natural man and the natural world always harkens back to Rousseau, who loved walking in the idyllic countryside and learning the lessons it had to teach. Like Shakespeare, he believed there were "tongues in trees, books in the running brooks/ Sermons in stones, and good in everything." But Rousseau was sure to walk in sunlight, not in a blizzard, and if he didn't watch his step he could be bitten by a snake. In his wanderings, he could have strayed into a swamp with mosquitoes carrying zika or encephalitis — or full of quicksand. He might have been swept away by a flood or been struck by lightning. And if he lay down for a tranquil sleep in yon sylvan glen, he could have wound up with poison ivy. In short, nature does not seem ideal in all respects, and we wonder whether human beings in a state of nature reflected the good aspects of the natural world or the brutal ones. Is Aristotle right, that to live the good life one must live in a great city?

Rousseau is supported in an odd way by the Scottish economist Adam Smith, also an 18th century thinker, the father of modern capitalism. Smith is usually thought of as seeing self-interest as fundamental to human nature, but in a convoluted way he claims selfishness is good for society, mirroring Rousseau's thinking.

In his *Theory of Moral Sentiments*, Adam Smith states that when the suffering of others is felt as part of our own experience, then their interests and ours are one. "How selfish soever man may be supposed, there are evidently some principles in his nature, which interest him in the fortune of others, and render their happiness necessary to him, though he derives nothing from it, except the pleasure of seeing it." If we identify with others as ourselves, then their happiness is our happiness.

More specifically, in *The Wealth of Nations* Smith supports the efficacy of the free market, which in an almost magical way ensures that individual self-interest will lead to economic prosperity for all. In his economic activity:

> [Every person] intends only his own gain, and he is in this, as in many other cases, led by an invisible hand to promote an end which was no part of his intention. Nor is it always the worse for the society that it was no part of it. By pursuing his own interest he frequently promotes that of the society more effectually than when he really intends to promote it.

Self-interest is the motive; prosperity for everyone is the result. As we pursue our own advantage, everyone will be better off; and as we fulfill the needs of others, we will be materially and morally enriched. The free market, unrestrained by government intervention, is the best economic system for general prosperity.

Although conservatives applaud this model, which could justify high profits for corporations and high individual wealth, there is controversy about its validity — especially for working people. The debate centers on the value of uninhibited capitalism versus regulated capitalism, "laissez-faire" economics as compared to a Keynesian approach, or another type of economy altogether. Does everyone actually benefit from each pursuing his own advantage? Does a rising tide raise all boats, or could the "invisible hand" be an invisible foot, kicking the poor? Does the hand of God bless capitalism, or could it be the devil's trick, making selfishness appear altruistic, a rationalization for greed? We could also ask whether the ends justify the means. Is there any merit in achieving a good result unintentionally, for society to be benefitted by the vagaries of the marketplace, because of individual selfishness?

Adam Smith believed he was on the side of the angels and that his economic system actually expressed our finest tendencies. He writes, "To feel much for others and little for ourselves; to restrain our selfishness and exercise our benevolent affections, constitutes the perfection of human nature." The economic foundation is always self-interest, but that can induce empathy and produce generosity, market activity that benefits everyone in the end.

The drama is ongoing in the world, and economists continually debate whether free market capitalism offers the greatest good for people at large, deliberately or not.

In the end we have to ask ourselves which vision of human nature is more accurate. Do we act rationally and kindly, or do our passions, especially the negative ones, overpower the angels of our better nature? And whether we are selfish by nature or not, does a free enterprise system, with minimum regulation, provide the greatest benefit to society?

## The Caring Gene

Recent research in neurology, experimental psychology, child development, and primate studies have suggested a "caring gene." Generosity seems had-wired in our brain, a built-in moral compass rather than being a social construct. Conscience appears to be inherent in human beings. Our moral awareness has a biological foundation, rooted in empathy - the ability to recognize and identify with someone else's perspective. Empathy is what enables us to feel another's pain, to exult in their achievements and share their joy. It is the reason for the "catharsis" that comes from identifying with characters in a play, novel, or film, projecting ourselves into their experience. We feel purged when the conflict is resolved, or even at having suffered their tragedy, and we feel a sense of personal relief at the ending

Instead of regarding all social behavior as driven by conditioning or coding, morality seems to come from within ourselves. A moral gyroscope apparently precedes the development of human society, even preceding the origin of the human species. It is visible especially in primates. For example, in one research study rhesus monkeys were trained to pull a chain for food. Then the experiment was changed so that some received food while others received an electric shock. When the rewarded monkeys observed this, they refused to eat, at least temporarily, preferring to go hungry than cause pain to others. This occurred even though they knew they would get food regardless. (The same behavior has been observed in rats.) In another experiment, monkeys were given cucumbers or grapes as a reward for completing a task; the grapes were their favorites. But when one monkey, who was receiving cucumbers, saw that another was receiving grapes, he would not eat or would throw the cucumbers out of the cage; apparently he thought it was unfair.

In the wild, chimpanzees have been observed trying to save their companions from drowning even though they themselves could not swim, and they have attempted to rescue others from leopard attacks. All bonobos will make injured monkeys comfortable by bringing them cushioning material, and they will console distressed members of the troupe, hugging and kissing them. Gorillas in captivity will open a door to allow a companion access to food, and give older apes water from their mouths; they will also help arthritic ones onto climbing frames. Capuchin monkeys try to obtain rewards for others, and after a fight, female chimpanzees will drag reluctant males together for reconciliation.

This moral sense seems to operate even in very young children. As the cognitive scientist Paul Bloom reports, studies in child development provide clear evidence of an imprint or "nativism." A fourteen-month-old will bring a crying friend to his mother, and one-year-olds prefer puppets who behave well to those who behave badly. In one experiment, both good puppets, who returned a ball to its owner, and bad puppets who ran away with a ball, were given treats. The children were then allowed to take one away, and almost all denied the treat to the bad puppet.

Bloom's conclusion is that every normal person has an innate sense of right and wrong,

> an understanding that helping is morally good, and that thwarting the goals of another person is morally bad. A rudimentary sense of justice..., a recognition that good guys should be rewarded and bad guys should be punished. An initial sense of fairness,... in particular that there should be an equal division of resources. And alongside these principles are moral emotions, including empathy, compassion, guilt, shame, and righteous anger.

Further evidence keeps appearing from child development centers. Two-and-half-year-olds can differentiate between genuine moral principles and those arrived at by consensus. The will respond that it is okay not to use a cubby for coats if everyone agrees to it, but it would not be okay to hit people even if the group consents. Morality seems "bred in the bone" as one psychologist puts it, a visceral response even before children have been acculturated. Apparently, babies and toddlers can judge the rightness and wrongness of other children's actions as well as their own.

A comparison is often drawn between our moral compass and our use of language. As we have learned from Noam Chomsky, the father of modern linguistics, the mechanism of the human brain includes the ability to acquire language, although the particular words we speak vary between cultures. The structure of language is "biologically determined in the human mind and genetically transmitted." All human beings, and to some extent the great apes, display the underlying organization of symbols, a universal syntax independent of any social context. Babies do not just mimic words or babble in their native language but come into the world equipped to understand the framework of language.

Likewise, our neural mechanism seems to include a moral response that is automatic and unconscious; it cuts across all cultures. We experience the emotions of other people vicariously, and we are drawn to alleviate their suffering. The result is our standard of conduct. A moral grammar seems encoded in our brain, and we appear predisposed to help rather than harm. St. Augustine was the first to claim that human nature is depraved and corrupt because of "original sin," and that this explains the presence of evil actions in the world. But perhaps we are innately good and inclined toward compassion. Perhaps we are genetically programmed to be kind. And as one researcher put it, "we cannot change our genes any more than a school of piranhas can decide to be vegetarians."

If we think of the accomplishments of civilization, the progress in science, medicine, and technology; our educational institutions; the structure and order of the state; the achievements in art; the rule of law; our communication and transportation systems; the humane treatment of the poor, the sick, and elderly; and so forth, we must conclude that reason and compassion is at our core. On the other hand, when we think of violent crime on the streets; the insurrections, rebellions, and wars throughout history; the corruption in government; the genocides; the slavery that still persists; cultural, racial, and gender oppression; global warming; nuclear, chemical, and biological weapons; the gap between the rich and the poor; and so forth, then we take a more pessimistic view and conclude that we are indeed cursed with inner aggression toward others, and perhaps ourselves.

But rather than thinking of human nature as good and rational, or malevolent or benevolent, some philosophers think of it as non-existent. In particular, a school of philosophy called Existentialism denies any pre-existing qualities to human beings. 20th century figures such as Jean-Paul Sartre and Albert Camus claim that each person creates himself anew by his choices and actions.

According to this position, we are thrown into existence without our permission and based on our decisions, we become a particular kind of person. This view is encapsulated in the slogan, "existence precedes essence." We come into existence blank and empty, without character or tendencies, and we then build our essential self through the commitments we make. What we are is a consequence of what we do, and there is no human nature. Our choices have dictated what we are; we do not choose from what we are.

Objects are the opposite: for them, "essence precedes existence." Some creator decides what an object will be — a knife, a painting, or in the case of God, a lamb or tiger. Its size, form, coloring and so forth are all selected in advance. Then the object is brought into existence fully formed, and it does not develop any further. Every squirrel and frog will act like every other squirrel and frog, because that is their nature. We cannot ever say that a squirrel made a mess of its life; it lives as it must.

However, in the case of human beings, first we exist, then we choose what we want to be. That implies, of course, that we are responsible for the kind of person we become, because we always had the ability to choose differently. Humans are entirely free and entirely responsible for who they are. Our nature is the result of what we do, rather than what we do being the result of our nature. Furthermore, the sum of all human choices make up human nature at any particular point in time, and it will change as our collective choices change. Human nature is mutable, and we are never what we used to be.

This is a theory of freedom because we are not restricted by a fixed nature that defines the boundaries of our aspirations. Of course, our environment imposes some limits so that the ghetto child is restricted in what he can achieve, and physical laws dictate that we cannot be in two places at once. We also cannot repeal the law of gravity, any more than we can reject the law of averages. Nevertheless, who we are is up to us.

This means that we are not forced to be rational, which the Greeks say defines us. In fact, one existential novelist named André Gide urges us to be impulsive and spontaneous, to act "gratuitously" because it is a more authentic response. Once we deliberate, then all of our history rushes in to affect our choice, and we are not making our own decision at all. In an anti-intellectual rant one of his characters says, "*Il faut...que tu brule en toi, tous les livres.*" You must burn inside of you all of your books. And Dostoevsky declares, "Twice two makes four without my will; as if free will meant that." If we can say, with deep chest tones, "Two plus two makes five today," then we are truly liberated.

In Existentialism we are also freed from the notion of original sin that is said to distort our thoughts and corrupt our actions. Whether we think clearly and act rightly is our free choice. In the same way, we are not compelled to be good but can take credit for deliberately choosing kindness over cruelty.

Sometimes our judgment of our species comes from watching children, either playing happily or refusing to share or take turns. We wonder whether they are little angels or little beasts, and whether we are seeing human nature undisguised. We also become introspective, wondering whether our own personal tendencies are toward sympathy or malice. Or we turn to accounts of early peoples. Were they competitive or cooperative? Did they go on raiding parties and slaughter their neighbors, or did they live in tranquil villages, their children gamboling joyously with the animals?

Parents make sacrifices and protect their children, but they also lose their tempers, react with harsh punishments, and resent the time and care that children require. The good witch and the bad witch are both mother on different days. Maybe George Orwell is right when he writes, "human beings want to be good, but not too good, and not quite all the time."

Our behavior seems to result from a complex interaction between hereditary factors, whatever they may be, and our social interactions. The existentialists would add to the mix the idea that we act out of our own free will, and are not the product of nature times nurture. If there is a basic human nature, its character remains unresolved.

The ball is now in your court, and you must play it as you see fit — but always according to what is reasonable.

# CHAPTER 3. ACQUIRING KNOWLEDGE: SHOULD WE LOSE OUR MINDS AND COME TO OUR SENSES?

Most of us assume we know the world by means of our senses. We use our eyes and ears principally, but also our sense of touch, taste, and smell. Through our primary sense of sight, we experience colors, hues, brightness, and forms; through our hearing we detect vibrations of loud and soft, high and low sounds; and through our tactile sense we feel textures of rough and smooth, hard and soft. We are also aware of being stroked, having an itch, and even being numb. Certain smells are repellent to us, such as the odor of a skunk, and others pleasing, such as the aroma of roses; and the sensory impressions on our tongue determine flavors of sweet, salty, sour, and bitter (accompanied of course by smell). Children seem to enjoy the taste of jam, and not because they once tasted some awful food; it is a natural pleasure in itself. In these ways we first come to recognize our mother's face, the agreeable sensation of being fed and warm, and later the more complex feelings generated by art, music, and literature.

In addition, we have extra senses that reveal the world, not a sixth sense but, for example, an awareness of balance, a sense of pain, and the kinesthetic sensation that makes us aware of movement in our muscles and joints. Is there a sense of danger, a sense of direction, a sense of being watched, or are those metaphors like a sense of humor?

As we mature, we learn the character of things through our senses, and separate reality from appearance, that is, what *is* so from what only *seems* so. We usually assume we know nothing at birth, but that we learn everything we know through sense experience as we live our lives.

All of this seems self-evident, but sometimes our senses fool us. For example, we regard a rock as the epitome of something solid and stationary, but the physicist tell us it is made up mainly of space, and its atoms are in constant motion. And the rock is hard only in the sense that an electrical repulsion is set up between the atoms in our fingers and the atoms in the rock, and the harder we press, the greater the resistance. In fact, we never touch "the rock" at all. We would also swear we see the sunrise and the sunset when all we see is the earth turn. What's more, it takes the sun's light eight minutes to reach the earth, so we are witnessing is how the sun was rather than how it is now. In fact, we never see the sun but only the light emanating from the sun as a result of electro-magnetic radiation due to nuclear explosions. Our senses also trick us into hearing the ocean in the spiral of a Nautilus shell, and perceiving purple mountains on the horizon when, close up, they are not purple at all. That raises the question of what is the ideal distance to view the color of things; sugar looks white to the naked eye but black under a microscope, so we don't know the actual color. White chocolate seems to taste brown...

Wagon wheels appear to move backwards; an amputee will feel pain in a "phantom limb"; railroad tracks seem to meet in the distance (although we know that parallel lines never meet); and in a magic act we would swear that the woman was sawed in half, and the rabbit materialized out of an empty hat. As in the case of the sun, we believe that we see the stars at night but that light may have traveled thousands of years before it reaches us, so that what we are seeing is a ghostly image of the past. The light from Polaris, the North Star, takes 430 years to reach us.

All of these mistakes make us question the reliability of our senses to transmit information. Maybe seeing is believing, but there are also cases of "hearing things" and "seeing things." Nevertheless, we ordinarily trust our senses, and many philosophers agree. Despite the errors, it seems self-evident that a correspondence exists between what we perceive and what is real. We simply must be careful to check our sense perception for false positives. If we hear voices where there is silence, or a lonely child has an imaginary friend, that is a hallucination, and if we believe there is a man in the moon, that is an illusion; the moon is simply earth's satellite, pockmarked with craters and human footprints. Are ghosts and ghouls, vampires and zombies (the undead) simply illusions or are they known through some special perception? Since their existence cannot be perceived in verifiable ways, we have to treat them as nonsensical, popular fantasies.

## Seeing Is Believing

*Empiricism* is the name given to the view that we can rely on our sense experience, and the most celebrated empiricists are the 17th and 18th century British philosophers: John Locke, an Englishman, George Berkeley, an Irishman, and David Hume, a Scotsman. In their separate ways, they championed the validity of our senses in establishing which statements are true. It is also the generally held belief as to how we know. We say, "Seeing is believing," or "Show me," and we mean that seeing, as well as hearing, tasting, smelling, and feeling, are the tests of genuine knowledge. In fact, by "proof" we mean the evidence of our senses and not a "gut feeling," guess, opinion, or hunch.

John Locke is usually classified as the first of the great British empiricists, and his defense of sense perception is contained in *An Essay Concerning Human Understanding*. Here he tries to determine the limits of our understanding, and he argues that all of what we know is ultimately derived from the senses. Human beings are always going beyond the power of the senses, "extending their Enquiries beyond their Capacities, and letting their Thoughts wander into those depths where they can find no sure Footing; [so]'tis no Wonder that they raise Questions and multiply Disputes, which never coming to any clear Resolution, are proper to only continue and increase their Doubts, and to confirm them at last in a perfect Skepticism."

According to Locke, our mind at the start is a "tabula rasa" or blank slate, written upon by sense experience. Our ideas are acquired by perception alone as we pass through life, and we then make connections, combine our associations, and recognize parts that coalesce into objects.

These sense experiences can be divided into two types: sensation and reflection. First-hand sensations provide information about things and events in the external world. Reflection takes those sensations, and through mental activity, organizes them into concepts. All of our ideas can be traced to sensations, but some are the secondary product of the mind combining, transposing, augmenting, and expanding those primary sensations into complex notions.

Locke denies the existence of "innate ideas," which was the mainstay of previous thinkers: Plato, as a prime example, held that concepts such as justice, truth, and beauty are contained in our minds at birth; Aristotle claimed the law of non-contradiction is pre-existent; Rene Descartes thought the idea of God is inborn; and Gottfried Leibniz argued for mathematical truisms such as 1+1=2, known before we encounter two sticks. Such ideas were believed to be "a priori," present in the human mind before birth. Our ideas were assumed to be too rich and complex to have arisen from our environment; there must exist inborn, self-evident truths.

As noted previously, some psychologists such as Noam Chomsky claim we have an innate ability to understand the structure of language. And as we've seen, some contemporary evidence points to an internal gyroscope, a moral gene that all people share. This view is opposed by psychologists such as B.F. Skinner who think all knowledge is the result of conditioning. Once again the debate is nature vs. nurture.

Many writers have spoken of the inherent wisdom of children, an understanding they lose as they become adults. In "Intimations of Immortality" Wordsworth writes, "Trailing clouds of glory do we come/ From God who is our home/...At length this Man perceives it die away,/ And fade into the light of common day." And e.e. cummings writes, "down they forgot as up they grew."

In conflict with this romantic tradition, Locke argues in his *Essay Concerning Human Understanding* that if there were innate ideas, common to all human beings, there would be universal agreement on those ideas. Instead, we have a welter of conflicting notions, sometimes even leading to war. We obviously do not have the same idea of God or Christian missionaries would not have to convert native peoples. Even children and idiots should be aware of such universal truths, Locke says, because "It seems to me a near Contradiction to say there are truths imprinted on the Soul, which it perceives or understands not; imprinting if it signify anything, being nothing else but the making certain Truths to be perceived."

Locke equates innateness with universal agreement, which may not be fair. False ideas, such as a square world, were held at one time by most people; and true ones, such as climate change, are not accepted by everyone. Even innate truths may not be universally believed, but people may have to be educated to comprehend them.

But to Locke, "the Understanding comes to be furnished with [ideas]" only through our natural faculties; there is nothing in the intellect that was not previously in the senses. It is up to the individual to judge things and their qualities according to his or her personal impressions. The government or academic "experts," superstitions or convention, should not dictate the truth. We must assess the evidence for ourselves, even rejecting the authority of institutions the way Galileo opposed the teachings of the Church. Genuine knowledge must be in accord with the reality of things, and that depends upon sense perception.

As a creature of the 17th century, Locke favored a monarchy, but as a man of the Enlightenment he advocated a limited one which was accountable for preserving "life, liberty, and property." These rights are not innate but in keeping with natural law. Similarly, the monarch's powers are not natural or absolute, any more than a father can beat his children if he pleases. Human rights are sacred, having been given by God, and they are held in trust by the monarch for the good of society; they cannot be abridged. Our Declaration of Independence largely copies this list, declaring "life, liberty, and the pursuit of happiness" as fundamental; Germany's principles are "*Einigkeit und Recht and Freiheit* (unity, justice, and liberty), and Canada extols "peace, order, and good government." Some states assume that government confers these rights, others, like Locke, that they are inalienable, basic to human dignity; they are to be safeguarded by the state.

To stand up for rights derived from natural law is odd for an empiricist, since those rights are not perceived, but Locke departs from his strict doctrine to recognize certain principles as self-evident.

George Berkeley (pronounced Barkly) was a bishop in the Anglican Church in Ireland, and although a fellow empiricist, he reacted strongly against Locke's version of the theory. His main objection, expressed in his *Three Dialogues Between Hylas and Philonous,* was the claim that the world is physical, as revealed by the senses. As a cleric, he took the fundamental reality to be "immaterial."

Locke did affirm the existence of God but his philosophy hardly left room for anything spiritual. We had rights but not a soul, and beauty, value, or heaven did not exist. Locke had described a mechanical arrangement of physical bodies in space and time, a system of clocks and engines, wheels and springs. These bodies operate on the sense-organs of people, which cause ideas to arise in the mind — ideas that reflect the actual, external, material reality.

Berkeley found this theory dangerous to the faithful and faulty in its logic. A world of physical objects has no purpose, meaning, or providence. And how could any observer, who can only contemplate his own ideas, know anything about a physical world? He only knows the ideas in his mind, and speculates that they come from an outside, material source. For all anyone knew, objects in the world may be unlike the ideas we have of them; worse still, there may not be any such objects. Our ideas do not need to have counterparts in the physical world, any more than there are real griffins or unicorns. This kind of empiricism, he thought, only leads to skepticism and solipsism — that only I exist.

In Berkeley's own philosophy he tries to remain an empiricist while rejecting the materialistic worldview, and to save the existence of God while affirming the reality of the external world. This is a tall order, and Berkeley's efforts are highly original, easy to ridicule but hard to disprove.

To Berkeley, to say that we perceive an object simply means that an observer has certain sensations, which implies that if there is no observer, then there are no sensations and the object cannot be said to exist. For example, when we claim "There is a tree," we mean that our mind is experiencing brownness and roughness, a certain form and height, an earthy smell, and the sound of wind through branches. Based on this, we form the idea of a tree, which is the sum of our perceptions. But we cannot say that the qualities continue to exist if no one perceives them. We cannot even say there is a physical tree there apart from its characteristics, when all we perceive are the characteristics.

Berkeley is therefore classified as an immaterialist and an Idealist, someone who thinks that only minds and their ideas are real. There are no material substances; ideas constitute the object, and those ideas are based on perception. We do not smell the flower but the aroma of the flower, and we do not hear a gong but the sound of a gong.

Berkeley breaks this down in terms of the various senses. With regard to touch, if we put our hand in tepid water after having had it in cold, we feel the water as warm, whereas if our hand was in icy water we feel it as warm. But the water itself has no physical temperature; our perception determines whether it is hot or cold. In fact, there is no such thing as a tangible substance called water; rather we feel a sensation of wetness and view it as colorless and transparent. To an Eskimo a 60˚ day may be balmy, while to a Hawaiian 60˚ is chilly. In the same way, if we stand too close to a fire we will get burned, but the pain as well as the heat is in us, just as there are no warm coats but only coats that keep us warm. To Berkeley, "the intense heat immediately perceived is nothing distinct from a particular sort of pain."

Likewise with regard to smells. To some people a horse barn has a disagreeable odor, to others a pleasant one, but the smell does not come from the animals; rather, we are perceiving certain smells and calling them stenches or perfumes. In the same way, we construct our idea of horse by combining a rectangular appearance, a warm touch, the sound of neighing, and so forth,. The enjoyment of our meals functions the same way. Food has no flavor, only taste, and taste varies between individuals. More generally, a sweet taste is pleasant and a bitter taste is unpleasant, but both the taste and the reaction are in the person.

The same analysis applies to colors. Whether the ocean is blue or green is a function of perception; it probably depends on how we learned to use the words 'blue' and 'green'. Besides, an object in darkness has no color because it cannot be perceived, or more accurately, we cannot claim it has any color because in the dark, our eyes are unable to perceive anything at all. If we are color blind, then red is grey to us.

But aren't there light waves of varying intensities that are actually generated, which we interpret as color? Berkeley would say such things are unknown since they are outside all perception, and in any case, there is no physical object giving off light waves. Besides, color depends on light, so if there's no light, then there's no color. From his perspective, if we put a red sweater in a drawer, we do not know that it remains red because it cannot be seen. Even if we view color as pigment rather than light, we have no assurance that the pigment remains in the sweater, unperceived. Worse still, once we close the drawer we cannot be sure the sweater is still there; after all, it is only a bundle of perceptions.

This brings us to the philosophic chestnut about sound: If a tree falls in the forest and there's no one there to hear it, is there noise? Berkeley, of course, would answer No, and on the grounds that he has laid out, it is difficult to prove otherwise. Without any ear to hear it, how can we say there was a sound? Setting up a tape recorder only extends our listening ability; it isn't the absence of listening. If we argue that sound waves must have been produced, detected or not, Berkeley would say that a spike might appear on a seismograph, or our body might feel vibrations, but sound means what is heard not what is seen or felt. What's more, a crashing sound does not come from the tree falling to the ground but consists only of a listener's perception. Without a listener, there is no sound.

But what about "primary qualities," as they were called, for example, motion? Can't we say that some things move while others are fixed and still, that a river flows over rocks while the rocks remain motionless? Berkeley's answer is that at the river's edge we perceive it as flowing while from a mountaintop the river is a silver ribbon. But what about figure or size; don't they remain constant as part of objects? Berkeley points out that objects look large close up and small from a distance. We know today that the moon has a rocky, powdery surface while from the earth it seems like a tiny disc we can cover with our thumb. Similarly, glass may be hard to a geologist but little boys know that baseballs break windows. Everything depends on our viewpoint, and a man can replace three panes of glass before he realizes there is a crack in his glasses. When we put a nautilus shell to our ear we are not hearing the roar of the sea but the flow of our own blood.

Based on this reasoning, Berkeley concludes, in his famous phrase, "Esse est percipi," to be is to be perceived.

Samuel Johnson, who compiled one of the first dictionaries of the English language, once kicked a stone and said, "Thus do I refute Bishop Berkeley." We can sympathize with his frustration, but Berkeley would answer that in kicking a stone we only experience a bundle of sensations; it doesn't prove the physical reality of the stone.

However, Berkeley faced more serious criticisms. If we each exist in our own circle of perceptions, then how is it that two people perceive the same characteristics called a tree and how is it that if we fall asleep in a room with a wood fire burning in the grate, when we awaken the coal will have become ashes? That suggests that the fire burned the coal even though no one was watching. Whether we are awake or asleep, life seems to happen.

In refuting this point, Berkeley reveals the complete, polished sphere of his system. He points out that he never said there isn't any external world, only that the physical world does not exist, and that things cannot exist unperceived. And more importantly, if the external world persists, and human beings are not observing it constantly, there must be a being that is. Obviously, that being is God. We must therefore assume the existence of God in order to account for the agreement in our perceptions and to explain the continuity of life. God exists everywhere and always, and all things exist, not as physical objects but as perceptions in the mind of God. In this way the world is maintained in being.

Berkeley's position and the opposition to it are neatly encapsulated in two limericks written by Ronald Knox, the 20th century cleric. The first is a challenge to Berkeley:

> There was a young man who said God
> must find it exceedingly odd
> when he finds that the tree
> continues to be
> when no one's about in the Quad.

But the reply on behalf of Berkeley reads:

> Dear sir, your astonishment's odd.
> I am always about in the Quad
> and that's why the tree
> will continue to be
> since observed by, yours faithfully, God.

Berkeley thus becomes a religious empiricist, analyzing the nature of reality to prove the existence of God. He uses perception against the common sense belief in the reality of the physical world.

While we admire Berkeley's cleverness, we are left wondering whether he is right. Couldn't an object exist apart from a perceiver, and be capable of being viewed even though no "being" had ever viewed it? Weren't there mountains on the far side of the moon before the astronauts saw them, visible but never witnessed by anyone before? Do we need God to be assured that wild roses in remote valleys are really blooming? And if everything must be perceived in order to be, mustn't God first exist in order to perceive himself into being?

In a sense, Berkeley views us all as a dream in the mind of God (probably a nightmare), and we can sympathize with this notion. We sometimes feel we are a reflection of another person's view of us, that we do not look out from our eyes but mirror the image in theirs. Or we have a sense that it is impossible for the world to remain in existence if we are not there to perceive it. Sometimes we don't care what happens after we die (although we do leave wills) because everything depends on us. Rationally, we realize that life will go on, but deep inside it seems impossible. Has Berkeley struck a chord?

Perhaps Berkeley is ultimately following his orthodox religious beliefs, and his theory of knowledge is an ingenious rationalization for his faith, a piety clothed in empiricism.

## The Empiricism of David Hume

The Scottish philosopher David Hume appears to be a more straightforward empiricist than Berkeley, but his reliance on the senses eventually led him to an equally radical position. He ultimately became a skeptic with regard to knowledge, specifically cause and effect and our personal identity, as well as miracles and religion.

In contrast to Berkeley, Hume was an atheist, which seems more consistent with trusting the senses to reveal reality. But his gentle kindness made him a beloved figure in Scotland, so that he was "canonized" by the people as St. David. The place where his house stood in Edinburgh was named St. David's Square. Throughout his life he longed for literary fame, and he is remembered for his *History of England* as well as his philosophic thoughts, especially his *Treatise of Human Nature*.

Like the other empiricists, Hume thought that seeing is believing, or more precisely, that we only know what we perceive through the senses, and that we do not possess any knowledge prior to experience. "Adam, though his rational faculties be supposed, at the very first, entirely perfect, could not have inferred from the fluidity and transparency of water that it would suffocate him, or from the light and warmth of fire that it would consume him."

Everything we know comes from the senses, and ideas are different from sense impressions only by being less lively or vivid. "An experienced feeling or emotion is more pronounced than any idea of it." When we recall the original sensations we may think we are re-living it, but in fact we can "never reach the force and vivacity of the original sentiment."

This implies that we cannot conceive of time or space since we have no impression of them. We can perceive events but not time, and we have sensations of objects in space but not space itself. For the same reason, there is no genuine idea of the self.

Now it might seem that we are wholly free in the ideas we can conjure up — imagining monsters or creatures with fantastic shapes, but in actuality we can only "compound, transpose, augment, or diminish" the material furnished to us by sense experience. A centaur simply combines impressions of a horse and a man, just as a sphinx combines a lioness with the wings of an eagle. Also, if we lack a sense such as seeing or hearing, we cannot form an idea related to it. Someone who is blind cannot conceive of blue, and we can never explain b flat to a deaf person; colors and sounds must be experienced in order to be understood, and that holds true of all other ideas.

We may also think that our ideas follow one another in random order but Hume claimed there are "principles of association" that account for the way ideas succeed one another in our minds. Sometimes ideas are connected by *resemblance*, as when a picture reminds us of the person himself; or *contiguity* when we see an anchor chain and think of the anchor attached to it; and *cause and effect* is used when we see a glass of wine and imagine the enjoyment of sipping it. The mind does not roam from one thought to another randomly but according to fixed connections.

The last notion of causation is especially important to Hume, not just with regard to ideas in our minds but in explaining sequences. The past is a record of causes and effects, and we study it for guidance. In our everyday lives, causation teaches us not to walk on thin ice, that some diseases are contagious, and that we should stay away from skunks and porcupines.

In analyzing cause and effect, Hume developed his most controversial theory. He first makes a distinction between "relations of ideas" and "matters of fact." An example of a "relation of ideas" statement would be 'All circles are round,' 'Murals are on walls,' and 'Three times 5 equals half of 30.' These propositions simply show the relation between parts of the sentence; they "unpack" the subject term in the predicate so we can see what it implies. Although we cannot deny the truth of these statements, at least not without contradicting the terms, we are only talking about ideas not the external world. That is, 'All circles are round' is a necessary truth and "Circles are not round" is meaningless, but only because of the way we define the concept 'circle' that is, how we use the word.

"Matters of fact" are more important, because they make claims about reality. For example, 'The sun will rise tomorrow,' 'Horses like to eat clover,' and 'There are skyscrapers in New York City.' These sentences refer to actual things, and although they could be false, they are still matter-of-fact types of propositions. We can tell because, even if they are not true, they are meaningful. "That the sun will not rise tomorrow," Hume writes, "is no less intelligible a proposition, and implies no more contradiction, than the affirmation that it will rise."

Hume then argues that the truth of "matters of fact" statements depends on cause and effect. To prove a claim we cite some fact. That someone is standing in a dark room is proven by hearing his voice; that a man is out of the country is proven by the fact that we received a letter from him. Therefore, everything depends upon the validity of causation.

However, when we think about it, we never perceive a cause, and since empiricists believe that knowledge depends upon sense impressions, cause is not a genuine idea! We may believe we see one event causing another but, strictly speaking, that is not true.

For example, we think we see the balloon burst because it was punctured by the pin, the glass shattered because it hit the ground, and the light went on because we threw the switch, but all we really saw was a sequence of events. The skin of the balloon was pierced by the pin followed by the balloon bursting; the glass struck the ground then shattered; and after throwing the switch, the light went on. We did not actually see cause and effect but assumed that a temporal sequence was a causal connection.

As an empiricist, Hume does not believe there is a mysterious "causal power" in one event that compels another event to happen. Rather, what we mean by cause is that one event always precedes another. This builds up a psychological expectation, a habit of thought, so that we come to expect the second event following the first. However, there is no inevitability to the sequence, no necessary connection. "After the constant conjunction of two objects, heat and flame, for instance, weight and solidity, we are determined by custom alone to expect the one from the appearance of the other."

This view of cause and effect, as regular succession, is certainly contrary to ordinary assumptions. If a child cries when it is hurt, that seems a natural response to the injury, and if we lose our appetite after eating, we assume the meal was responsible. As Tom Stoppard remarked, St. Sebastian did not die of fright. To Hume, however, "If we believe that fire warms, or water refreshes, 'tis only because it costs us too much pain to think otherwise."

Regardless of its correctness, Hume's view of causation does not change science or our daily expectations. Nature is consistent and falls into predictable patterns, *although the explanation is different* for what happens. We cannot be sure of the future because events are not necessarily connected but we can have sufficient confidence that nature is uniform and regular. When we hit a nail with a hammer, we can expect that the nail will then go deeper into the wood.

Hume may not be right, but on empiricist grounds it is hard to refute the notion that causation is a mistake.

## Keeping Our Wits About Us

On the other side of the divide are the *rationalists* who distrust the evidence of the senses. In addition to the errors already cited, the rationalist points out that we perceive the earth as stationary. In point of fact, the planet is constantly moving, in several directions, and at enormous speeds. It rotates on its polar axis at 1,040 miles per hour, and rotates around the sun at 67,000 mph. The earth is also whirling on the spiral arms of the Milky Way galaxy at 490,000 mph, and as part of the expanding universe, it is traveling at a rate of 244,800 mph. But we do not perceive any of this motion; when we get out of bed in the morning, we do not need to steady ourselves. And we do not feel the earth wobble on its axis, or the way space stretches, making more of itself.

Not only are the senses untrustworthy, but they are also narrow. Life may be wider than what the senses reveal, or differently put, there may be things worth saying that cannot be proven empirically. Love, morality, soul, conscience, deity, mind, and so forth may be real but they are all beyond our perception. If we think straight, using our rational faculties, that could be a far more reliable method of knowing. Einstein relied heavily on *Gedankenexperiment* or thought experiments, such as riding on a beam of light, which led him to special relativity theory. We have never seen dark matter but it its existence is postulated to explain the spin of galaxies.

Certainly mathematics uses pure reason more than sense perception. In stating that $2x^2 + 4x^2 + x^2 = 7x^2$, there is no reference to anything that is squared. Science needs mathematics, but pure mathematics does not need science. Some mathematicians do believe that numbers are real. They do not mean "real numbers" as opposed to "imaginary numbers" such as the square root of -1, but that numbers are as real as rocks.

Plato is the arch rationalist, believing that our senses only reveal shadows, a physical world of imitations, and imperfect copies of an underlying reality. When we descend within our own minds we reach the truth, which we can then bring to light.

As Plato conceives it, there are two realities: the world of Sense, which means the physical world accessed by the senses, and Ideas or Forms or Universals, which are known to the mind. Surprisingly, he claims the latter is more real.

Every class of things has an Idea that corresponds to it. For example, there are horses in the world but there is also the Idea of a horse. Particular horses come into being, then pass out of existence, but the Idea of a horse remains. Even if horses became extinct, as happened to dinosaurs and dodo birds, we would still have the Idea of what a horse is.

Ideas, in fact, are eternal. They continue into the future even after a particular thing exemplifying it has vanished. And they not only succeed but precede the existence of things. For how could we recognize an object unless we already had the Idea of it in our minds? How could we separate a horse from other creatures without first knowing the meaning of horse? Whether we label it 'horse,' 'chevalle,' or 'caballo,' we could not identify objects as being horses without first understanding the concept of horse.

Not only are Ideas eternal, but they are also perfect. When we think of a horse we imagine one that is ideal in all respects, the perfect form of a horse, and because we have that model in mind, we are able to rate those we see. We can judge a specific horse as having a shallow chest, a sway back, poor conformation, and so forth. That assessment would be impossible unless we possessed the Idea of a perfect horse.

Plato doesn't just apply his analysis to horses. More importantly he argues that we recognize a beautiful object when we come across it because we already have an innate Idea of beauty, just as we know that kindness is better than cruelty because we understand the concept of goodness. Likewise, we can judge a statement as true because our brain can separate what is true from what is false. We can also imagine what a good form of government would be, by comparing existent ones to the ideal. This is the basis for his ideal state, as described in *The Republic*.

Ideas are therefore more real than physical things because they are eternal and perfect. Objects, which are finite and imperfect, are not unreal but contain a lower mode of reality. A painting is not as real as the object it depicts, and an object has less reality than the Idea it represents.

Plato maintained further that we never learn anything new. Rather, everyone is born with the fundamental Ideas embedded in their souls. What we call learning is actually remembering, that is, recalling to our consciousness what we already know. All learning is recollection.

But if our mind contains these notions, which are eternal and perfect, why is there disagreement between people (which is Locke's point)? Why are there constant conflicts about religion, politics, and morality, for example? Plato's answer is that although there is only one truth, some understand it more clearly, others dimly. By engaging in philosophic argument, we can get closer to the essential truth.

Plato illustrates his theory with his celebrated "allegory of the cave," expressed through the mouth of Socrates in one of his dialogues. He writes,

> Let me show you in a figure how far our nature is enlightened or unenlightened. Behold! Human beings living in an underground den, which has a mouth open toward the light and reaching all along the den; here they have been from their childhood, and have their legs and

necks chained so that they cannot move and can only see before them, being prevented by the chains from turning round their heads. Above and behind them a fire is blazing at a distance, and between the fire and the prisoners there is a raised way; and you will see, if you look, a low wall built along the way, like the screen which marionette players have in front of them, over which they show the puppets.

And do you see men passing along the wall carrying all sorts of vessels and statues and figures of animals made out of wood and stone and various materials which appear over the wall... [the prisoners] see only the shadows.

[Glaucon, the person to whom Socrates is speaking, remarks, "You have shown me a strange image, and they are strange prisoners." Socrates replies, "Like ourselves."]

And now look again, and see what will naturally follow if the prisoners are released and disabused of their error. At first, when any of them is liberated and compelled suddenly to stand up and turn his neck around and walk and look toward the fire light, he will suffer sharp pains; the glare will distress him, and he will be unable to see the realities of which in his former state he had seen only the shadows... Will he not fancy that the shadows which he formerly saw are truer than the objects which are now shown to him?

The prison house is the world of sight, the light of the fire is the sun, and you will not misapprehend me if you interpret the journey upwards to be the ascent of the soul into the intellectual world...The immediate source of reason and truth is the intellectual, and this is the power upon which he who would act rationally either in public or private life must have his eyes fixed.

It is not the material world that possesses the highest reality but the world of Ideas, the light that is known by reason. Everything else is shadows.

## The Rationalism of René Descartes

The French philosopher René Descartes is considered the father of modern philosophy which may seem strange since he is a 17th century thinker. But he refused to accept ideas based on authority, whether from the church, traditional thought, or celebrated books. In his major work, the *Meditations*, he expresses his need to prove things for himself, using reason as his touchstone. The senses are fallible but if we use reason and think straight, rejecting the warmed-over ideas of our teachers, then we will arrive at the truth of things.

For example, he used the example of wax to illustrate the superiority of rationalism over empiricism. Although a piece of wax can change in smell, color, shape, size, heat, and sound (when struck), we still recognize it to be same piece of wax. Since the sense qualities change, we cannot know it is the same wax by using our senses; we can only know it by our understanding. The rational mind apprehends reality.

Descartes passionately wanted knowledge that could not be doubted, certain, indubitable understanding. In this quest he was like a man whose head is being held under water, struggling for breath. He was desperate to find ideas so clear and distinct that they were indubitable. So he embarked on a program of "systematic doubt," questioning everything that could be doubted, including what had been taught as well as the evidence of his senses.

The *Meditations* are presented as a journal, inviting the reader to reason along with the writer in searching for the truth of things. He begins by examining the most obvious perceptions, his awareness that he is sitting in his chair in front of a fire with papers in his hands. Although this seems self-evident, nevertheless dreams can have a similar vividness, so he is not sure if he is awake or asleep. This is reminiscent of the Chinese sage, Lao-Tze who wrote, "The other night I dreamt I was a butterfly, flitting from flower to flower, and now I do not know if I was a man dreaming I was a butterfly, or if I'm now a butterfly dreaming I am a man."

Nevertheless, he reasons, even if he is dreaming, what he is dreaming about must be real. We cannot dream of anything we have not experienced in real life. But he stops himself again. Suppose that an evil demon were in charge of the world; he would delight in fooling us, making the content of our dreams an illusion. And even if God ruled the world, we still had no guarantee that we were in touch with actuality. For his own purposes, God could conjure up visions that would be indistinguishable from real life. So whether the deception is malicious or benevolent, we cannot be certain that our experiences are reliable.

In doubting everything Descartes is even led to question his own existence, declaring that maybe he does not exist. But here he draws the line. He reasons that if he thinks, then he must exist. Even if he is doubting or being deceived, he must exist to doubt or be deceived. Therefore this proposition, drawn from reason and not the senses, is necessarily true: "Cogito ergo sum" — I think, therefore I am.

Descartes then asks "But what am I?" He exists but what is his nature, and he answers "A thing which thinks...which doubts, understands, [conceives,] affirms, denies, wills, refuses, which also imagines and feels." And this conclusion too is impossible to doubt; we affirm it in the act of denying it.

But is "cogito ergo sum" a sound foundation on which to build a philosophic structure? It seems that Descartes has not proven that his whole self exists, including his body, but only his thinking mind, and then only when it is thinking. We certainly do not think all the time; as the old man said, "Sometimes I sit and think, and sometimes I just sit." Many people watch television, day dream, send text messages, and stop thinking altogether, and we do not think when we are asleep. Even if dreaming is considered a form of thinking, we do not dream the entire night.

Descartes, incidentally, never explained the relation between mind and body in a satisfactory way but divided the two in a doctrine known as "Cartesian dualism." Ever since, philosophers have been trying to show how two such radically different entities can interact to form a complete self.

In any case, Descartes' basic principle may be undeniable but it turns out to be rather trivial: that our mind exists while it is thinking. Perhaps we should choose rationalism over empiricism, but this argument does not prove it. Descartes avoided the weaknesses of sense perception, but sometimes we are so afraid of making the same mistakes that we make different ones.

Rationalism too has its problems because some truths of physics defy logic. That time can be slowed down by gravity makes little sense, any more than postulating "black matter" that we cannot see or explain. The best known, rational impossibilities come from quantum theory. According to experimental evidence, atoms and molecules exhibit the properties of both a particle and a wave. These are two disparate elements which together explain the phenomenon of light. But how can two contradictory ideas both be true? What's more, matter has been proven to go from one place to another without traveling through the intervening space. This is mind-boggling data that make us question whether the mind can be trusted to understand reality.

Niels Bohr, the Danish physicist, once said that the opposite of a correct statement is a false one, but the opposite of a profound truth is another profound truth. This implies the universe is not logical.

Empiricism and rationalism are usually considered the fundamental means of knowing, and when they conflict we have to make a choice. We must trust either what we see or what we think. Bertrand Russell, the 20th century British philosopher opted for empiricism saying "If you are an empiricist you will be partly right, but if you are a rationalist, you can be entirely wrong." He meant that Plato's system, for example, is internally consistent but it might not diagram reality at all.

However, maybe being confined to two choices is limiting, and we might want to break out of that binary box. We may prefer trusting our feelings or emotions, intuition or revelation, our instinctive reactions. Maybe we "just know" in a rush of understanding. We certainly don't decide where we want to live, what we want to do in life, or whether we love someone based on rational arguments. We seem to make choices outside of both ways of knowing.

The ball is now in your court, and you must play it as you see fit — but always according what makes sense.

# Chapter 4. The Existence of God: Are We Here By Chance Or By Design?

The philosophy of religion is the field that examines the claim that God and a spiritual world exists, along with a host of heavenly angels who will battle Satan at the End of Days. It evaluates the reality of this supernatural realm stretching beyond our natural one, the reliability of the Bible, the relation between faith and reason, and the nature of life after death. The philosophy of religion also asks whether prayer actually works, and how we can tell, and whether ethics is independent of religion or based on it. That is, it poses the question of whether a secular ethic has any foundation; and if non-believers can be good people, and if believers can commit atrocities. Is atheism a belief the way not collecting postage stamps is a hobby, or being bald is a hair color? Did Christ point to virtues that would nourish us, and did we, like a dog, look at his finger?

And how can we distinguish between "God spoke to me in a dream," and "I dreamt that God spoke to me"? The British philosopher Bertrand Russell, who was an atheist, was asked what he would say to God if they ever met, and he replied, "Not enough evidence, Lord, not enough evidence." We can't just believe what we want to be true, but what kind of evidence counts to prove or disprove God's existence?

We also wonder if God created us in his own image, and we returned the compliment. If triangles had a God, would it have three sides? This thought is expressed in Rupert Brooke's poem "Heaven":

Fish (fly-replete, in depth of June,
Dawdling away their wat'ry noon)
Ponder deep wisdom, dark or clear,
Each secret fishy hope or fear.
Fish say, they have their Stream and Pond;
But is there anything Beyond?
This life cannot be All, they swear,
For how unpleasant if it were!
One may not doubt that, somehow, Good
Shall come of Water and of Mud;
And, sure, the reverent eye must see
A Purpose in Liquidity.
We darkly know, by Faith we cry,
The future is not Wholly Dry.
Mud unto mud! — Death eddies near —
Not here the appointed End, not here!
But somewhere beyond Space and Time,
Is wetter water, slimier slime!
And there (they trust) there swimmeth One
Who swam ere rivers were begun,
Immense, of fishy form and mind,
Squamous, omnipotent and kind;
And under that Almighty Fin,
The littlest fish may enter in.
Oh! Never fly conceals a hook,
Fish say, in the Eternal Brook,
But more than mundane weeds are there,
And mud, celestially fair;
Fat caterpillars drift around,
And Paradisal grubs are found;
Unfading moths, immortal flies,
And the worm that never dies.
And in that Heaven of all their wish,
There shall be no more land, say fish.

According to the Bible and Judeo-Christian theology, the Western God is a perfect being, with every positive attribute. He was not born but always was, existing eternally; he is far beyond our understanding but also resides within us, maybe as our conscience; he is a person-like being rather than an abstract force, a father who has a son; and he is the only God in heaven and earth, a holy, sacred being who must be regarded with reverence. In addition, he is omnipotent or almighty, able to create heaven and earth, as well as being omniscient or completely wise. Above all, he is considered wholly good, loving his creatures on earth unconditionally.

But some problems immediately surface about these attributes, especially the last three.

If God is all-powerful then he can do anything, but could he make a square circle, or create the world and not create the world simultaneously? Can he do what is logically impossible? In this connection, logicians have posed the stone paradox: Could an omnipotent God make a stone so large he could not lift it? Whether we answer yes or no we find ourselves in a tangle. If he could not create such a stone, or if he could not lift such a stone, then he is not omnipotent. Perhaps God can perform feats of strength that are uncanny but cannot do what is logically contradictory. But it would be odd if an all-powerful God were limited by Aristotelian logic.

As for God being all-knowing, which means totally aware, could he ever do anything unexpected, surprise himself, or be shocked by human behavior? Also, omniscience implies knowledge of the past, the present, and the future, so God foresees both our actions and his own. But if he really knows what we will do, then we cannot do otherwise and we have no free will. He may not be forcing us to act, but what we do is fixed and inevitable or he could not foresee it. This implies that human beings we have the illusion of freedom but not the reality, and shouldn't be held responsible for their actions.

Christianity usually assumes we have been given free will, and that we are responsible for our decisions. But if the above analysis is correct, we cannot help what we do, and should not be condemned to hell or elevated to heaven because of our behavior. According to doctrine, the devil lets us satisfy the desires of the flesh and only asks that we forfeit our soul, and God will save our soul if only we surrender the pleasures of the body. But if providence governs everything, we have no control over our choices, neither the mortification of the flesh nor the purification of the spirit.

What about divine goodness and love, which seems the very essence of God. Here we encounter the stumbling block of "the problem of evil." The issue is that if God is completely powerful, wise, and good, then why do people suffer on earth from natural causes? Of course, some of our pain we bring on ourselves — cirrhosis of the liver from excessive drinking, a heart attack because of being overweight, STDs as a result of unprotected sex. But some of our suffering comes from the conditions we have been given on earth. We are subject to disasters such as earthquakes and hurricanes; to sickness such as leukemia and multiple sclerosis; attacks by dangerous animals such as bears and rattlesnakes, and some of the planet's terrain consists of jungles, swamps, and desserts. Here, we cannot blame ourselves, but if the world is God's creation, then he is accountable for it all. Why would a benevolent loving Father give his children an environment that causes so much misery? And why would he allow so much cruelty in his name — the Inquisition, the Crusades, religious wars, the burning of witches, slavery and human trafficking, terrorist attacks, the conversion of native peoples at the point of a gun. It is said of the Pilgrims that "first they fell upon their knees, then they fell upon the aborigines." Wouldn't a loving God want to intervene, at least in child abuse and atrocities?

We will discuss the proposed solutions to the problem of evil at a later point, but it stands as the greatest obstacle to faith.

## Does God Exist?

The primary question in the philosophy of religion is the existence of God, and there is a long list of arguments trying to prove that he is in fact a reality, arguments that arose principally during the Middle Ages. The "natural theologians" assumed that faith and reason were compatible, that "philosophy is the handmaid of theology" proving the truths of religious revelation. If belief and reason did conflict, then so much the worse for reason, but luckily there is no basic tension.

Some of the arguments are formal and complex, others natural and persuasive, appealing to our common sense. Let's begin with an example of the first, the "ontological argument," originally formulated by the medieval theologian St. Anselm in his *Proslogion*.

Anselm argues that he has an idea in his mind "than which none greater can be conceived." In other words, that he is thinking of a perfect being. And if he is thinking of such a being, which cannot be denied, then that being must have attributes of eternality, omnipotence, omniscience, and so forth. In addition, the idea of a perfect being must include existence; otherwise it would not be that than which none greater can be conceived. The conclusion, therefore, is that this being, or God, must exist.

At the time, some thinkers objected that this idea might exist in Anselm's mind alone, like imagining a unicorn or centaur. Today we could include Santa Claus, the Easter Bunny, and the Tooth Fairy as fictions that do not correspond to anything; they are real words that do not refer to real objects. But Anselm answered that if it his idea is imaginary, then he would not be thinking of a perfect being. He would then exchange his idea for one that has existence, and then we would have to admit that such a being is in fact existent. To argue that a perfect being might not be, would be like saying we can imagine water that isn't liquid, or a square without four sides. If we conceive of a perfect being, which is God, that perfection must include existence.

To put the point another way, a being that exists in reality as well as in our minds is greater than one that exists in our mind alone. So if we have the idea of a perfect being, that being must exist in fact and not only in our imagination. Perhaps we cannot conceive of absolute perfection, but whatever else it includes, existence must be part of it.

This is the kind of argument that makes our head spin, but Anselm thought that by working our way through the logic, every person can prove God's existence to himself.

But is his reasoning sound? Various philosophers have challenged the "proof" on the grounds that Anselm is confusing an idea with what it represents. The *idea* of a perfect being must contain the notion of existence or it would not be perfect as an idea, but that does not imply there is an existent being behind the idea. Anselm is confusing thought with reality, but they are on different levels. A word is not a thing, a map is not the land, and we cannot satisfy our appetite by reading a menu (unless we have an emotional problem). In the same way, we cannot argue that because existence must be part of the idea of a perfect being, the being that the idea stands for necessarily exists.

## The Cosmological Argument

St. Thomas Aquinas presents a more straightforward and accessible argument, in fact, he offers five arguments in two paragraphs of his Summa Theologica. Most of the arguments revolve around the idea of cause and effect. Everything that occurs is caused by some event that preceded it. We can always ask what caused this to happen, and what effect will it have. In fact, a cause-effect chain stretches backwards and forwards through time.

However, St. Thomas argues, the causal chain cannot go back and back forever. There cannot be an "infinite regress" of earlier causes, and prior causes, and still more ultimate causes. a "primum mobile" or prime mover must exist, and that initial force can only be God. He flicked the first domino that made all the other dominoes fall.

Aquinas, the "Doctor Angelicus," is the major theologian of Catholicism, exerting a tremendous influence on Church doctrine. He is the scholastic mind of religion, embracing the Greek thinker Aristotle and, in fact, "canonizing" him retroactively. He is himself considered a saint, receiving inspiration directly from God, and in Catholic education, if Aquinas did not write on something it must still be taught in conformity to his thought.

St. Thomas presents a series of "ways" of proving God's existence, some mentioning causation explicitly, others implying it. His first way is that of change, for anything that changes must be changed by something else, and that must be changed by something earlier. But this cannot go back endlessly. We are "forced eventually to come to a first cause of change not itself being changed by anything, and this is what everyone understands by *God*." The Lord is the unmoved mover.

With regard to the second way, Aquinas says "a series of causes cannot go on forever," that is, we cannot have a succession of earlier causes in an endless backwards chain. "So we are forced to postulate some first cause, to which everyone gives the name *God*."

The third way is somewhat more sophisticated, making use of the distinction between "contingency" and "necessity." A contingent thing depends upon something else in order to be. For example, a tree would not exist if it were not for moisture, sunlight, and nutrients in the soil; factories would not be built unless there was a demand for their product, the availability of bricks and mortar and personnel to operate it; and each of us would not have been born if our parents had not met. However, everything cannot be dependent on other things; something must exist necessarily, carrying the reason for its existence within its own being. "So we are forced to postulate something which of itself must be, owing this to nothing outside itself, but being itself." This, of course, is God. He is the ultimate reason for everything.

The fourth way stretches causation to include the existence of the *ideal* that then produces lesser qualities in objects. That is, "there is something which is the truest and best and most excellent of things, and hence the most fully in being." We grade objects according to this perfection, as in judging the worth of a person's life relative to the ideal human being. "Now when many things possess a property in common, the one most fully possessing it causes it in the others; fire, as Aristotle says, the hottest of all things, causes all other things to be hot." Aquinas therefore concludes, "So there is something that causes in all other things their being, their goodness, and whatever other perfections they have. And this is what we call *God*."

Aquinas's fifth way has a different character, acknowledging the concept of function. He asserts that all things appear to have a purpose in being. "Goal-directed behavior is observed in all bodies in nature, even those lacking awareness... But nothing lacking awareness can tend to a goal except it be directed by someone with awareness and understanding...and this we call *God*."

These arguments sound persuasive, but philosophers have not treated them kindly. The main criticism of the cosmological argument is that it rests on a self-contradiction. If everything has a cause, then so does God. And if God is an exception, then the world might also be an exception, in which case we have no need for God. In other words, to call God an uncaused cause contradicts the premise of the argument that all things have a cause. Why is the first cause exempt from this rule? Why must everything require an explanation but claim God's existence is self-explanatory?

This is not a sophisticated criticism but a child's question. If a child asks "Where did everything come from?" the religious parent answers, "God made it." The bright child is not satisfied and asks, "Who made God?" And if the parent says "No one made God, he always was," then the truly precocious child will say, "Then maybe everything always was, and God did not make it."

Furthermore we could ask why there cannot be an infinite regress of causes, just as there can be an infinite series of effects. The argument seems based on the common assumption that there had to be a start to everything but the arrow of time could be double-ended, going backwards as well as forwards, just as a mathematical series can be infinite. There is no first or last number, especially if one considers fractions and negatives. Similarly, there might not be a beginning just as there might not be an end; both are theoretically possible. Besides, events could be arranged in a loop, with the last effect being the first cause, like a snake swallowing its own tail.

Another criticism is that if there must be a start to the process, why identify that start with God? Couldn't there be a natural explanation, such as "big bang," a spontaneous, physical explosion of sufficient magnitude to create the universe? Do all natural events require a supernatural cause, or is that superfluous? And if we insist that something divine had to light the spark for big bang, then we can ask what caused that. This, of course, brings us back to square one, the infinite regress of causes.

But what are the chances of the universe developing as it did? In other words, why is there something rather than nothing? Stephen Hawking declared that "If the rate of the universe's expansion one second after big bang had been smaller by even one part in a hundred thousand million million, the universe would have collapsed into a hot fireball." However, if there were billions of big bangs, then it is more likely that one would have the conditions necessary for the development of the universe. In other words, chance can imitate order if the numbers are large, and Astronomical numbers are enormous.

### Earthly Design Implies a Divine Designer

A third major argument purporting to prove the existence of God has been labeled the teleological argument, and it is attributed to Aquinas as well as to a later thinker, William Paley.

When we look out at the world we do not see chaos and randomness but an orderliness characterizing everything. In fact, we have physical laws describing the rules governing matter, and we predict events as following from these laws. We know the apple will fall from the tree in accordance with the law of gravity, that a magnet will attract iron filings, and a stone on a string will whirl outwards by centrifugal force.

When we regard the stars and planets, we see them arranged in a system, and our planet is positioned in just the right relationship to the sun. Any closer, we would sizzle; any further out, we would freeze to death. If the earth were too hot, water would vaporize; too cold, it would become ice. And if our planet were too large a rock, it would collapse; too small, it would spin off into space. What's more, we need the right gases in our atmosphere in order to breathe, and we have those gases; we need an atmosphere with moisture to sustain ourselves, and we have the perfect amount of precipitation; and we need to eat to live, and edible plants and animals have been provided. The beauty of the earth alone shows the brush strokes of God.

Animals need various characteristics in order to survive, and each creature has what it requires. The giraffe has a long neck to reach the leaves at the tops of trees, whereas the turtle has a short neck that it can retract into its shell in case of danger; birds escape predators because they can fly, whereas gazelles rely on their speed; chameleons can change color as camouflage, whereas the zebras have stripes that enable individual animals to blend into the herd; and the rhinoceros and elephant have thick hides which are a protective armor. Every animal has been given its own particular qualities that enable it to live.

Our own bodies are wonders of perfection, the parts working in ideal harmony. The nervous system, digestive system, muscular system, respiratory system, skeletal system, and so forth, all mesh together, as do our liver, kidneys, heart, brain, lungs, and other organs. The human eye alone is a marvel that allows the perception of light and the ability to gauge depth and distinguish ten million colors.

Since we see evidence of design wherever we turn, this implies that there has to be a cosmic designer responsible for making everything. The harmonious order of the parts, and the degree of complexity could not have come about by chance. An intelligent mind must have constructed the whole, and it governs all of creation. As the astronomer Fred Hoyle puts it, to attribute the structure of the universe to luck is like thinking a Boeing 747 was assembled by a hurricane from a scrap yard.

This argument is presented most effectively by William Paley in his famous "watchmaker analogy." He argued that if we found a watch on the ground in perfect working order, we would be forced to conclude "that the watch must have had a maker ... who formed it for the purpose which we find it actually to answer."

> In crossing a heath, suppose I pitched my foot upon a *stone*, and were asked how the stone came to be there, I might possibly answer, that for anything I knew to the contrary it had lain there forever; nor would it perhaps, be very easy to show the absurdity of this answer. But suppose I had found a *watch* upon the ground, and it should be inquired how the watch happened to be in that place, I should hardly think of the answer which I had before given, that for any thing I knew the watch might have always been there. Yet why should not this

answer serve for the watch as well as for the stone; why is it not as admissible in the second case as in the first? For this reason, and for no other, namely that when we come to inspect the watch, we perceive — what we could not discover in the stone — that its several parts are framed and put together for a purpose, i.e., that they are so framed and adjusted as to produce motion, and that motion so regulated as to point out the hour of the day; that if the different parts had been differently shaped from what they are, or placed after any other manner or in any other order than that in which they are placed, either no motion at all would have been carried on in the machine , or none which would have answered the use that is now served by it. The inference we think is inevitable, that the watch must have had a maker — that there must have existed, at some time and at some place or other, an artificer or artificers who formed it for the purpose which we find it actually to answer, who comprehended its construction and designed its use.

By analogy, when we encounter the intricate structure of the world we must infer that it too had a maker; the parts could not have fallen together by accident in just the right combination. If there is a perfectly functioning system, that has to be more than chance. "There cannot be a design without a designer," Paley wrote, "contrivance without a contriver; order without choice; arrangement without anything capable of arranging." That is, unless we assume "the presence of intelligence and mind" the world in its orderliness cannot be explained.

Such reasoning seems undeniable, almost too obvious. By contrast, the assumption that everything occurred by some stroke of luck, strains all credibility. Nevertheless, the argument's validity has been challenged by a number of philosophers, especially following the writings of Charles Darwin. In his *Origin of Species*, Darwin offered an alternative model, a simple, natural explanation for the order that exists. His writings caused a paradigm shift in modern thought; his book changed the world.

Darwin argued that natural selection provides the explanation for the structure of the world and everything in it. With regard to animals, each creature that is alive today has the traits it needs, because if it didn't, it would not have continued to live. Those that were fittest, through chance mutations and adaptations, were able to survive and to pass their characteristics on to their offspring. Those that were not fit, perished in the struggle for survival. Many species became extinct — as many as 99% or 5 billion. Therefore it is not surprising that every animal we know has what it needs to maintain itself in existence.

To regard this as uncanny would be like being surprised that all Olympic winners are good athletes, or that all major cities are located near water. If the winners were not good athletes, they would not have won the Olympics, and major cities developed because they were built on large bodies of water. It is not a remarkable coincidence that it takes the earth exactly one year to orbit the sun, and that a day is exactly twenty-four hours...

Evidence continues to be amassed of natural selection through survival of the fittest, so that Darwin's theory of evolution is a virtual law today, assumed by almost all scientists. "Missing links" continue to be discovered to fill in the picture, making the still photographs into a film. Evolution can even account for the extinction of species such as dinosaurs and the flightless dodo bird. Dinosaurs were deprived of their source of plant food by an asteroid strike; it sparked a conflagration and threw up a cloud of dust, obscuring the sun's light and killing all vegetation. The dodo bird did not have sufficient defenses against hunters as well as against the predation of rats, pigs, and monkeys. Today we know about extinct species, because of fossil remains, and each species died out because it could not meet the challenges of the environment.

The explanation that God called back certain creatures at various times seems less convincing. An omniscient God would not change his mind and recall the triceratops, stegosaurus, and tyrannosaurus in order to try mammals instead. Similarly, it seems improbable that God made the earth with dinosaur imprints, or scattered other fossils on earth to test our faith. It is possible that this happened, just as *for all we know* oysters are doing differential equations, and hibernating bears are reviewing the periodic table of the elements, but *as far as we know* these things are not true.

As for human beings, Darwin presented evidence that humans descended from primates according to the same laws of natural selection. Favorable adaptations occurred due to chance variations. Our limbs were once a pseudopod protruding from protoplasm for locomotion and grasping; our eyes were light-sensitive cells; our hand was once a scaly fin or hairy paw. We evolved from human-like apes, flaking obsidian for sharp spears all the way to astronauts rocketing to the moon and manning space stations. The human brain now contains 80 billion neurons — as numerous as the stars in a galaxy.

Some theologians have suggested that man might have originated from primates but was quickly adopted by God; however, this seems like a rear-guard action. What's more the human body does not seem a perfect mechanism, one that an all-knowing God would produce. It contains a number of imperfections, from the time of birth through ageing and death. Otherwise, we would not have such an enormous medical establishment as well as corporate laboratories and pharmaceuticals.

The medical evidence of fetal development also lends credence to evolutionary theory. At various stages of gestation, the fetus has gill indentations in its neck, webbed fingers and toes, fine body hair called lanugo, a tail that drops off (in most cases), and a depression below the nose called the philtrum, the relic of a snout. This is why biologists have said "ontogeny recapitulates phylogeny"; the fetus in its growth goes through all the stages of human evolution.

With regard to the earth, there would not be life on the planet if it were not 93 million miles from the sun, have a protective magnetic field, atmospheric gases that can be breathed, and plants and animals to eat. Earth happened to be perfectly positioned, not too hot or too cold, a Goldilocks phenomenon. Other planets were not so fortunate, although there are 17 billion planets in our galaxy of similar size and composition that might have sustained life. Asteroids with icy tails bombarded the earth, and water was released by the impact, creating oceans, lakes and clouds; without an envelope of water surrounding our planet, no organism could exist. Asteroids also brought amino acids and carbon that are the building blocks of life. Again, the argument for divine creation seems to be upside down. It is not remarkable that the earth has ideal conditions for life, but that if the conditions had not been ideal, there would be no life.

There was also a dispute concerning time. Sir John Lightfoot claimed that the universe began at exactly 9:00, October 23$^{rd}$, 3927 B.C., but Darwin maintained there had been an evolution over millions of years. Contemporary scientists have confirmed this through techniques such as radioactive decay. Astronomers now estimate the start of the universe at about 13.8 billion years ago, the sun as forming 9 billion years later, and the earth as 4.5 billion years old. Our planet will continue to exist for another 5 billion years, then be obliterated when the sun becomes a red giant and swallows the earth.

The oldest skeleton of the genus *homo* was carbon dated as 4.4 million years old. *Homo sapiens* (or homo but not very sapien) originated some 200,000 years ago; the cave paintings at Chauvet alone date from 35,000 years ago. And species were not made through a single act of creation at a fixed point in time, but new species developed over millions of years. The higher apes, specifically bonobos, are our closest relative, as shown by hominid fossils.

There are other criticisms of the teleological argument, as there are of the ontological and cosmological proofs, but evolution is the major one. Maybe God has many names, and we are distracted by the multiplicity of Churches; the U.S. alone has at least 48 denominations and 350,000 religious congregations. But critics say that if we accept creationism, we should also accept the stork theory of birth.

In any case, each of the arguments faces serious objections. Some philosophers believe, in fact, that defending an idea always breeds a doubt of it. No one ever questioned the existence of God until St. Thomas tried to prove it.

But where does this leave us? Should we believe in God until it is disproven, or should we not believe until it is proven? Which is the default position? And what would be admissible evidence for establishing the existence of a being beyond our understanding? If we believe by faith, that gives us no protection against mistakes and could lead to violence. Terrorists who flew planes into the World Trade Center, and suicide bombers who kill hundreds of innocent people are motivated by blind faith. We don't want to think the universe is cold and dark, and that the earth contains neither justice nor meaning, but neither can we construct reality closer to our heart's desire.

## Can We Reconcile Human Suffering and Divine Love?

As indicated earlier, an equal difficulty in the philosophy of religion is the problem of evil. For there to be a problem we must assume that God is omnipotent, omniscient, and omni-good, and that some aspects of the earth cause suffering to people. If God is all-powerful, he could prevent the misery; if he is all-knowing, he would be aware of whatever happens and if he is wholly loving, he would not want people to live in pain. Why, then, is there suffering from natural causes?

There is, in fact, very little peace, even if there is order in the universe. The Big Bang was violent and so was the inflation during the first second of creation. Stars explode, meteors bombard the surface of planets, and our sun provides heat and light through continual nuclear explosions. The cosmos is not only creative but destructive; the music of the spheres is probably a dissonant roar. And according to chaos theory, disorder, randomness, and turbulence are rampant, interfering with scientific prediction.

Natural evils can be sorted into several categories but they all concern the physical world we inhabit rather than man's inhumanity to man. As the Christian writer C.S. Lewis said, "It is men not God who have produced racks, whips, prisons, slavery, guns, bayonets, and bombs." The atrocities of human history can be accounted for in terms of free will, which we can use for good or ill. If we choose to abuse it, that is not God's fault, although he might be guilty of neglect or complicity; because of free will, his hands were not tied. But we are concerned with natural evils which are part of the earth that God gave us as our home. This is the world that must be explained because it involves considerable suffering from our natural surroundings that are ultimately attributable to God.

One category of natural evils is *catastrophes and disasters*. People are afflicted by hurricanes, tornadoes, floods, earthquakes, tsunamis, avalanches, blizzards, droughts, volcanic eruptions, landslides, lightning strikes, forest fires, killing cold, burning heat, and other "acts of God." For example, 300,000 people were killed in a cyclone in India in 1839; 900,000 were killed in the Yellow River Flood in 1887; 136,000 when Krakatoa erupted in 1883. More recently, a cyclone killed 500,000 in Pakistan in 1970, 655,000 were killed in the Chinese earthquake of 1978, and in 2005 some 200,000 were killed in the Indonesian tsunami, and 23,000 in a Pakistan earthquake. In 2008 a cyclone in Burma killed 100,000. The Haiti earthquake in 2010 left 200,000 dead, and Hurricane Katrina left 2000 dead in New Orleans. These figures do not include those injured or who lost their homes or their livelihood. Some 20 million were affected by the floods in Pakistan in 2010 when a quarter of the country was underwater, and that same year floods and landslides in China affected 300 million. The toll in human misery is enormous, and invites questions as to why such disasters happen if a loving God governs all.

*Sickness and disease* constitutes another class of evils when they are not caused by people themselves, that is, by smoking, drugs, alcohol, junk foods and so forth. In this category we can place the illnesses that naturally afflict us: polio, smallpox, tuberculosis, epilepsy, cystic fibrosis, rheumatism, glaucoma, hepatitis, measles, Parkinson's disease, malaria, multiple sclerosis, influenza, cancer, cholera, typhoid fever, pneumonia, crippling arthritis, and so forth, as well as genetic disorders of blindness, deafness, deformed limbs, and brain damage such as anencephaly. The Bubonic plague (the Black Death) killed 25 million people in 1330, one third of Europe's population; the Great Plague of Seville in 1696 killed 700,000; the Great Plague of London in 1665 killed 100,000, 20% of the population. About 13,000 people died of Yellow fever in 1878; and up to 100 million Americans died in the 1918–19 influenza epidemic. Malaria kills 300 million people a year, 10,000 died of the Ebola virus in Africa, and one and a half million die of AIDS, originally contracted from the blood of monkeys. Eight million people get cancer every year. The Bible is filled with accounts of plagues and pestilences that destroy whole peoples.

Watching the suffering of anyone we love can have a profound effect on our faith, and from the standpoint of civilization, we wonder why outstanding people should suffer. Why should Beethoven go deaf and Monet go blind? The most agonizing cases, of course, are those of the young, the most innocent and vulnerable members of the human race. Parents are desperate to protect their children, but even infants suffer injuries as well as genetic defects, disabling diseases, and physical and mental handicaps. The earthly parent does everything in his power to alleviate the pain, and wonders why God does not do more to help — and why the sickness had to happen in the first place.

*Hostile environments* make up a third classification of evils. Here we can include deserts, jungles, swamps (with quicksand), Arctic wastes, and barren land not fit for crops, herds, or livestock. We can get cancer from the sun and from radon in the ground; some people have allergies to plants and animals; and some plants, such as poison ivy, oak, and sumac, are toxic to most people. The earth is 70% water and we are land mammals who have not been given gills. What's more, 97% of that is salt water, with fresh water available only in lakes and rivers; fresh water is inaccessible to us in underground streams and frozen ice, glaciers, the Arctic, and Antarctic.

There are also *wild animals* on earth that attack us if we invade their territory, threaten their young, or cross their paths when they are hungry. There are lions, leopards, tigers, cougars, and panthers; grizzly, black, and polar bears; the rhinoceros, elephant, and hippopotamus; wolves, hyenas, and wild boar; sharks, octopus, barracuda, alligators, and saltwater crocodiles; rattlesnakes, copperheads, king cobras, coral snakes, and bushmasters; scorpions, centipedes, tarantulas, the brown recluse, and the black widow. Animals will trample, claw, gore, maim, and kill us; a myriad of insects will sting and bite us, transmitting diseases such as malaria, Dengue fever, and West Nile virus; and microscopic bacteria and viruses can be deadly to the human body. No place on earth is free from animals that are destructive to man, any more than there are places immune to disasters or disease. "Nature is red in tooth and claw," Tennyson writes, "So careful of the type she seems, so careless of the single life." We wonder why there should be predators and prey, carnivores as well as herbivores when meat-eaters causes so much bloodshed.

Finally, we have the natural evil of *death and decay*. We wonder why human beings must be mortal, living only "four score years and ten," and why dying often involves anguish and pain, depriving us of our dignity. And we wonder why so much of our lives must be spent sleeping. If we sleep 8 hours a night, and live for 60 years we spend 20 years asleep. As Byron phrases it, "Death, so called, is a thing which makes men weep/ And yet a third of life is passed in sleep." Furthermore, we wonder why we must undergo the metamorphosis of ageing, where our skin becomes wrinkled, our body is disfigured, and our face becomes a caricature of ourselves. Our arteries too begin to harden, affecting the functioning of our brain. As Rochefoucauld writes, "The defects of the mind, like those of the face, grow worse with age." And the fact that someone we love will one day be a skeleton makes our love poignant and tragic.

As one writer said, it would be better for God's reputation if he did not exist, because he has a lot to answer for.

The goodness of God and the pain of people seem incommensurate, but several theologians have tried to reconcile the two. One proposed explanation is that our suffering is punishment for our sins. Beginning with the story of Adam and Eve in *Genesis*, we have repeatedly disobeyed God, rebelling against his commands. He created us "from the dust of the ground, and breathed into our nostrils the breath of life," and gave us the paradise of Eden, asking only that we not eat from a particular tree. But man defied the will of God, and through the enticement of the devil speaking through a snake, ate the forbidden fruit. With that, the first human beings were expelled from the Garden of Eden and, ever after, their descendants have to endure a world of hardship and death. "In Adam's fall/ We sinned all." And if we are not saved through works, grace, or the sacrament of baptism, we could burn in hell for all eternity

Was Eve tempted by the snake or by the fruit, usually considered an apple? The snake could be "that serpent reason," or a phallic symbol, suggesting sexual temptation, especially since Adam and Eve were suddenly ashamed of their nakedness. Or the apple could represent possessions, on a Marxist interpretation, private property. Customarily it is considered forbidden knowledge, especially the knowledge of good and evil.

An immediate question about this account is why subsequent generations should have to suffer because of the sins of their great, great grandparents? In our criminal justice system, One person is never be punished for the crimes of another; that is unjust and would never hold up in court. So why should anyone today be cursed with original sin and have to endure a world of punishment in the form of catastrophes, sickness, deformity, decrepitude and so forth? The Bible does say, "I the Lord thy God am a jealous God, visiting the iniquity of the fathers upon the children unto the third and fourth generation," but this seems vindictive and unfair. What's more, Adam and Eve should not be punished before they knew good from evil, and a loving parent would never dangle the forbidden fruit in front of their children, then punish them for yielding to temptation.

Some theologians treat the Fall as a "felix culpa" or happy fault, planned and foreseen by God. He operated on the assumption that a redeemed world is far better than an innocent one. But if it were planned and foreseen, why penalize the human race.

Another version of this explanation has to do with present day sinfulness, which also deserves to be punished. The wars and genocides, violence on the street, rape and theft, torture and exploitation — the whole catalogue of assaults, justifies retribution by a just God. We see examples of God's retaliation for sin in the Flood, in Sodom and Gomorrah, and above all in the notion of Hell, and this shows the model for the disasters that afflict us.

In fact, one 17th century philosopher, G. W. Leibniz, maintained this was the best of all possible worlds, one that has the precise amount of suffering needed relative to man's sinfulness. This "optimism" was parodied in *Candide* where Voltaire wonders, if this is the best possible world, what can the others be like? A retributive system is also expressed in the Hindu law of karma whereby people are reincarnated in a higher or lower caste depending upon the moral quality of their previous lives.

To think of suffering as a response to wrongdoing seems in accord with our experience as children. If we go outdoors in winter without a coat and then get sick, our parents might tell us that it serves us right; it's what we deserve, poetic justice. We all carry a weight of actual or pathological guilt within us, so that every sickness means we have atoned for that much. And using the paradigm of our courts, we know we have been condemned to death, and working our way backwards, we wonder what we have done to deserve this. It is then easy to imagine a paradise that was lost because we disobeyed our heavenly father.

However, this answer does not seem sound, mainly because the distribution of punishments is askew. The worst people are not punished most severely, and may not suffer at all, whereas the best people can undergo a series of misfortunes. We try to make our institutions fair, but as we sometimes say to one another, life itself is not fair. Hospitals are not filled with sinners, and those on the street are not the most virtuous. We cannot say that only awful people are drowned by tsunamis, buried under avalanches, or struck by lightning. In Robert Frost's verse play, *The Masque of Reason*, God visits Job and says, "I've been meaning to thank you these thousands of years for teaching mankind a very valuable lesson: that people do not always get what they deserve."

The minister Jerry Falwell claims that the destruction of the World Trade Center was punishment by God for "pagans, abortionists, feminists, gays, lesbians, the A.C.L.U., and banning prayer in schools." But did the three thousand people in those buildings really deserve to die, any more than those on the streets? Would a benevolent God be that vengeful? And wouldn't a lightning rod on a church steeple show a lack of confidence?

Another proposed explanation is that suffering builds character. If a person works hard, faces challenges, and overcomes obstacle, then they develop into fine people, whereas if life is always comfortable, then there's no incentive to grow. Stumbling blocks are stepping stones, problems are really challenges, difficulties offer opportunities. As Machiavelli said, "soft climates produce soft men." God in his wisdom knows this; therefore he has made the earth a place of "soul making." The environment is hard but not overwhelming, and the evils that exist are stimulants to succeed.

This is in keeping with conventional wisdom. We sometimes think that Whatever hurts is beneficial, while pleasure is decadent, threatening our character. The worst tasting medicine does the most good, and people in northern states welcome snow and ice; it is the secret of Yankee discipline. G. B. Shaw writes in *Man and Superman*, "The British always think they're being moral when in fact they're only uncomfortable." Athletes know if there's no pain, there's no gain, and they must not only want to win but want to practice in order to win. And we have the examples of Stephen Hawking, Itzhak Perlman, Franklin Roosevelt, Ray Charles, and others who would not have become outstanding people if it weren't for their handicaps.

This explanation seems sound, but is it true that whatever doesn't kill us makes us stronger, or does it sometimes make us weaker? Do people always improve if they lose their home in a tornado or if they contract cancer, or can they become embittered or crushed by the experience? It seems that some are made better by suffering but others are made worse, and probably more people are ruined by suffering than elevated by it. Trial by fire can cause fatal burns, and to argue "whom God loveth he chasteneth" smacks of Stockholm syndrome.

If someone is drowned in a flood, including the biblical Flood, they cannot then learn the lesson that pain teaches, and if having a paralyzed child makes the parents better people, that is an awful means to a beneficial end — even if the parents then contribute to research in cerebral palsy. Tennyson writes, "That not a worm is clove in vain... Or but subserves another's gain," but why must the good of one creature depend on the death of another? Sacrificing some to improve others is not a moral system. What's more, there is also the problem of distribution. Those who would benefit from problems may not experience many, and those who cannot bear very much are sometimes overwhelmed.

Besides, even if we need difficulties in order to grow, our psychological makeup could have been designed differently. Our character might have been improved by being drawn upwards toward greater achievement, not goaded by pain. The donkey can be led forward by the carrot; it does not need the stick. What's more, many people in history have developed fine characters without experiencing much suffering — Aristotle, Shakespeare, da Vinci, Shelley, and so forth. It is possible, therefore, to develop a fine character without overcoming great obstacles.

Another suggested explanation is that contrasts are necessary for appreciation We cannot appreciate a sunny day unless we've experienced rainstorms; we cannot appreciate a solid meal unless we've gone hungry; and we cannot value our health unless we've been sick. Without a comparison, we take life for granted. In other words, we are only thankful for our blessings in contrast to our afflictions. Since God wants us to enjoy our lives, he has introduced evils so that we can recognize the good when we experience it.

This also sounds like a plausible answer, but do we need the negative to appreciate the positive? Infants appear to enjoy milk without having first tasted castor oil, and not just because they are hungry; they would not relish sand or vinegar nearly as much. Milk has a naturally pleasurable taste that does not require a comparison to be enjoyed. Similarly, if we were burned at the stake we would recognize that as bad, and not just in contrast to a cool, summer breeze.

We might appreciate the good *more* relative to the bad, but that's not to say we could not appreciate it at all. And if we had the choice, we would rather appreciate our health less and do without awful diseases.

Furthermore, we have far more pain on earth than we need in order to value pleasure. An occasional cold may be necessary to appreciate good health, but we do not require tuberculosis, muscular dystrophy, cancer, Alzheimer's, and so forth. In other words, the evil on earth is excessive relative to the benefit it provides.

And even if contrasts are necessary for appreciation, opposites are not. That is, having partly clear days with temperature in the 60°s might be required for us to value sunny days in the 70°s, but we do not need sub-zero temperatures. In other words, contrasts can occur among shades of good, and the least good does not become bad. A taco dinner is not awful in comparison to fine French cuisine; it is simply not as good it would be bad if we came down with Ptomaine poisoning.

At this point we might want to throw up our hands and say, "We cannot comprehend these things." Since we are finite, limited, earth-bound, skin-bound creatures, we cannot hope to read the mind of God. Humans are simply unable to judge, but we must believe that the world is good in ways that are beyond our understanding. From the standpoint of eternity, *sub specie eternitatis*, the universe has a benevolent purpose; the symphony is richer for having some dissonance. We simply must have faith that the scheme is good.

This response is understandable, but it does not help us escape the problem. For if we cannot judge, then we cannot judge the scheme as good or bad. If our brain is too feeble or corrupt to understand, we cannot reach any conclusion. It is self-contradictory to say that we are unable to judge, therefore God is good. All we can conclude from "We do not know" is, "We do not know." That is, if we undercut our ability to comprehend, we are left empty-handed. We cannot even say there is a God, much less a benevolent one. Things might be even worse than we imagine.

The problem of evil therefore remains a problem, and one that we must work through if we are to believe in a supernatural order. Robert Browning said, "God's in his heaven, all's right with the world," which implies that if all's not right with the world, then God's not in his heaven.

Should we believe in religion because it offers comfort? But it is only comforting if we are convinced it is true. We can't persuade ourselves that we don't know what we do know, even for peace of mind. In the end, lying to ourselves is never satisfying; self-deception collapses of its own weight. If we are to believe, it must be for good reasons.

The ball is now in your court, and you must play it as you see fit — but always according to what is reasonable.

# Chapter 5. The Fair Distribution of Wealth: Freedom vs. Equality

Except for hermits, solitaries, and monks, most people live amongst others in society. Aristotle, in fact, defined human beings as political and civic animals. And since we interact with our fellow creatures, our actions often have consequences for them as well as ourselves. This fact is obvious, but it implies that our decisions as to how to live are public as well as private. We do not exist in a vacuum or a hermetically sealed box but affect others by our behavior, and we must decide what would be good for them as well as for ourselves. Our well being is connected to the welfare of others, for the world is an interconnected network.

One area that concerns us is the equitable distribution of wealth and income — wealth meaning everything a person owns, income referring to what a person earns from work as well as from dividends, interest, rents, and royalties. It is no secret that wealth and income are not evenly distributed. We also know that the economic disparity has increased in our nation and among countries of the world. Norway, the world's richest country, is 496 times richer than Burundi. In our country the gap between rich and poor is, in fact, the widest since the 1940s. For nearly three quarters of a century the rich have gotten richer, the poor have gotten poorer, and the wealth of the middle class has slowly eroded. According to a PEW poll in 2012, the middle class is shrinking, having lost 40% of its net worth and almost 18% of its housing equity over the past 10 years. Joint family income has also decreased over the same period.

Within the U.S. economists report that the top 1% of earners received 17% of all national income in 2003, and the figure rose to 21.3% in 2006. Compared to 1982, that is an increase of 12.8%. Their annual income climbed by 86.2% while their tax bill decreased by $50 billion. Meanwhile, the Center for Economic and Policy Research reports, the poorest fifth of American families became 8% poorer. The median income across the country fell, so that the period between 2000 and 2010 was a "lost decade" for most Americans. The top 0.1% — that's 160,000 families — have more combined income than the poorest 120 million people.[1]

Over the past 10 years the compensation of chief executive officers has increased almost 300% while production workers have gained 4.3%. According to *Business Week*, the ratio of C.E.O. pay to that of a factory worker rose from 42:1 in 1960 to 531:1 in 2000. This is a far larger ratio than any other developed country. In Europe, by comparison, the ratio is about 25:1. As of 2010 the median compensation for C.E.O.s in the U.S. rose to $3.9 million.

The Nobel Prize winning economist Paul Samuelson used the following metaphor to dramatize the difference: "If we were to make an income pyramid out of child's blocks with each layer representing $1000 of income, the peak would be far higher than the Eiffel Tower, but most of us would be within a yard of the ground."

In 1986 the 18 million poorest families received $93 billion while the 18 million top families made $903 billion — nearly ten times as much. According to the U.S. Bureau of the Census, the families in the top 20% income group now take home 43.5% of the national income, which is the highest level ever. Meanwhile the income share of the bottom 60% has fallen to 32.4% — its lowest level since 1947 when figures were first collected — and 46.2 million people fell below the poverty line in 2014.[2]

In terms of wealth ownership, the top 1% of households owned 34.6% of privately held wealth, and the next 19% (the managerial, professional, and small business owners) hold 50.5%. This means that 20% of the people own 85% of the nation's wealth, leaving only 15% for the bottom 80% (wage and salary workers). Financial wealth, that is, total net worth minus the value of one's home, reached 42% for the top 1% of households.

Furthermore, "The top 1% hold 38.3% of all privately held stock, 60.6% of financial securities, and 62.4% of business equity. The top 10% have 80% to 90% of stocks, bonds, and trust funds, and over 75% of commercial real estate. Since financial wealth counts as far as the control of income-

[1] Johnston, D. C. *'04 Income in U.S. Was Below 2000 Level. New York Times*, Nov. 28, 2006, p C-1.
[2] Wolf, E. N. *Recent Trends in Household Wealth in the United States - an Update to 2007. Working Paper No. 589.* Annandale-on-Hudson, NY: The Levy Institute of Bard College, 2010.

producing assets is concerned, we can say that just 10% of the people own the United States of America."[1]

As far as the rest of the world is concerned, only Switzerland, at 71.3%, tops the U.S. in the degree of wealth held by the top 10% of the people. By comparison, America's top 10% owns 70.8% of the wealth, Denmark 65.0%, France 61.0%, Sweden 58.6%, U.K. 56.0%, Canada 53.0%, Norway 50.5%, Germany 44.4%, and Finland 42.3%.

## Does Economic Inequality Indicate an Unfair System?

Clearly, wealth and income are distributed unequally, but that in itself does not prove the system is unjust. Neither does the growing gap between rich and poor. The system would only be unjust if everyone did not have the same chance to succeed, if the American promise of equal opportunity was not a reality. Positively put, the distribution is fair if wealth and income depended upon an individual's ability, effort, skills, discipline, and similar factors within the person's control, that is, if economic success was equally available to all in a free and open market.

In considering the question of distributive justice, we know that different people are born with different traits. Furthermore, we cannot control this biological inheritance short of a *Brave New World* where people are genetically engineered to match society's needs. Fertility clinics are beginning to offer embryos with a certain eye or hair color, hand-eye coordination, intellectual capability, keen sense perception, artistic talent, and a clean bill of health, but so far the choices in the DNA databanks are limited. Aside from tinkering with our DNA, the ethical question is whether individuals of equal ability have an equal opportunity. If a bright, energetic, skilled and motivated person works hard in school and on the job, does he or she have the same chance to succeed as an able person from a privileged background? Is the American dream still alive and well, a society in which opportunities are available to all, and people receive what they deserve?

The foundation of our society is the ethical assumption that people should get their just deserts. It is a retributive system of rewards and punishments, meted out fairly. If someone is convicted of grand larceny, say armed robbery, then a sentence should be handed down that is commensurate with the offense. Allowing for previous convictions, the age of the offender, and so forth, the person is given the appropriate prison sentence. On the other hand, if someone has been law-abiding and industrious, exhibiting virtues of enterprise, initiative, and skill, then the person should be rewarded for his or her efforts. In our society that means not only respect but the benefits that accrue to wealth and status. The person has fulfilled his part of the

[1] http://www2.ucsc.edu/whorulesamerica/power/wealth.html

bargain, played by the rules of the economic game, and therefore deserves financial success. Bad luck and the vagaries of the marketplace might present obstacles, but the system generally should work in his favor. In moral terms, people should benefit from their achievements.

We might have adopted other economic models. Instead of giving people what they deserve, we might have chosen a Marxist approach and given people what they need. A welfare state could have provided a more comprehensive safety net for the poor, the sick, the disabled, and the old. That would have been more charitable, less Darwinian and more Christian.

In a Marxist system the governing principle is "from each according to his abilities, to each according to his needs." The fact that you have a naturally high intelligence does not entitle you to a larger slice of the pie. Rather, it places a greater responsibility upon you to give to society, precisely because you have more to give. This system is frequently accused of eliminating any incentive to work since your income is not a function of your efforts. However, the Marxist replies that material self-interest may not be the only incentive for work. People can also be motivated by recognition, job satisfaction, creativity, group comradeship, appreciation, interesting jobs, and a feeling of accomplishment. They might also want to seek the good of all, not just themselves. Even if people always do what they want to do, what they want to do could be to help others.

In point of fact, we now have a mixed capitalist/socialist economy rather than a pure laissez-faire system. We have welfare payments, Social Security benefits, public schools, workmen's compensation, Medicare and Medicaid, low income housing, food stamps, disability insurance, and unemployment compensation. In addition, we have government agencies such as the Federal Trade Commission, the Interstate Commerce Commission, and the Bureau of Consumer Protection; there is the F.A.A., the I.R.S., the E.P.A., and the F.D.A. Even minimum wage laws and child labor laws protect the public from exploitation.

But by and large, our economy is a free one, with private ownership of property and the means of production, all driven by the profit motive. We have competition more than cooperation; companies, not just industries; and reliance on personal ingenuity, not central planning. We grant each person the freedom to compete in the open market, insofar as their capabilities permit. The government steps in to regulate industry, banks, and the financial markets when they use their power to restrain competition and take advantage of the public, but the economy is basically an open one. Debate occurs over the extent of government regulation, that is, how much the need for protection should restrain the free market, but essentially capitalism embraces the virtue of freedom.

But is our capitalist system a genuine meritocracy? Do the wealthy deserve their wealth by virtue of their greater abilities, and do the poor deserve to be poor because they are not the most capable? Does the disparity reflect the relative merits of the rich and poor, so that the poor simply have not worked hard enough? Does everyone stand an equal chance of success, so that the unequal distribution of wealth is fair?

## The Forces Opposing Equal Opportunity

As we all know, various factors militate against equal opportunity. Within our nation about half of our major wealth holders inherited their wealth; and since wealth gives people an edge in the market, that means everyone is not starting even. And by receiving an inheritance, the children of the rich have an advantage in acquiring more wealth. In addition, inheritance taxes — called "death taxes" by conservatives — have been repeatedly lowered, and the wealthy often hire "creative" accountants to find loopholes in the laws.[1]

We cherish the freedom to acquire as much wealth as we (legally) can, and the freedom to pass that wealth on to our children, but the result is that some people have an initial advantage over others. The distribution is unequal at the outset, and that inequality is perpetuated over generations. We do not prosecute a child for what his father did because that would be unfair. Should we reward a child because his father did well?

Race and gender also factor into the analysis. Certain racial and ethnic minorities, excluding Asian-Americans, are more likely to be poor in our society. Blacks especially are concentrated in menial, low paying, dead-end jobs, and they experience substandard housing, inadequate schooling, weak family support, and poor health care. All of this translates into fewer opportunities to succeed. Even if discrimination were not a factor in employment or college acceptance, blacks are not as "plugged into" personal networks. They have been systematically excluded, and for that reason alone cannot compete with white applicants.

To insist on strict, high standards for employment or admission for people who are disadvantaged at the start, merely perpetuates the status quo. As President Johnson said, you don't take someone who has been shackled all his life, put him at the starting line of a race and say, "You are now free to compete with all the others."

With respect to gender, the median full-time salary for women is 77% that of men. Discrimination (the glass ceiling) accounts for most of this disparity, although in all fairness, women are less likely to engage in dangerous occupations which often pay more, and less willing to travel or

---

[1] Madoff, Ray. *Immortality and the Law: The Rising Power of the American Dead.* New Haven: Yale University Press, 2010.

relocate; they are more risk-averse and reluctant to start new businesses. In various ways, marriage and pregnancy also account for some of the disparity when women "stop out."

One of the main reasons for the difference in economic level between rich and poor is education, which is connected to wealth and income in both obvious and subtle ways.

Sociologists tell us that admission to colleges, especially to the elite universities, depends heavily on wealth. This is because wealth correlates with high academic achievement — 12 points on the SATs for every $20,000 of family salary. Therefore, admitting the highest achievers simply maintains the hierarchy of affluence because they then command the higher salaries.

Specifically, wealth confers academic advantages initially, that is, at the grade school level or earlier. If children are raised in an affluent home, their schools will be superior, with better instruction and more AP courses; their parents will be better educated and there will be what Pierre Bourdieu calls "cultural capital" in the home, as well as family contacts and networking. They will have access to tutors, more co-curricular activities, experiences abroad, learning camps, and exotic vacations. Students from better zip codes will also have the psychological advantage of greater self-confidence, motivation, and an expectation of success — — which cannot be overestimated. All of this translates into higher scores on tests for college admission, and it allows privileged families to pass on their social position to their children. The comfortable remain comfortable.

Lower income children, by contrast, have a higher drop-out rate in high school, especially in the inner city and particularly among blacks, and if they stay in school they will have lower test scores. They are not adequately prepared for learning. Also associated with low income are criminality, unemployment, obesity, malnutrition, debt, high infant mortality, drug use, and mental illness. These young people are not well connected but "unhooked," according to the Admissions Office phrase. Disparities in income also correlate with statistics on sickness, accidents, teenage pregnancy, and life span. The child poverty rate is 20% in the U.S. — the highest of any industrial country, and blacks are three times more likely to be poor. A high birth rate does not cause poverty; rather, poverty causes a high birth rate.

The diversity movement has not offset the advantages of privilege since the wealthy still dominate; students of modest backgrounds are under-represented in colleges, especially the select ones.[1]

The difference in the quality of secondary schooling is especially noticeable, and it correlates with affluence. Wealthy children are also more

---

[1] See Meighan, R. and Siraj-Blatchford, I. *A Sociology of Education* (London: Cassell, 1997), and Karabel, Jerome *The Chosen: The Hidden History of Admission and Exclusion at Harvard, Yale, and Princeton* (New York: Houghton Mifflin, 2005).

likely to attend private school and be "legacies" at colleges, the children of alumni — 54 percent overall and 75 percent at some colleges today. This is not as unbalanced as it used to be: Between 1906 and 1932, some 400 boys at Groton applied to Harvard, and virtually all were admitted; in 1932 Yale accepted 72 percent from blue-ribbon schools.

Admission preferences are still badly skewed. At Phillips Exeter Academy, for example, 15 percent were recently admitted to Harvard, Yale, and Princeton. In addition, the number of legacies has increased at those colleges. The "big three" are, in fact, the least academically diverse with a disproportionate number drawn from the top-tier.[1]

Elite colleges will also set aside slots for students who excel at the "tonier" sports such as riding, fencing, and crew racing, which are offered at private schools. The upper-class also marry within their own ranks and set up trust funds for their children. Social scientists call it the "systematic preference of privilege" or "structural functionalism": society tends toward equilibrium rather than rewarding ability.

It is also well known that heavy donors to colleges as well as the offspring of wealthy alumni receive special consideration, in effect buying places for their children. To a lesser degree, the same is true of parents who can pay full tuition. The Admissions Office always has an eye on the Development Office, and the institution wants to come in on budget. Since the number of places is limited, poorer children are often left out. The wealthy as well as the powerful, famous, and politically connected receive preferential treatment.[2]

A more subtle factor that is affected by wealth is IQ — assuming intelligence or the 'g' factor is something genuine and not just knowledge of American culture. According to neurobiology, neurons make connections with neighboring neurons until the age of 16, during which time environmental stimuli are critical to intellectual development. After that the capacity of the brain to adapt its connections begins to diminish.

Some psychologists such as Howard Gardner argue for multiple intelligences, such as spatial, bodily-kinetic, musical, interpersonal, mathematical, and so forth, but the general psychological community affirms an IQ that can be measured.[3]

However, this inherited intelligence is not immutable; to some degree it is plastic. It can be affected by various environmental elements: nutrition,

[1] Soares, Joseph *The Power of Privilege*. Stanford: Stanford University Press, 3007, 89.
[2] Golden, Daniel, *The Price of Admission* (Three Rivers Press, 2007). See also Stevens, Mitchell *Creating a Class: College Admission and the Education of Elites* (Cambridge: Harvard University Press, 2007). Stevens refers to "the tendency of privileged families to hand privilege down to their children."
[3] See Gardner, Howard *Frames of Mind: The Theory of Multiple Intelligence*. New York: Basic Books, 1983.

gestation, birth weight, exposure to toxic chemicals (lead, alcohol, or drugs), peer groups, early education, and even music (the Mozart effect). Above all, the richness of the home life will strongly influence a student's cognitive ability and, in turn, his or her score on intelligence tests.[1]

It seems clear that if you are a middle class youth or minority from modest circumstances, you have little chance of getting into an Ivy League school. Students from the top 25 percent of wealthy households account for over 67 percent of all slots in the top 150 universities. There is a thumb on the scale for class-based affirmative action. The road to substantial wealth and status runs through America's elite universities, such as Harvard, Yale, and Princeton, and those who are admitted come from families that already occupy a high socio-economic rank. In this way the elite perpetuate their position and upward mobility is stifled.[2]

If access to universities depends on high scores on standardized tests, and the high scorers are those from wealthy homes with academic advantages, then equal opportunity becomes an illusion. And if the gap between rich and poor is widening, then an increasing number of students are being denied the chance to compete equally and to achieve success.

## The Consequences of Inequality

The effects of this inequality are often hidden, but they can be substantial. In *The Spirit Level: Why Greater Equality Makes Societies Stronger*, Richard Wilkinson and Kate Pickett identify some of the consequences. They see strong links between inequality in wealth and rates of obesity, mental illness, drug and alcohol abuse, imprisonment, lower life expectancy, crime, and teen pregnancy. These problems are not just the result of poverty but are increased at all levels according to the *degree of inequality* in society.[3]

In a recent book by Joseph Stiglitz, a recipient of the Nobel Prize in economics, the author argues that greater equality benefits everyone, for even the rich "need a functioning society around them to sustain their position." Therefore it does not pay for the wealthy "to help themselves in the short term rather than help society over the long term."[4]

There is evidence that when greater equality exists, nations have enhanced cohesion, mutual trust, and a sense of community. More equal

---

[1] Neisser, U; Boodoo, G; Bouchard, Jar, T.J.; Boykin, A.W.; Brody, N.; Cecil, S.J.; Halpern, D.F.; Loehlin, J.C.; Perloff, R.; Sternberg, R.J.; Others, "Intelligence: Knowns and Unknowns." *Annual Progress in Child Psychology and Development*, 1997.
[2] Karabel, Jerome, *The Chosen: The Hidden History of Admission and Exclusion at Harvard, Yale, and Princeton*. New York: Houghton Mifflin Harcourt, 2005.
[3] Wilkinson, R. and Pickett, K. *The Spirit Level: Why Greater Equality Makes Societies Stronger*. N.Y.: Bloomsbury Press, 2010. 352ff.
[4] Stiglitz, Joseph. *The Price of Inequality*. NY: Norton, 2012.

societies also display longer life expectancy, health, and lower violence, in both developed and developing nations. With regard to violence, over fifty studies conclude it is more prevalent in societies where income differences are larger, and this is especially true of homicides.

In larger, macro-economic terms, the case for greater equality was made by the 19th century philosopher John Stuart Mill, and it has been repeated by modern thinkers.[1] Mill argued for flattening the economic pyramid on the grounds of "decreasing marginal utility." For example, when a person buys a car it generally makes him happy. Cars provide mobility and control, increasing our freedom of movement. And if that person buys a second car, that will also increase his happiness, but not as much as the first. Therefore, if everyone owned a car rather than some people having several, that would increase the total happiness quotient for society as a whole. Another example is that of houses. A summer home will yield less utility to a single millionaire than a primary residence will to a homeless family of five.

In other words, each addition to a person's wealth yields less satisfaction than previous additions. And a dollar spent by a poor person will buy things of greater usefulness, such as food, shelter, and health care, than a dollar spent by a rich person, which is likely to purchase luxury items. If wealth and income were spread more equitably, then more of people's wants would be satisfied and the aggregate of happiness would be increased.

It seems common sense that wealth is related to power, but although that connection is obvious it may not be all that visible. Social scientists have analyzed the relation, and reaffirmed that a correlation does exist between the two.[2]

For one thing, wealth influences power in donations to political parties, lobbyists, and candidates, and in contributions to "super-pacs," which are exempt from limitations on campaign spending. Corporations, that are now considered persons under the law, are free to spend millions of dollars to influence political decisions.

Second, the ownership of stocks can control corporations, which are the dominant institutions in America today. In 2001 the top 1% owned 33% of stocks, in 2004, 36.7%, and in 2010, 38.3%; since then, the percentage has only increased.

Third, wealth and power interpenetrate, so that those in power can generate more wealth, for themselves or their friends. A government position can be used to feather one's nest, for instance, with a land deal, laws in favor of certain industries, or a contract to a corporation. Among government

---

[1] Pigou, Arthur Cecil. *The Economics of Welfare.* London: Macmillan, 1932.
[2] http://www2.usc.edu/whorulesamerica/power/wealth.html

employees, there is a revolving door between regulators and the industries they regulate.

Lastly, running for public office can be very expensive, so candidates must be independently wealthy (as Donald Trump was in the 2016 election), or beholden to wealthy contributors. Lawmakers generally fall into both categories. About two thirds of Senators are millionaires, with an average net worth of almost 14 million dollars.[1]

In short, the wealthy have strongly influenced public policy in their favor, and this has steadily increased inequality in the United States. Historically, it seems true that economic inequality leads to political inequality, and when wealth controls politics, then democracy is threatened.

## A Suggested Solution

It would be naive to expect the rich and powerful to relinquish their position voluntarily. Marx thought it would take a revolution to achieve justice. In our society where wealth is life's report card and "doing well" means having a high income, people will cling to their financial and social status. Nevertheless, change can occur — and by peaceful means.

In particular, the government could intervene to bring about a more equitable redistribution of wealth. If business will not be self-regulating, then external controls is necessary. This is what happened during the early 20th century when unregulated capitalism led to the creation of trusts, cartels, and monopolies. President Teddy Roosevelt, followed by Taft and Wilson, engaged in "trust busting" of large corporations that functioned in restraint of trade. These corporations would sell their product below cost until their competitors were driven out of business or were forced into takeovers. Once the dominant firm eliminated its competitors, it became a monopoly and could set whatever prices and wages it pleased. The "robber barons," such as John D. Rockefeller, J. P. Morgan, and Andrew Carnegie, thereby controlled such industries as railroads, oil, cigarettes, and sugar refining. Free-market capitalism had led to a concentration of wealth and power, high barriers to open competition, the exploitation of workers, and a general economic inequality. The federal administration had to step in for the health of the free market and the public good.

Taxes are the main method used by government to affect economic redistribution, and values determine tax policy. One of the main instruments within the tax system is the graduated income tax on individuals. Here, a sliding scale is used whereby the tax rate increases in relation to the level of income. The poorest pay the lowest percentage, the richest, the highest — at least in theory.

---

[1] *The New York Times*, May 16, 2012

In actuality, the progressive tax has scarcely altered the differences between rich and poor. As income has increased, progressivity has slowed, then stopped. It then slipped backward for the top 1%. This is due to numerous factors including loopholes in the tax law that astute accountants can discover. These loopholes mainly pivot round deductions, write-offs, overseas investments, off-shore accounts, charitable donations, and municipal bonds. Some 1500 millionaires have not paid any taxes for the past three years; the same is true of 30 major corporations, including General Electric, Boeing, and DuPont. G.E. had an income of $10.3 billion in 2009 but paid nothing in taxes.

The wealth of the rich has also increased as a function of the tax rates on capital gains and dividends, which the Bush administration lowered to 15% in 2003. Overall, this tax rate fell by 7% during the Clinton administration, and another 6% during the George W. Bush era.[1]

Most modern economists, such as Paul Krugman, Peter Orszag, and Emmanuel Saez, argue that tax policy after World War II has increased economic inequality significantly. The wealthiest citizens have been given far greater access to capital than lower-income Americans.[2]

Apart from its efficacy, the graduated income tax is a mixed blessing. On the one hand, it seems unfair to those who are industrious and enterprising, who freely and legally acquire their wealth. On the other hand, we must recognize the role played by social advantages in financial success, and make allowances for the disadvantaged being handicapped.

In terms of the equitable distribution of wealth, the graduated income tax seems a positive measure. Everyone does not start even; the privileged have a head-start. Therefore, in the interest of social justice, some portion of the wealth of the rich should be channeled to the poor; it will allow them to catch up after being socially restricted. It seems a fair way of restoring the American dream of equal opportunity and upward mobility. We need an effective tax structure that will reduce the inequality in wealth and income, and promote greater economic access for all members of the society.

Wealth is not wholly the result of effort and ability, and insofar as it has been acquired in ways that have nothing to do with merit, that wealth is not justly owned. Standards of fairness and the public welfare require that it be more evenly distributed. Financial inequality should only be the result of natural differences in skill and talent, and an individual's hard work.

---

[1] Piketty, Thomas, and Saez, Emmanuel. Income Inequality in the United States, 1915-1998. *Quarterly Journal of Economics, Vol. CXVII, 2003.* See also Picketty's *Capital in the Twenty-First Century* which argues the return on capital is driving economic growth.
[2] http://www2.ucsc.edu/whorulesamerica/power/wealth.html

The more fundamental debate is whether equality or freedom is more important. Is equality the correct rendering of fairness and justice? Is freedom valuable in itself or only as an instrument to secure happiness, self-realization, or enjoyment? Is the conservative economist Milton Friedman correct in saying, "A society that puts equality before freedom will get neither. A society that puts freedom before equality will get a high degree of both"?

As we have seen, if the government allows unfettered freedom in the marketplace, then wealth becomes concentrated in the hands of the few, but if the government intervenes to equalize wealth, then individual freedom is severely reduced. The libertarian wants the first, the socialist the second, and the two cannot exist simultaneously in absolute form.

We therefore have a mixed economy, and political parties argue endlessly about the proportion and the balance. However, given the extraordinary inequality today, greater government action may be needed to reduce injustice as well as social unrest. At this point, action must be taken to bring about greater equality; otherwise, the system is morally bankrupt.

The ball is now in your court, and you must play it as you see fit — but always according to what is reasonable.

## Chapter 6. Nature Times Nurture Equals Behavior: Do We Ever Make a Free Choice?

Usually we assume we are personally free, the "masters of our fate," "the captains of our soul," but academics in various fields have questioned this assumption. Everyone from theologians to behaviorists has raised doubts as to whether we can think what we please and do what we choose. They suggest that freedom may be an illusion that we maintain for our self-respect. Our pride depends on it, and to think we are programmed robots, or string marionettes, or characters in a book is an assault on our dignity.

Technically speaking, free will means the ability to decide what to do, whereas freedom means the ability to do what we decide. This is the reason Oscar Wilde wrote in *The Ballad of Reading Gaol*, "Stone walls do not a prison make/ Nor iron bars a cage," and it is why the Greek philosopher Epictetus said, "Fetter me? You may fetter my leg, but not Zeus himself can get the better of my free will." They were both denied freedom, but they still possessed free will.

### Our Fate Is Sealed

The belief that we are at liberty to choose is denied completely by the doctrine of destiny or fate, and almost every culture has this notion embedded in it. The Spanish say "que sera, sera," what will be will be; the French phrase is "c'est écrit," it is written; the Arabs use the word "kismet"; the Greeks refer to "moira," which even circumscribes the gods. The common meaning is that everything is predestined to occur as it does, and no one can escape the machinery of fate. The future is as fixed as the past, frozen and unalterable; we live in a bloc universe.

Just as things that are done can't be undone, what will happen must happen because all events occur inevitably.

In Greek mythology, destiny is personified by the Fates and Furies. The Fates or Moirai are three sisters: Clotho, who spins the thread of life, Lachesis, who measures the length of life, and Atropos, the inevitable, who cuts the thread. The Furies are three goddesses who exact revenge for violating social rules. They personify vengeance, jealousy, and anger; snakes writhe in their hair while blood drips from their eyes.

In literature the best known example of fate occurs in Sophocles' *Oedipus Rex*, a drama in which the title character is a "plaything of the gods," destined to kill his father and marry his mother. This was the limit of horror to the Greek mind. Everything Oedipus does to avoid his fate is the means fate uses to fulfill what has been ordained. Sigmund Freud, of course, uses the Oedipus myth as a prototype of the maturing process, claiming it is played out in the psyche of every boy in his sexual development. He wants to murder his father, and possess his mother himself.

Among the Greco-Roman philosophers it is the Stoics who most stress the role of fate in human life — figures such as Seneca, the slave Epictetus, and the emperor Marcus Aurelius — the only philosopher king in history. Named for the Stoa or porch in the marketplace, Stoicism flourished in the ancient world, perhaps because it preached inner tranquility during turbulent times.

Epictetus is probably the major representative of the movement, and he proclaimed that destiny rules the universe, governing every physical occurrence. Nothing happens by chance or luck, including the events in our lives. We may think our decisions shape our future but nothing is outside the iron law of inevitability. Everything occurs as it must and we have no choice in the matter. Whatever we do is a thread in the tapestry of destiny, and the design cannot be altered.

But to the Stoics, the gods are at the heart of things, suffusing the rational machine with a benevolent spirit. Everything that occurs happens for the best, as well as being unavoidable. In fact, nothing in nature can be evil ultimately, because positive, vital energy permeates the universe. From our earthly perspective, epidemics, droughts, and earthquakes are disasters, banishments and starvation are misfortunes, but when viewed from on high, they are necessary and beneficial. Events occur with a mathematical inevitability, but they also tend towards the good.

If this is the nature of reality, then we ought to support whatever happens. As rational beings we should accept the inevitable, even approve of it. Events are predestined but our reaction to them lies within our own power. We could rail against our fate but that would be foolish and pointless; it might even be blasphemous because we would be criticizing the gods. Rather, we should remain calm, using our good sense to control our emotional reactions. *Sustine et abstine*, endure and abstain. Since we cannot do anything to avoid the disease or disaster, we should maintain our poise and equanimity, even in the face of catastrophe. If we adopt *apatheia* or an attitude of serene indifference, then we will be in control of our lives, acting rationally. "It is not what happens to you," Epictetus writes, "but how you react to it that matters," and "Ask not that events should happen as you will, but let your will be that events should happen as they do, and you shall have peace."

The other main source of the destiny belief is Christianity, both in direct and indirect ways. First, there is the central notion of God's providence, which means his plan for the world and everyone in it. Many theologians accept this view that God is completely sovereign, which implies a pre-determinism. Here God controls and directs all things, "brute creatures and the affairs of men"; "not [a sparrow] shall fall to the ground without your Father's will," and "even the hairs of your head are all numbered." If God has written the book of life, then none of his characters can step off the page and decide what they want to do.

Calvinism in particular asserts God's complete control of the world. To claim that man is free would reduce the deity's strength, circumventing his power. God decides at birth who will be elected to glory, which is a call that cannot be resisted, and who will be damned to hell for all eternity, without hope of mercy, The doctrine is called "double predestination." To allow man to win his own deliverance through good works reduces God's power to save our souls through grace; it makes him less than almighty. In order to retain the Lord's perfection, he must govern all happenings, especially man's salvation.

Second, destiny is implied by God's omniscience. As we discussed earlier, if God foresees everything that we will do, then in some sense the future is unalterable. If he knows what will happen, then it must happen and could not be different. God himself may not be compelling events but they must be unavoidable or he could not predict them. This means we are not free, although we might have the illusion of making choices. If the future is open ended, then God is not all knowing; conversely, if God is all-knowing, then the future is predetermined. What will happen is as unalterable as what has happened.

The paradox is that Christianity also maintains that human beings are free and responsible for their actions. If we cannot help what we do, then we do not deserve heavenly rewards or damnation in hell.

This paradox arises in *Genesis* in connection with the Garden of Eden. Did Adam and Eve have any choice in the matter? As an omniscient being,

God knew beforehand that they would yield to temptation, and if he knew it would happen, then the future is already written. That means the Fall was inevitable, and Adam and Eve did not freely sin. They therefore did not deserve to be punished — much less have their sin infect all of humankind.

A parody of this dilemma appears in *Penguin Island* by Anatole France. Here God says,

> [M]y foreknowledge must not be allowed to interfere with their free will. So as not to limit human freedom, I hereby assume ignorance of what I know. I wind tightly over my eyes the veils which I have seen through, and in my blind clairvoyance, I allow myself to be surprised by what I have foreseen.

But does destiny rule our lives? Today we tend to dismiss this notion, and champion free will and freedom. Fatalism has not been refuted so much as abandoned, probably because the evidence is lacking. We only fall back on fate at times of stress such as war, when we have no power over events. Soldiers will sometimes comfort themselves by thinking, "Unless this bullet has my name on it, I will be safe; if it does, there's nothing I can do about it." This resignation could also occur on a very bumpy flight where the weather and the skill of the pilot determine whether we live or die. Here we might try to regain control by vowing, "Get me through this and I'll build a cathedral"!

## Causal Determinism

In addition to this pre-determinism, which has a cosmic or spiritual dimension, the theory of determinism also has a scientific version. The scientific theory also denies that people are free, but uses Newtonian mechanics to argue the case. Everything that happens is caused by prior factor in an unbroken chain of causes and effects (as the cosmological argument assumes and Hume denies). No event is uncaused; the dominoes do not fall because they choose to. Once we know the antecedents, then we know the consequents. There is no chance, randomness, or luck, but compulsion and inevitability, not because of supernatural forces but earthly laws.

What caused the tree to crash? The hurricane-force wind. What caused the train to move? It was pulled by the locomotive. What caused the snow to melt? The warm sunlight of spring. In the same way we can ask, why did an individual act the way he did? and the answer lies in his heredity and environment. The past dictates the future by rigid, natural principles, and once we know all the determinants, we will be able to predict human choices as accurately as the behavior of rats in a maze. "Nature times nurture equals behavior," the behavioral psychologist says, and in poetic terms, the flower was in the bud, the ending in the beginning, the child is father to the man.

Our background will determine our thoughts and actions, including the occupation we select, the clothes we wear, the car we drive, the entertainment we like, and the friends we choose (people like ourselves). We generally follow the religion and politics of our family, and if we rebel against them vehemently, that too shows their power over us. Vehemently opposing our family, society, country, and so forth is a left-handed compliment.

When we say that we know someone, doesn't that mean we know how they will behave? We depend upon them to act in predictable ways, to stay in character. If we are uncertain as to what someone will do from moment to moment, then we can't say we know them. In fact, people who are wholly unpredictable probably have a mental disorder; they act like a set of random numbers rather than being the same, consistent self through time.

This causal, deterministic theory is sometimes called "the billiard ball" theory. Once the cue ball is struck, and all other billiard balls are in place, a necessary sequence is set in motion. At the cosmic level, once the initial conditions of the universe are established, the rest of history will follow inevitably. A theoretical intelligence, who knows the complete range of possibilities, could predict all events, from Big Bang to Big Crunch. This holds true for human life as well, because we are a part of the natural world and our actions are the effect of prior causes. Whatever we think or do is dictated by biological, social, and environmental factors.

This even applies to our tastes. We may be free to do what we like, but we are not free to decide what we like. We cannot will ourselves to find someone attractive, or to love someone we hate. Can we control our preferences in food? It seems that we either like tofu or Brussels sprouts or we don't; it depends in part on the foods we ate as a child. Octopus tastes better as calamari, and eating snails is more sophisticated if they are called escargots. Some types of music appeal to us, others do not, and we can't force ourselves to like classical music if we find it boring. Similarly, some people enjoy fall more, others spring; some enjoy baseball, others football; and some prefer texting to talking. Whether we like or dislike something does not seem a matter of choice, and cannot be changed by making an effort; our will power seems irrelevant.

In business, market researchers assume that various demographics can be targeted for certain products. Upscale consumers will consume single malt scotch, young women buy cosmetics and perfumes, and medicine and prosthetics should be advertised to the elderly. "Data mining" is used to predict demand, a rifle not a scattershot.

But predicting consumer behavior is an inexact science, not absolutely accurate. Doesn't that mean we are free in our choices? The determinist replies that, at present, the responses of a particular demographic are only probable because we don't have enough data, but as we make finer discriminations, we will become more accurate about target markets. Once we gather sufficient information about consumer habits, we will know what everyone will buy. According to some scenarios, advertisers will soon be able to call out to people on the street with programmed loudspeakers, reminding them to purchase their favorite brands. If we were free to do whatever we please, we could not be manipulated this way.

The debate, then, is between the determinist and the libertarian, and whether we are compelled or free makes a difference. We like to think of ourselves as autonomous, of having "agency" to affect our lives. We take responsibility for our actions, accepting praise or blame because the decision came from us. We feel proud of our accomplishments, ashamed of our mistakes, in both cases standing behind our conduct. We tell people what they ought to do, which assumes they are free to do differently. As the philosopher Immanuel Kant said, "Ought implies can." We must be capable of choosing one action over another; otherwise the "shoulds" make no sense. In short, if all of our decisions are made for us, life would lose much of its meaning.

But what prior conditions are identified by scientists as compelling our behavior? For one thing, we have physical traits we inherit as part of our genetic endowment; they contribute substantially to who we are and what we do. At birth we are given our sex, race, IQ (the "g" factor), our sense organs for seeing, hearing, tasting, smelling, and feeling, as well as our nervous system, skeletal structure, metabolism, and musculature. If we have high secretions of adrenalin we will be quick to fight or flee, and with an overactive thyroid our speed of living will resemble a racehorse or race car. Our level of testosterone will determine whether we are aggressive and have a strong sex drive, whereas estrogen will make us more passive with a patient disposition. Our biological makeup also includes body type which can be divided into *ectomorph*, a slender, angular, fragile, light build; *endomorph*, a round, soft body with a tendency toward fat; and *mesomorph*, a muscular, large-boned frame. What's more, our DNA will create a predisposition to cancers, obesity, alcoholism, and cardiovascular disease.

Accordingly, an ectomorphic female who is short, with a slight build and light musculature, poor motor coordination, an underactive thyroid and a low energy level, is extremely unlikely to become a professional football player. In the same way, someone with an endomorphic male body, with slow reflexes, a low IQ, and poor hearing and eyesight has a slim chance of becoming an astronaut. In other words, according to our body type, we will be qualified for certain fields and would not be fit for others; in fact, we would be unlikely to choose anything contrary to our biological capabilities.

Climate and geography are two other factors that are said to be responsible for both social and individual actions. Referred to today as environmental determinism, this theory claims that our physical surroundings also help explain and predict our development. The temperature, weather, and topography in the northern temperate zone lead to industry and achievement, a vigorous work ethic and a higher level of civilization. There is greater inventiveness and efficiency, and superior political, economic, artistic, and educational institutions. People are more organized, invigorated, and productive. Tropical climates on the other hand, produce lethargy, even laziness, slack morals, decreased ambition, and little discipline. People live sensuously rather than intellectually, they move slower, are less active, "relax, submit, and enjoy" life, without having to earn their pleasures or justify their existence. As one theorist put it, "Those in warmer climates are more physiologically comfortable due to temperature, and so have less incentive to work to increase their comfort level."

Tropical regions are plagued by infectious diseases such as trachoma, sleeping sickness, and malaria, which are transmitted more easily in warm climates. Workers are sick more often and are less productive. Also, the soil is less fertile for crops with high evaporation and an uncertain supply of water. Even after accounting for variables such as labor, machinery, investment, and irrigation, the productivity in agriculture is 30% to 50% lower in the tropics. The average GDP per capita in 1995 was $3326 compared to $9027 in higher latitude countries. In Africa, income has declined steadily over the past 40 years, especially in the sub-Sahara where the rainfall is low and the soil is poor.

The location of a country, and of the population within a country, is also identified as a determinant. Coastal regions tend to be developed far more than inland areas. On the coast, marine life and seaweed are available to eat or sell, there is more opportunity for trade and commerce, transportation costs are lower and consequently, financial centers are formed. (Austria and Switzerland are outliers.) This is why the population tends to cluster along seas and oceans. And here they are exposed to a variety of peoples with diverse ideas, making them more open, liberal, and tolerant. The heartland is the center of conservatism and patriotism as attitudes are confirmed by like-minded people.

People in mountainous regions are more independent and self-reliant, quiet, strong, and introspective, whereas those on the plains are more gregarious, extroverted, and social. People in landlocked countries are inclined toward isolationism and fundamentalist religion,

Some of these points are subsumed under the "equatorial paradox" — the view that 70% of a country's economic development can be predicted by its distance from the equator. The further away, the greater the growth (until one reaches the poles). In the U.S. for example, the northern states are more developed than the south; Europe is further ahead than Africa; and North America is more advanced than South America.

Environmental determinism is largely a 19th and early 20th century theory, and it has been criticized as racist and Eurocentric. One advocate of this view said "You can lie in a hammock and pick bananas" rather than develop agriculture. On these grounds, colonialism has been rationalized because certain societies are uncivilized. It is "the white man's burden" to save these people and institute a superior Western culture. This is clearly patronizing and presumptuous.

In opposition, some scholars have pointed out that the Tigris–Euphrates Valley does not lie in a temperate zone; neither does ancient Egypt, Greece, or Rome. The first human came from the African continent, and Africa has contributed significantly to world culture, especially in art, music, dance, and sculpture.

Environmental determinism has been harmful, nevertheless there seems to be a grain of truth in it. As one commentator said, it has not been disproved so much as disapproved because of the way in which it was used. To some extent, climate, geography, and topography do affect us.

Society's effects on the individual seem undeniable. A feral or wild child is raised outside of society as reported in scientific accounts and in legends. Examples would be the Tarzan books by Burroughs, Kipling's Mowgli, and Romulus and Remus, the mythical founders of Rome who were suckled by wolves. But most of us are brought up within society, in fact we are scarcely human in isolation, and that carries an imprint. As discussed. We are hard wired for language, but the development of language is age-specific, and if there is no verbal interaction with other people, we lose that ability.

Every society puts its stamp on its citizens. We do not live in a vacuum but are a microcosm of our culture, absorbing its traditions, mores, religion, politics, and *Weltanschauung* or world view. To be raised within a society, the determinist argues, means being the product of that society, having that nation's identity and being subject to its determinants. People will act in different ways depending on their country, family, schooling,

For example, someone raised in India as a Hindu, speaking Urdu and living in a rural village with a tradition of farming, would probably not consider following the Protestant ethic and becoming an arbitrageur on Wall

Street. Similarly, a person brought up as "lace curtain" Irish in a working-class district of Dublin, with a parochial education and blue-collar attitudes, would hardly be tempted to emigrate to India and become a guru. It makes a difference whether one attends a village school in Afghanistan or a *lycée* in Paris, whether one is a graduate of a technical training institute in Nairobi or a Midwestern American university. Informal education also forms the person, for the books and magazines we read, the films, video games, and television programs we watch, our social media, text messaging, laptop and cell phone usage — all affect the type of individual we become.

Our society also dictates the kinds of food we eat, what we consider beautiful, the sports and entertainment we like, the jewelry we wear, and our style of dress, that is, how we package our bodies. In the U.S. we do not generally wear a toga, burkha, or loin cloth. It also selects our moral code, our religion, and our politics, as well as the type of person we find attractive. Depending on our sex, race, and socio-economic status, we are regarded in a certain way and given opportunities or denied them. The language spoken in our society also affects us, for all languages possess built-in values and attitudes toward the world. Ideas that are Temptations of thought in English are almost unthinkable in Chinese. In fact, The *Sapir-Whorf hypothesis* maintains that language determines thought much more than thought determines language.

Of major concern today is the way women are treated in a society, whether suppressed or encouraged to flourish. These attitudes affect a woman's self-regard as well as the chances she has for self-development.

In these and other ways, our social background severely defines our options and makes our choices for us. According to the determinist, each individual is formed by his heredity and environment. This is why the Jesuits say, give me a child until the age of seven, and I'll show you the man; why B.F. Skinner, a founder of behaviorism, says, "It is a mistake to suppose that the whole issue is to free man. The issue is how to improve the way he is controlled"; and why Max Planck declared, "The assumption of an absolute determinism is the essential foundation of every scientific enquiry."

## The Hidden Fracture Lines

The determinist presents a convincing case, but what are the criticisms of the doctrine by libertarians or indeterminists? The opponents maintain that we are free to choose between alternatives, not compelled in our thoughts or actions. They argue that, despite the numerous forces impinging on us, we can always decide what we ourselves want to do. These forces are influences, not determinants, and ultimately our choices are our own. Once we are aware of the forces influencing us, we are able to decide which ones to accept and which ones to reject. Influences only become determinants when we are unconscious of their power. Once we realize how they operate on us, then we are no longer compelled. With awareness comes control.

For example, people raised in a city would be inclined to continue living an urban life, but they need not do so. They could reject this influence and decide to move to the country. Or people raised in a religious household would be inclined to be religious, but at some point of reflection they might assess their faith and conclude that atheism is more sensible. Someone raised communist could choose a capitalist system; a New Englander might decide to live in Hawaii; and if our parents are Democrats, we can still decide to register with the Republican Party. Peoples on the equator can choose to resist or yield to the lethargy of a warm, humid climate; and mesomorphs might decide to become accountants rather than Olympic weight lifters.

As these examples illustrate, libertarians do not deny the importance of climate, psychology, geography, biology, and so forth in their affirmation of a free will position. Rather, they deny that these are irresistible factors. A large part of the function of education is to make us knowledgeable about the forces operating on us. Then we are empowered and do things voluntarily, taking charge of our lives.

Another way of putting the objection to determinism is that There can be *reasons* for actions, not just *causes*, and having reasons implies some process of deliberation, where a person weighs the alternatives and chooses between them. Cause and effect assumes a strict, mechanical model, such as the instinct that impels a bird to weave a nest, but human beings decide for themselves whether to build a home. For human beings, all causes can be "becauses," actions done for some reason.

Another argument against determinism is that it argues backwards. It explains why a person did something, but cannot predict what a person will do. To take an example from science, If gravity is a sound theory, then a rock should fall to the ground when it is released from our hand. Predictive power is part of the proof of a scientific theory. In the same way, if determinism is valid, then it should foresee what decisions a person will and must make. But that element is weak or missing from determinism.

Suppose that a boy named Mike, whose father is a businessman, decides to attend business school. The determinist would attribute this decision to his wanting to be like his father. If, however, Mike decides to study engineering, then the determinist would say it was because of a favorite uncle who is an engineer. And if Mike dropped out of school, to play guitar in a rock band, then the determinist would say he was rebelling against his background. In other words, anything Mike chooses can be made to fit, but the real test of a theory is whether it can predict what a person will do given his options and background.

The libertarian also accuses the determinist of committing the fallacy of *post hoc, ergo propter hoc*. As discussed previously, the fallacy lies in assuming that if one event follows another, the earlier event must have caused the later one. But sometimes there is only a temporal sequence, not a causal connection. For example, the fallacy would be committed if we thought that because someone died after going to a hospital, that the hospital killed them, or that hospitals are places where people go to die. In the same way, the determinist assumes that because we can identify prior factors, that those factors necessarily caused the event. But the burden of proof is on the determinist to prove that the prior events forced people to act as they did. Otherwise we're justified in our customary view — that people are free to think what they like and do as they please, despite preceding factors.

One of the strongest arguments against determinism is that it is self-contradictory. That is, when determinists try to convince people to change their minds and agree with them, they give the game away. For they are assuming people are free to think differently, regardless of their social upbringing, biology, the climate, and so forth, And the more the determinist tries to persuade people of the truth of determinism, the more convinced they should become that determinism is not true. In other words, the determinist cannot preach his doctrine, without contradicting his assumptions. All he can do is remain silent, because once he argues for his position he cuts off the branch on which he sits.

Another way of putting the point is that, by their own admission, determinists cannot help but believe in determinism because, like all other ideas, they has been determined to believe it. That is, if all our thoughts are the product of prior causes, this includes the idea of determinism. The determinist has not freely decided his theory is true but believes it because he cannot help it. And on determinist grounds, the libertarian has to believe in libertarianism; he is compelled to believe he is free. All discussion is therefore useless. The only way the argument could make sense is if the parties were free to be convinced otherwise.

One type of determinism deserves to be mentioned with some respect — a specialized form called logical determinism: All propositions or statements, past, present, and future, are either true or false. The proposition that the New England Patriots will win the Superbowl did not *become* true when they won; it was *always* true; we just didn't know it. What did people breathe before oxygen was discovered in the 18th century? Oxygen. It was there all along. This means that statements about the future have truth value in the present, which implies the future is already determined. As one writer put it, "The future is certain. It is just not known."

This is a specialized category, of course, but There is one way of trying to resolve the free will controversy, and that is by affirming a version called soft determinism.

Hard determinism claims that since all of our actions are caused by prior factors, we do not have free will. To speak of freedom and personal responsibility makes no sense when all of our actions are part of an iron causal chain. But soft determinism, also called compatibilism or self-determinism, maintains that even though all actions are caused, nevertheless people are free because they participate as causes of their actions. If an act proceeds from the individual's personality or character rather than from external forces, then the act is both free and caused.

Soft determinists therefore claim that free will is compatible with determinism, since the person can be the original source of action. On this reading, the universe is admitted to be a system of physical laws embracing all things, including human beings, but people are free agents within that system. The person can make any number of choices, but the cause lies within them, and once having chosen, the events must play out according to natural law.

Ethicists tend to affirm free will, endorsing either soft determinism or libertarianism. They believe we can choose among alternative ways of living, and they use rational arguments to prove it. Furthermore, the free will position can be recommended to other people without contradiction, and they are free to accept or reject it.

An interesting question in this connection is whether reason can force us to the conclusion that we are free, and if so, whether that means we are not free As Dostoevsky points out, "Twice two makes four without my will. As if free will meant that!"

Subtle distinctions aside, perhaps we ought to trust our sense of having free choices, especially since it is supported by logic. We assume responsibility for our actions, and that means we could have acted differently. Feelings of regret and shame, pride and self-respect would be irrational sunless they were based on free decisions, just as praise and blame, rewards and punishment would make no sense. In some circumstances we cannot help doing what we do — if the brakes fail on car, for example, but for the most part, we are at liberty to make decisions, and we are accountable for them.

"Man is not fully conditioned and determined," Victor Frankl writes, "but rather determines himself whether he gives in to conditions or stands up to them...Man does not simply exist but always decides what his existence will be, what he will become in the next moment."

The ball is now in your court, and you must play it as you see fit — but always according to what is reasonable.

# Chapter 7. Honesty and Integrity: Should Truthfulness Depend Upon the Situation?

## Honesty

Honesty is generally considered a virtue, but its meaning can be confusing. Honesty does not mean saying what is true. It means saying what we believe to be true. We can make an honest mistake and not be lying, even though what we say is not true. We could be fooling ourselves, or just be mistaken in our convictions. But the honest person intends to tell the truth, aiming to say what he believes is in fact the case. Lying, conversely, means the intention to deceive people. A liar can tell others what they want to hear, or what is to his own advantage, or something that happens to be true by accident, but that he does not believe it himself. Lies are always deliberate; one cannot lie accidentally.

The opposition is between being truthful and lying, rather than true and untrue. Bearing false witness is different from making a mistake and inadvertently saying something false.

This is the point of the story told by Salman Rushdie in *Satanic Verses*. A man is about to be released from a mental institution but the doctors are not quite sure about him. So they give him a lie detector test (a polygraph) and ask him if he is Napoleon. The man answers No, but the polygraph shows he is lying.

Was he, in fact, Napoleon? No, but he thought he was, and lied while telling the truth.

Honesty is valued in most societies, and to call someone a liar is a stinging charge. This is because the person is being accused of cowardice, of lying his way out of a situation; he did not have the courage to tell the truth. Liars must have a good memory because they must remember the stories they tell rather than the actual facts. The liar must further hide his lie, and becomes involved in an edifice of deceit. As Sir Walter Scott wrote, "Oh what a tangled web we weave when first we practice to deceive."

The person being lied to also feels demeaned because he was treated as an obstacle to be overcome rather than being given full dignity as a human being. The liar intentionally manipulates information, treating the other as an impediment rather than a person deserving respect.

In addition, society as a whole is damaged by lying because the social fabric depends upon trust between people; otherwise, it unravels. We must rely on each other's word and have confidence that what we are told is true, insofar as the speaker believes it to be true. Society would break down if we could never trust what people say. As sociologists point out, truth-telling has great social value. It promotes security and cohesion. This is why the lies of government officials are particularly corrosive, breaking down confidence in a country's leadership.

For these reasons lying has negative consequences to the liar, the person lied to, and to society generally. This applies to deceit and general dishonesty as well. For example, a used car salesman omits mentioning that a car has been in a serious accident, leaving the impression that the car is perfectly sound. Here the salesman is not lying but deceiving the buyer, leaving a false impression. It is a vice of omission rather than commission, but it can be equally harmful. By not disclosing important information, the buyer is being cheated.

Of course, there is a philosophic question as to whether there is such a thing as the truth and, if so, whether we can ever know it. "Truth?" asked Pontius Pilate, "What is that?", and Shakespeare writes, "There is nothing either good or bad but thinking makes it so." Many people, in fact, feel that everything we say should be qualified, that life is too complex to reveal any simple truth much less the whole truth.

Does the issue of objective truth affect the issue of truth-telling? It seems like a red herring. Even if we all determines our own truth, there would still be lying in the sense of people saying what they themselves do not believe to be true.

But aren't there conditions under which it is morally permissible to lie, in fact, times when we are morally obligated to lie? Suppose a young child asks whether there is a Santa Claus, or a painter on his death bed asks whether his latest exhibit was a success when it was an awful failure, or a friend who is grossly overweight asks how she looks in that red dress? Or more significantly, suppose someone comes running up to us with a smoking gun and asks "Which way did my wife go?" If we were truthful, we could be an accessory to murder.

Shouldn't we lie in those circumstances? In other words, aren't there "white lies" or beneficial lies that do no harm and can do real good? Can't we fool ourselves for the sake of peace of mind, have national myths of innocence, think positively to keep up our spirits, and maintain varieties of untruths that are useful? The moral question is whether we should lie whenever it would be advantageous to do so. Is truth-telling situational?

Although there are exceptions to telling the truth, those exceptions do not undermine the basic principle. In fact, they may reinforce it because, by and large, the principle holds true; the exceptions are few and far between. In general, it seems the conventional view can be trusted; telling the truth is better than telling a lie. Exceptions overturn scientific theories but reinforce moral generalizations.

What's more, we are inclined to lie if the outcome is favorable for ourselves. This makes a relativistic definition of truth-telling highly suspicious. Most probably, we are rationalizing, convincing ourselves that the rule can be bent or broken in our case. But unless an overriding reason exists, we should respect the principle of truthfulness and try to be honest in our dealings with one another.

As the philosopher Sissela Bok declares, we should rule out deception whenever honest alternatives exist. If there are other ways to accomplish our ends besides duplicity or treachery, they should be used.[1]

## Self-Deception

One interesting question in this context is whether we can or should ever lie to ourselves. Are we able to convince ourselves that we don't know what we do know, and are we ever right to pretend that a fiction is a fact?

From a psychological standpoint, we do seem able to deceive ourselves, especially when driven by emotional need. As Demosthenes wrote, "Nothing is easier than self-deceit. For what each man wishes, that he also believes to be true." He is referencing the constant temptation to lie to ourselves, selecting what we want to believe and blocking whatever is unpleasant. Rationalization and self-deception do seem commonplace, and the only real question is to what extent we can be willfully ignorant before it becomes a serious case of denial.

One of the easiest forms of self-deception is to fool ourselves about who we are, having a higher self-regard than is warranted. We accept distorted memories that are favorable to our self-image, and choose to forget humiliations or embarrassing moments from the past. For the sake of our ego,

[1] Bok, Sissela. *Lying: Moral Choice in Public and Private Life*. NY: Vintage, 1999.

pleasant memories are kept alive; painful memories conveniently disappear. We defend against our vices, exaggerate our virtues, and treat our motives as higher than they really are. When it would threaten the reality we have constructed, we can refuse to admit what we know to be true; it is a matter of self-protection.

For example, we might find it unbearable to think that we are not very loveable, or that we have a low IQ, that we have chosen the wrong occupation, or the wrong mate, or that we have failed to become the person we aspired to be. None of us wants to believe we have wasted our life. We find it painful to recall the cruel or violent things we have done, the choices that were stupid or thoughtless. We would just as soon forget the times when we disappointed our friends or let our parents down. We might feel ashamed of the things we like, or find our sexual fantasies inconsistent with our self-image.

A woman may know her husband is having an affair but not admit it to herself, refusing to accept the truth in order to protect her marriage. A man might want to believe he is a successful at his job and at relationships, not a loser. And it might be psychologically important to believe that prayer works so that the world is somewhat under our control. Regardless of the reality of God, people long for a divine being to exist so that their lives make sense. Religion renders life meaningful, and promises life after death. This is why Voltaire declared, "If God did not exist, it would be necessary to invent him."

Similarly, we may refuse to believe in our own death, although we will accept that other people die. The proposition 'Man is mortal' is an undeniable truth, but we distance it as an abstraction that has nothing to do with us; inside we feel we're not the type. If our lives are threatened by a horrific event — a fire, an assault, a car accident — we may protect ourselves from the trauma by saying, "This isn't happening to me."[1] And if someone we love dies, we may want to believe in a heaven where everyone will meet again; otherwise that love might be thought meaningless. Rochefoucauld said we can no more look at death directly than at the sun.

Whether healthy people would want to know how long their life span will be is an open question. If science could predict when our biological clock will run down, would we welcome that news so we could make our plans, or would we rather remain ignorant? Many people would prefer not to read the printout of their genome, or have a fortune-teller reveal their future.

Self-deception therefore seems commonplace. We will accept the comforting illusion and act as if it were true, preferring to live in a fool's

---

[1] This dissociation is one explanation for "out of body" experience," where people claim to have watched themselves dying from a corner of the room.

paradise. We want to be stronger, wiser, and more competent than we really are, and so pretend we are in fact our ideal self, making ourselves the hero of our imagination.

However, despite our emotional needs, we ought not to override our rational understanding. What we know to be true should not be forbidden to our conscious minds. In a larger sense, our psychological health, maturity, and self-respect depend on facing the truth. One philosopher, W.K. Clifford, even claims it is a moral obligation: we have no right to believe anything on insufficient evidence.

We may deceive other people for their good, but it seems weak to seek such consolation ourselves. No matter how charming and satisfying the illusion, if we choose to believe what we know to be untrue, we are not treating ourselves with dignity. Unless we face up to reality, our worldview and self-concept will be founded on cowardice. And as Bertrand Russell has pointed out, since we are ashamed of cowardice in other spheres, there is no reason to admire it with regard to self-understanding.

## Lies in Politics

Politicians have a bad name for telling half-truths, distorting the truth, and outright lying. Socrates once said, during dangerous times, "I was really too honest a man to be a politician and live," and Plato refused to enter politics because the state put Socrates to death. In their speeches politicians use tactics of evasion, distortion, exaggeration, misdirection, emotional language, and misleading claims. They employ tricks of concealment of facts, the twisting of statistics, and taking quotations out of context. They also commit fallacies in reasoning precisely because they are effective — attacking the messenger not the message (*argumentum ad hominem*), appealing to national pride (*argumentum ad populum*), setting up a straw person, poisoning the well, and so forth. Sometimes the lies are blatant, and the liars are caught red-handed; at other times they slant the truth. Bertrand Russell once declined the adjective 'firm' as "I am firm, you are obstinate, he is stubborn, they are pigheaded." The connotation of words can have a strong emotional effect, as in "I have reconsidered, she has changed her mind, and you have gone back on your word."

Journalism, the third estate, used to be a bulwark against political deceit, but the neutrality of the broadcast press was undermined when Republicans repealed the Fairness Doctrine, which required reporters to be balanced and objective in their political coverage. As a result, a host of radio talk-shows and networks, such as Fox News present a heavily partisan viewpoint that reflects conservative Republicanism. Currently, print and broadcast journalists will often slant or filter the news according to their political viewpoint. Selection of newsworthy items can be biased, and what is covered can be a matter of free advertising for favored people. For this reason, the public has lost a great deal of confidence in the media to present the news fairly.

The level of honesty today may not be worse than in the past, but it does not seem any better. To focus just on the recent past, Rod Blagojevich, the former governor of Illinois, devised a plot to sell the Senate seat that had been vacated by Barack Obama. Although he consistently denied the charge, he was convicted of conspiracy to solicit bribes. Presidential candidate John Edwards at first concealed then admitted that he had an extra-marital affair and fathered a child out of wedlock. Marion Berry, the mayor of Washington, D.C., insisted he had never used drugs, then acknowledged that he did take cocaine but not crack. He was forced to resign his position and served six months in prison, after which he was re-elected mayor. In a homosexual incident reported by an undercover officer, Senator Larry Craig tried to pick up a man in a stall of a public restroom. His defense was that he touched the man's shoe because he had "a very wide stance." And Mark Sanford, the governor of South Carolina, disappeared for four days to visit his mistress in Argentina. He claimed not to have spent any public money for the trip (or other trips, but he later reimbursed the taxpayers for the expense.

With regard to recent presidents, in the 1970s President Richard Nixon lied about the Watergate affair, as proven by the White House tapes. Nixon and the Committee for the Re-Election of the President had authorized illegal spying of the Democrats at the Watergate complex. During the presidency of Ronald Reagan in 1986 the Iran-Contra scandal broke, in which arms were sold to Iran in exchange for American hostages. The profits bought weapons for the Contra rebels in Nicaragua fighting against the Sandinistas. This transaction was illegal because there was an arms embargo against Iran and a prohibition against secret wars. It was unclear how much Reagan knew about it. A large number of documents were destroyed or withheld from investigators. Certainly the Reagan administration deceived Congress about the affair.

In 1988 President George Bush said, "Read my lips, no new taxes," but he did increase the old ones. In 1998, while Bill Clinton was president, he had an affair with Monica Lewinsky, for which he was impeached by the House of Representatives. Publicly he denied the accusation vehemently: "I did not have sexual relations with that woman." In defending himself, he parsed his language carefully, saying, "It depends on what the meaning of the term 'is' is." And George W. Bush announced that Saddam Hussein "had gone to elaborate lengths...to build weapons of mass destruction" that threatened the United States. This was just after 9/11, when emotions ran high and Americans were eager for retaliation. The result was the Iraq War in which over 100,000 people were killed. No weapons of mass destruction were ever found. The evidence was selectively read. If this was intended to punish the perpetrators of 9/11, we got the wrong man. As Julius Caesar said, "Beware the leader who bangs the drums of war in order to whip the citizenry into patriotic fervor, for patriotism is indeed a double-edged sword. It both emboldens the blood, just as it narrows the mind." War, as we know, does not determine who is right but who is left.

Other notable untruths that have been told in recent years include the following: Sarah Palin said she visited Ireland and Iraq (her plane refueled in Ireland), and that, as governor, she never accepted earmarks (actually she accepted $450 million); Al Gore was falsely accused of claiming he discovered the toxic waste site at Love Canal and invented the Internet; and Michelle Bachmann perpetrated the fiction that HPV vaccine can cause mental handicaps. Lies about President Obama abound: that he described Sarah Palin as "lipstick on a pig," that he supported sex education for children in kindergarten, that he would raise taxes on the middle class (actually 80% of Americans received a tax cut), that he is a Muslim, and the "birther issue" — that he is not a U.S. citizen (despite the fact that his birth certificate has been authenticated).

In the 2016 presidential election Hillary Clinton claimed that she came under sniper fire in Bosnia; that her email practices were allowed; that we now have more jobs in solar energy than in oil; and that the Benghazi probe is the longest-running congressional investigation. But Donald Trump far exceeded her in "misstatements." He claimed we do not screen immigrants to exclude terrorist; that a judge hearing his case is Mexican; that Hilary Clinton wants a ban on all guns; that large numbers of Somali refugees have joined ISIS; that the Orlando terrorist was born in Afghanistan, and so forth. According to PolitiFact, 15% of Trump's statements are half-truths, 16% are mostly false, and 40% are clearly false; the Daily Wire lists 101 lies told by Trump.

It is common knowledge that politicians often do not keep their campaign promises, and that they misrepresent their opponent's views. Negative advertisements, criticizing the other candidates, are frequently distortions of the person, his statements, and his policies. And when lies are told, the target of the lie is placed in an impossible position. Geoffrey Stone, Professor of Law at the University of Chicago, writes "If he ignores the false accusation, it gains traction; if he disputes it, he dignifies it, gives it greater publicity, and makes it sound suspicious. If he calls a lie a lie, he comes across as accusatory and mean spirited."

If our political leaders lie, this can have devastating consequences to the nation. We do not demand complete openness about the activities of government; some surveillance systems and military movements, for example, must remain secret. But if those we trust with inside information deliberately lie for a political agenda, then we feel betrayed and manipulated. The harmful effects range from soldiers that are wounded or die needlessly, convinced they are fighting for freedom, to children learning that public lying is acceptable: "That's just politics," they are told. The message is that lying is to be expected in the adult world.

We cannot hope for a nation of saints, and sometimes there are no decent alternatives to telling lies, but lying should not become part of the culture of politics. It ought not to be considered normal and routine. And the more widespread lying becomes, the stronger the pressure to participate in the deceit. Eventually, we become callous to misrepresentation, treating it as endemic to politics.

The truth will not always triumph, but lying is usually corrosive. As a people, there should be outrage at the extent of lying in business and politics, and the seriousness of the lies told by our leaders to advance their own interests. When Richard Nixon said to David Frost "When the President does it, that means it is not illegal," the implication is that his actions are above the law. This is in opposition to the Constitution, and to our democratic principles. The actions of the head of state should reflect our founding documents and be answerable to our courts.

## The Level of Rhetoric

The present level of political rhetoric has caused cynicism among the public as well as disaffection and alienation from government. Thirty percent of the electorate identify themselves as Independents, not just because the Republicans and the Democrats have been gridlocked in Congress, arguing rather than solving problems, but because of the absence of basic civility in discussions. The language used is often disrespectful and negative toward opponents, and duplicity has become prevalent. The debates are more about the person advocating a position than about the position itself.

Rhetoric is a term with deep roots, stretching as far back as ancient Egypt and China, extending especially to ancient Greece. Witness the "rhetoric" in *The Iliad* and *The Odyssey*. In Athens, Aristotle in his book *Rhetoric* defines it as speaking skill or effective writing that convinces an audience of a point. This is done mainly through "oratory" that makes a persuasive appeal.

Aristotle breaks down rhetoric into three modes: pathos, which appeals to an audience's emotions, ethos which convinces people of the authority, honesty, or qualifications of the speaker, and logos, which is reasoned discourse or rational argument. (Logos also means everything divine; the Bible states "In the beginning was the logos," and Christ is considered logos incarnate.)

However, rhetoric acquired a bad name because the first two types, emotional and personal persuasion, were used by a group of itinerant teachers called Sophists who went about from city to city teaching techniques for self-advancement. The Sophists, who included figures such as Protagoras and Gorgias, taught practical skills for success. They were thought to use deceptive, clever-sounding arguments that were illogical, or to employ intellectual trickery, in order to win at any cost. Their defense was that they taught virtue or excellence, which was not true, and they were regarded as charlatans, unscrupulous individuals who were more interested in the fees than in honest argumentation.

This is the thrust of Socrates' objection to the Sophists. He thought that they used rhetoric to motivate or persuade people, not to prove their point through a train of logic. They had no respect for truth, but believed that every argument can be countered by an opposing one, and that an effective debate can only be judged by how convincing the speaker was. Protagoras, for example, said "Man is the measure of all things," that what is true is subjective, a matter of opinion. Facts are flexible, and beauty is in the eye of the beholder. The sophists thought that discourse shapes reality, and perception is everything. As a philosopher, Socrates believed that a good argument is based on knowledge not the appearance of knowledge, and that an argument should prove some truth according to standards of reasoning.

Increasingly today, rhetoric is being used in the way that Socrates deplored, that is, in the manner practiced by the 5th century Sophists. Advertisers, for example, will conceal facts, exaggerate claims, make misleading statements, fake free offers, and have tricky trade-in allowances. They will create artificial desires through the endorsement of glamorous celebrities, divert people's attention from the main features of products, and put important information in small print; as consumers we are told to always read the fine print, which means the advertisers deliberately try to deceive us.

Public relations firms are also prone to sophistry since they are dedicated to a positive image for their clients. That comes down to highlighting the good and downplaying the bad, or "spinning" the truth for a favorable effect. Lawyers too can be sophistic, and the negative part of a lawyer's image is derived from that reputation. In our advocacy system, both the prosecution and the defense try to make the best case possible, but that could mean that the most persuasive argument will win and not that justice will prevail. Since the lawyer's reputation and income depend on winning, there is a built-in temptation to use any means possible, provided it is legal. Emotional persuasion can trump logical discourse in trying to influence a jury, cleverness matters more than decency..

In the same way, politics is infected with sophistry from "spin doctors" and damage control, to attack ads and the use of opinion polls to determine policy. As well as serving the public good, politicians need to impress their constituency so they will be elected or re-elected. This aspect of the system opens the door to abuses of rhetoric.

Rather than using the model of the academy, where the evidence is weighed and arguments assessed, the candidate is considered a product and the voter a customer. It takes smart advertising, publicity, and selling to get the largest market share. Market research, focus groups, sampling, and polling are used to determine the public's wants, and actual demand is more important than what people express they want. It shapes campaigns. Even when people agree with one party's position on issues, they will be swayed by a political/advertising campaign that appeals to the emotions. The sad fact is that a strategy of persuasion is more successful than reasoned discourse.

Images are often regarded as more effective than ideas, especially in the television/laptop, cell phone age. Issues of foreign policy, health care, and even the economy pale beside a likeable face, an agreeable manner, a winning personality. TV images of a candidate matter almost more than what is said, particularly if the image is accompanied by a quotable sound-bite. Perception can manufacture attitudes, and repetition works. Even a lie is believed to be true if it is repeated often enough.

As mentioned previously, language is also important in evoking the right emotional response, which is why so much care is taken with semantics. Words do not just refer to things or their characteristics; they have emotional associations or connotations. How people respond to an issue often depends on the language in which it is clothed. Words such as 'security,' 'freedom,' 'God,' 'country,' 'success,' 'family,' and 'traditional values' elicit a favorable reaction in Americans; conversely, we respond badly to 'communist', 'atheist', 'immigrant', or 'Muslim'. Liberals refer to conservatives as reactionaries, and to conservatives the phrase "tax-and-spend liberal" has almost become one word.

The coloring of language is used in more and more sophisticated ways to influence our opinions. Is it an 'uprising,' 'an insurgency,' a 'conflict,' or a 'civil war,' and are the fighters 'rebels,' 'revolutionaries,' 'guerillas,' or 'freedom fighters'? We shouldn't 'cut and run' or 'retreat from a fight,' but we can make a strategic withdrawal and 'chart a new course.' Anyone who opposes a war is 'unpatriotic,' and whoever raises the issue of economic inequality is fomenting 'class warfare.' If someone is against prayer in school, he is 'godless,' and if a member of Congress opposes a piece of legislation, then he is being 'obstructionist.'

A filet mignon is much tastier than a first-class piece of dead steer.

Emotional appeals, whether through loaded language or visual images are not bad in themselves. In fact, some thinkers maintain that pure reason will never motivate us to action. It seems legitimate, for example, to show pictures of starving children to evoke pity and encourage donations to charity; this is a fair way to evoke pity, but for students to ask for higher grades because they studied hard or broke up with their girlfriends is irrelevant to the grade they have earned. Emotional arguments are wrong when they subvert logic, and that seems to be the intention of a great deal of political rhetoric. We need to use our heads, not our hearts, when considering whether someone is fit for public office. Political propaganda only gets in the way of rational judgment.

As Elvin Lim writes, today "speeches are designed to maximize applause lines, stroke the emotions, and appeal to our intuitions, while being lean on substantive content." The arguments ought to be rich in analysis and educated references, in the style of the Lincoln-Douglas debates that went on for 7 hours at a high level. In contemporary speech, politicians prey on our fear, pride, envy, and hatred, a practice which does not promote reflection but is cynical manipulation.[1]

In public discourse and in our personal lives we should practice honesty, and only make exceptions when a higher value would be threatened

The ball is now in your court, and you must play it as you see fit — but always according to what is reasonable.

---

[1] Lim, Elvin T. *The Anti-Intellectual Presidency: The Decline of Presidential Rhetoric*. NY: Oxford, 2008.

# Chapter 8. Good Taste and Bad Taste: Is Beauty In the Eye of the Beholder?

Commonly, we tell each other that whatever a person likes is art to them, that one man's trash is another man's treasure, that it's all a matter of taste. As the Romans declared, *De gustibus non est disputandum*, about taste you cannot dispute.

But that would mean the paintings in the Louvre do not deserve to be there but only reflect the taste of the curator, that the music played at Lincoln Center is not good music but just popular with the elite, and that Greek architecture is not admirable but merely reflects a style the ancients preferred. This subjectivism would throw out most works of art that civilization admires, claiming it's all personal, not a reflection of the qualities inherent in the work. Is aesthetic judgment a matter of whim, fashion, and idiosyncrasy or is there such a thing as excellent art? Are paintings of dogs playing cards, or Elvis paintings on black velvet, as good as the masterpieces of the masters?

Most aestheticians begin with the assumption that there is better and worse art, meaning by art: painting, poetry and prose, sculpture, music, architecture, theater, and dance. Some works of art are judged intrinsically valuable, and the business of aesthetics is to explain why a piece of art deserves to be admired. On what grounds can we justify saying that a landscape painting or a musical composition is actually a wonderful work of art? How can we judge that a time-lapse photograph of a rose unfolding is beautiful? In his relativistic view of art Picasso said, "truth is multiple, otherwise how could there be a thousand paintings of a tree," but there could be numerous versions of a tree, some closer, others further away from the truth of it. Maybe Cézanne comes closer than a child's lollypop tree, or brings out an essence that no one else had revealed.

## Distinctions In Aesthetics

A number of vexing questions should be addressed before art is evaluated. How do we distinguish between art and other objects, such as machines? Does art have to be beautiful or at least attractive, or can it be ugly, moving, whimsical, depressing, exciting, or reflective? Is there a difference between noise and music, and must painting be done with a brush or could we drip paint onto the canvas as in the works of Jackson Pollock? Are all beautiful objects works of art — an orchid, a rainbow, a waterfall, snow-capped mountains, coral and tropical fish, bird songs and whale songs, or does art need to be man-made? Could intricate bird's nests or the bee dance be considered art, or a chimpanzee or elephant painting? Can natural things such as seashells be art, if we select one at the beach and put it on our mantle piece? (It seems odd that the shell was not a work of art lying on the sand but becomes one when we display it.) If we carve a hole in a rock, thereby modifying a natural object, does it then become sculpture? Most artists, of course, use preexisting material, then put the stamp of their personality on it. Even poems are written on paper made from pulp, and architects use quarried stone and wood as well as concrete made from crushed rock; glass comes from silica, and steel is a combination of iron and carbon - all natural elements.

Another question is whether an object must be intended as art to be considered art, or can something like a clay pot qualify, even if it was originally made to store grain or carry water? What about lighthouses, office buildings, tents as shelters, and cathedrals meant for worship? Paleolithic cave paintings had a magical purpose: gaining power over bison, horses, and deer, as did drawings on Egyptian sarcophagi, intended to be used by the pharaoh in the afterlife. Even the Parthenon was built as a temple of worship dedicated to the goddess Athena, and its beauty is part of the devotion. Nevertheless, the result is exceptional. Can we say, "By their fruits ye shall know them, not by their roots"? Maybe marches by John Philip Sousa might qualify as art, although it's sometimes said that military music bears the same relationship to music as military justice does to justice.

We certainly cannot say with deep chest tones that anything fashioned by man is art because that would include coal mines, missiles, and mathematical formulas (although mathematicians do speak of "elegant proofs"). If art must be intentionally made, then the earth is art only if we believe in a divine designer. Only then can we say that the sky at sunset shows the wonders of God, that the Lord fashioned everything from plants to planets to beautify his creation.

And does the symphony that's never played still count as music, the manuscript that is never published still be a fine literary work, and if not, is there any purpose to them, any more than flowers that are never seen?

In addition, the difference between art and craft is a matter of controversy. The usual distinction is that craft originated in usefulness and is still connected to utility, whereas art is useless for all practical purposes; it has no ulterior purpose but is appreciated for its own sake. Also, craft cannot express as much feeling as art. An oil painting conveys a greater range of emotions than a vase or bowl; ceramics is cruder, with a more limited range. Expressiveness is always constrained by the medium, the way a piano can say more than a harmonica, a violin more than a drum. In addition, craft stresses the skill of the craftsman, while art emphasizes the creativity of the artist. The technique seems to obtrude itself and monopolize our attention. In craft we also know at the beginning what we want the end to be, whereas art is less predictable, more spontaneous and open-ended. At the outset, we have only a tentative plan in mind. To quote John Hospers,

> Let us suppose you are a carpenter, and that you receive an order for a thousand classroom chairs, with the exact specifications indicated — the kind of wood to be used, the height, width, and so on, and the color they are to be painted. The *end-in-view* (the thousand completed chairs) is already fully known in advance... Your activity is that of a craftsman... On the other hand...the poet doesn't know when he begins to write his poem what the final poem will be like... if he did, he wouldn't have to go through the creative process, he would only have to write the words down.

Based on these differences, art usually includes the fine arts — painting, sculpture, music, and so forth. Under crafts are listed leather work, quilting, jewelry making, weaving, mosaics, ceramics (pottery), photography, printing, carpentry, cooking, glassblowing, basket weaving, sewing, viticulture, perfume making, spinning (textiles), and so forth. If we buy a painting because it matches the couch, then it becomes decoration.

Craft seems peripheral to the arts, occupying a marginal area like cheerleading as an Olympic sport, or calling NASCAR drivers and racehorses athletes. An animal notices food, mates, predators, but when people experience art we do not want anything from the object; even the painting of a nude does not incite lust but is a celebration of the human form. Craft may grab our attention but art tends to keep it, gaining in interest over time, and the work is not good because it has lasted but it lasts because it is good. Perhaps art is distinguished by being intrinsically interesting.

But it is difficult to know how to handle the "practical art" of architecture, which builds structures for people to live in, for playing, working and praying, and the "craft" of photography, seems closer to fine art than a family album of snapshots (although taking a picture is different than making a picture). Weaving can rise to the level of fiber sculpture, and stained glass seems like a form of painting, just using another medium. Chiseling in stone can produce a statue or a grave marker, and the work of masons is akin to the physical labor of sculptors. Artisans can be difficult to separate from artists.

We are also uncertain how to classify secondary artists or executing artists — actors, musicians, singers, and dancers whose originality is limited by playwrights, directors, composers, conductors, and choreographers. Chopin was a primary artist who wrote music for solo piano, but the pianist Emanuel Ax performs them superbly; Shakespeare wrote *Hamlet* but Laurence Olivier is renowned for his portrayal of "the melancholy Dane." Most of the performing arts are mixed or collaborative efforts such as theater and films; opera in particular involves a range of artists and craftsmen including the chorus, dancers, the orchestra, lighting technicians, conductors, and set designers.

It is interesting that in the "lower" modes of expression, that is, the useful or practical crafts, we use our sense of smell, taste, and touch; in the "higher" forms of *beaux arts*, seeing and hearing, predominate. This is because humans have developed the greatest sensitivity to sight and sound; most animals live in a world of smells. Perhaps the sensations of taste and aroma and touch are too difficult to arrange being ephemeral and transitory, whereas fine art is enduring. Chefs and perfumers can form beautiful creations but, as one critic put it, there are no "smell symphonies."

In recent centuries a cult of personality has developed, especially in pop' culture, and it is a question whether actors, electric guitarists, and rock singers deserve that much attention. Whom a culture celebrates says a great deal about that culture. We experience the work of art through the performers but they seem secondary to the original creators — the dramatist, poet, novelist, composer. Still, the musical score would be dead notes on the page without the concert, and the written play comes alive in the drama on the stage. In that sense, the chef who prepares an excellent meal may be as important as the person who originated the recipe.

Some affinity does exist between art and morality, so that it's difficult to say that a work of pornography could ever be judged a masterpiece. The writings of Jean Genet or the Marquis de Sade fall into this twilight realm, the first describing criminal homoeroticism, the second celebrating sadomasochistic sexuality. Tolstoy wrote that the best literature unites mankind, and illustrates wholesomeness, poetic justice; the good end up happy, the wicked defeated. But the writings of Genet and de Sade are good as literature, while the social effects could be harmful; they are aesthetically admirable but morally decadent. Are the two mutually exclusive, or could there be an obscene work of art? Of course, the connection between pornography and sex crimes is hard to make; 65% of perpetrators have been viewed obscene material, but 80% have read the Bible.

It does seem that some art is both admirable and deplorable in different respects, so a decadent masterpiece might be possible. And if an internal conflict occurs, should it be banned for its negative consequences, such as vulgarizing people, or allowed for its artistic merit? This is often the problem of censorship.

In examining the issue of art another question is the relation between the arts. Is each field independent of the others, or are there connections that can be recognized? Those who claim uniqueness for each of the arts say that music best expresses our sense of time its continuous flow punctuated by occasions, the feeling of resistance and breakthrough. Literature best displays human emotions — jealousy, yearning, fury, exhilaration, and so forth; sculpture and dance celebrate the human body, the one inanimate, the other dynamic; architecture is about mass and weight, volume and space; and painting reproduces nature or an alternative reality, enabling us to better appreciate the world we see.

But we can also identify relations and cross-fertilizations. In one, circular scheme, if we begin with painting, that can shade over to sculpture if there's enough paint on the canvas — low (bas) relief, high relief, or free-standing. If sculpture is used to house, as in the buildings of Antoni Gaudi, it becomes architecture, and architecture has been called frozen music (although music is not melted architecture). Music merges into poetry if the rhythm, meter, and tones are emphasized, and poetry becomes prose when the meaning of the words is paramount. Literature is a word painting, which completes the circle.

Another scheme is to arrange the arts according to their liberation from physical material and their ability to express the human spirit. Architecture is most embedded in materials as well as being compromised by the function it must serve, the costs involved, and the technical requirements of engineering; buildings should not be made to perform acrobatics. Sculpture has greater liberty since it can use materials more freely and has no utilitarian purpose; it is only meant to be admired. Painting renders three dimensions in two dimensions, introducing a representational element. The literary arts take abstraction one step further, using language to depict people, objects, and events instead of literally showing them. And music might be the most liberated of the arts because it is the most abstract, using sound to appeal directly to the mind.

Still another scheme is to divide the arts into two categories: physical and temporal. The physical arts include painting, sculpture, and architecture; the temporal, music, dance, and literature. It is true that paintings, for example, take time to view, but they are primarily material objects, made to endure; they are constructed as monuments, designed to outlast the artist. And it is true that dance is physically seen but it is basically an art of performance extended through time; it occurs, then comes to an end, and it is remembered as a series of moments. In the same way, music has a score and literature has a text, but neither art consists of the markings on the page. The musical notes or the typography are not the art, although the spacing of a poem can add to its effect; Some poems are made like pyramids or hearts. But when we experience the classical ballet or modern dance, the symphony or concerto, the novel, poem, or play their nature is revealed through time.

Aside from recognizing art as distinct from other things, trying to separate art from craft, the question of artistic value and moral value, and the relation between the arts, the main problem in aesthetics lies in evaluation: What justifies the judgment that a work of art is good?

First of all, we know that a distinction can be made between what we like and what we value. We might enjoy an escapist movie, a horror, monster, or adventure film with lots of superhero action, but in the end we often admit to ourselves that it was a bad film. Conversely, we might not like a serious film that leaves us despondent and reflective, but be forced to acknowledge that it was an excellent film. And sometimes we like a work for extraneous reasons — because the play has an actor we enjoy, or the scribble drawing was done by our Little Johnny, or the seascape reminds us of that summer vacation in Maine. We are responding to our personal connection. To call a work of art worthwhile we need to focus on the work itself, and to justify our judgment with good reasons. (And to get more subtle still, what we value may not be valuable because we may not have good taste.) We should not praise Picasso's "Guernica" because we dislike violence and it is a political protest against the Spanish Civil War, or value Hugo's "Les Miserable" because its setting is the French Revolution, a period we appreciate. Neither should Dickens and Alcott be called good writers because they write happy endings.

We must also keep in mind the distinction between art and good art. Little Johnny's scribble-drawing may qualify as art; it is not a bicycle or a peacock, and was created intentionally to express his feelings, but whether it is good art is another matter.

## Good Art As Faithful Representation

Over the years aestheticians have developed theories as to what makes good art good, and the principal debate in the philosophy of art is over which standard is closest to the truth. The traditional theory is that of representation: a good work of art is one that faithfully imitates its subject. If a painting captures the actual landscape, a story is a slice of life, a bust is the exact image of the person, or the music creates a picture in sound, then the work is valuable. Sometimes this is called the mimetic theory, photographic theory, or simply naturalism or realism.

Plato first described it in *The Republic* saying the poet or painter —

> can create all plants and animals, himself included,
> and earth and sky and gods and the heavenly bodies

and all things under the earth and in Hades [by]
taking a mirror and turning it round in all directions.

Shakespeare repeats the image when Hamlet declares that the end of acting is "to hold as 'twere the mirror up to nature," and Leonardo da Vinci describes painting as "the sole imitator of all visible works of nature...That painting is the most praiseworthy which is most like the thing represented."

On this view, if the artist honestly imitates people or objects, moods, thoughts, attitudes, or emotions, then he has created a good work of art. As Aristotle remarked, "it is natural to delight in imitation," and children especially like miniatures — toy soldiers, doll houses, tiny cars and farm animals. We want the representational work to be so accurate that we recognize the object or the person, that it is rendered "warts and all."

In ancient Greece, the story goes, a contest was held as to which of two artists could paint more realistically. One of the artists painted a bowl of cherries that was so exact birds flew down from the trees to eat the fruit, but when the judges tried to draw aside the curtain to view the other picture, they found it was painted on the canvas; the second artist obviously won because he fooled the judges, not just birds.

Representation is the usual, common-sense view, the response of the person in the street. What the public wants from a picture is that it look like the thing depicted, not a fragmented image broken up into planes of light. If a still-life of flowers does not look like actual flowers, then the average person regards it as a bad painting. The same holds true of panoramas and family portraits. We use this criterion when we judge children's artwork, praising them as they progress from lollypop trees to realistic depictions of oaks and willows.

We even appreciate classical music that has a flute duplicating bird songs, the harp for the sound of running brooks, the cello for the human voice, and trumpets and timpani for the noise of battle. Bedřich Smetana's symphonic poem "The Moldau" represents a river beginning at its source, flowing through the countryside, and emptying with a roar into the sea, and when Tchaikovsky's "1812 Overture" is performed, canons are sometimes brought onto the stage for greater realism.

When we read a novel, we expect the story to be true to life, the setting believable. We realize it is fiction, of course, and we can only suspend our disbelief so far, but the characters ought to come alive. "The imaginary garden must have real toads in it." The plot should have an inner logic; it should ring true. We identify with the individuals in a story, play, or film, and as Aristotle says, we undergo a "catharsis," vicariously experiencing what they experience and finally feeling emotionally purged. This is why tragedy is so enjoyable, even though there might be misery and bloodshed. We empathize with the characters while being protected from the dangers they face, and our anxieties and terrors are purged in the end. We feel relief, as if waking from a nightmare.

Dance, the most ancient art, also represents human experience but through a sequence of body movements, usually performed to music using steps and gestures. Dance can be professional, ceremonial, erotic, sacred, or social, and used to incite warriors to battle or to summon the gods. Figure skating and gymnastics incorporate dance movements, but the movements of birds, even in mating rituals, are too repetitive to qualify as art. In general, dance offers a story in mime or interprets the music, expressing and evoking emotion. Dancers cannot speak but use the language of movement, pattern, and choreography to communicate their meaning. The silence itself contributes to the art, making it a purely visual experience.

An example of a simple, representational poem is Longfellow's "The Village Blacksmith":

> Under a spreading chestnut tree
> The village smithy stands;
> The smith, a mighty man is he,
> With large and sinewy hands;
> And the muscles of his brawny arms
> Are strong as iron bands.
> His hair is crisp, and black, and long,
> His face is like the tan;
> His brow is wet with honest sweat,
> He earns whate'er he can,
> And looks the whole world in the face,
> For he owes not any man...

Is it the representational element that pleases us and makes us admire a work of art? Perhaps, but that would mean photography is superior to painting since it offers a more exact replica (although it distorts life since the photograph is frozen and time never stands still). And what about science fiction, fantastic drawings, or surrealism, all of which are non-representational? What's more, this theory would make painting, literature, and dance more of a skill than an art, copying nature and rendering these media a form plagiarism. Art would be a matter of technique, the ability to draw, describe, or move one's body rather than the creation of something original.

Also, does the reproduction of just anything in the actual world create good art? If we placed a tape recorder at the average breakfast table, that would probably not make for interesting dialogue; daily conversation is not the stuff of fiction. Would bathroom functions make a good play because they're real, or would we rather not see that on stage? Would it improve statues to have them skin-colored? Even a flat, literal photograph taken by an amateur photographer may be dull; ordinary life can be inane and formless. We wonder about Warhol's paintings of Campbell's soup cans or Marilyn Monroe, which was justified as part of our culture and therefore worthy of representation. Are there better and worse subjects for art, fit or unfit topics, or is it just a matter of how the subject is treated? Is everything that is natural worth capturing?

E. H. Gombrich in his celebrated *Art and Illusion* questions our belief that we see the world as it is, and if our perception is flawed, then we have no accurate basis for comparing the art work to reality. To Gombrich, everything we see is "filtered by the mind, which organizes and interprets the data in certain ways...depending on past habits, emotional predilections, temperamental bias." And if we assimilate the artist's "schema," we then see objects through his eyes. We see real life events through the characters we read, the images presented to us, which is what is meant by "life imitates art."

Besides the problem of knowing reality, we cannot reproduce the entire world. We must select a portion of it, and that requires discrimination to enhance interest. The only, truly accurate map of the world would have to be the size of the world. We have all seen statues of perfectly proportioned Greek men and women, but even the Greeks did not look like the Greeks; these are idealized figures with the defects removed. Similarly, an author must decide on the events, characters, setting, period, theme, organization, language, and so forth when he begins writing. Life may not have a plot, no beginning, middle, or end, or possess any purpose, but a novel or short story requires meaning, which implies that life might have to be falsified for the sake of artistry. Modigliani painted women with elongated necks; Giacometti stretched his sculpted figures out of all proportion to make a point. Even photographers have to decide on exposure, lenses, subject, definition, scale, still or movie film, color or black-and-white, tricks in the dark room, and so forth. In an interior shot the furniture might be staged to form the best design, and even nature must be composed to be appreciated. We do not take a photograph with a bush in the way but arrange the shot with mountains in the distance, plow furrows in the foreground, and that cluster of daffodils to the left. The camera lies, and there is no innocent eye.

In addition, some fields of art do not lend themselves to imitation, particularly architecture. Maybe minarets were invented by cypress trees, houses by cave dwellings, towers by phalluses, and church spires are fingers pointing to God, but by and large the features of buildings are not found in nature. This includes triangles, circles, and squares which do not appear in pure form. Architecture is inventive, which can produce inspirational or grotesque structure. Architects' buildings are successful or unsuccessful based on their imagination; while doctors bury their mistakes, architects can build theirs.

In short, art is not a photocopy of nature but an imaginative transformation of experience. It can be true to life without being life-like, and it reflects a dialogue between the creator and his subject. Art is not a clay tablet bearing impressions of the world, rather the artist uses his mind and senses for an interpretation of reality. We either respond to his vision or we don't, but we should not judge his work on whether it accurately copies something real.

## The Standard of Significant Form

Representational art appeals to us directly, but it does not hold up well under scrutiny. Copying is not creating anything original, and nature itself can be more interesting than any copy of it. And in selecting what portion of nature to reproduce for a good result, the artist uses some other criterion besides realism. He will choose a particular arrangement for greatest affect, even if it entails distortion, and will select an order, setting, figures, and so forth that will best express the subject matter.

Based on considerations like this, some aestheticians argue that what appeals to us in art is not verisimilitude but the form of the work, the relationship of elements. It is the proportion, measure, balance, and symmetry that we find attractive. As the English critic Clive Bell put it,

> What quality is shared by all objects that provoke our aesthetic emotions? What quality is common to Sta. Sophia and the windows at Chartres, Mexican sculpture, a Persian bowl, Chinese carpets, Giotto's frescoes at Padua, and the masterpieces of Poussin, Pierra della Francesca, and Cézanne? Only one answer seems possible — significant form. In each, lines and colors, combined in a particular way, certain forms and relations of forms, stir our aesthetic emotions. These relations and combinations of lines and colors, these aesthetically moving forms, I call 'Significant Form.'

Each of the arts has formal elements that can be organized in an appealing way. Architecture has features of materials — stone, glass, concrete, steel, marble, and wood; the interior design; the floors, ceilings, lighting, and stairways; the height of the building in relation to its width; the placement and type of windows and doors; possible arches, columns, domes, cantilevers, courtyards, and so forth. The architect must also account for volume and mass, and consider whether the structure will appear like an organic secretion of the land or stand opposed to nature, man flexing his muscles. The composer likewise must arrange his musical elements of melody, harmony, and rhythm, key and chords, tempo and beat, meter and cadence. He must orchestrate the composition by shifting the melody between instruments — the violin, the oboe, the cello, the trumpet, varying the timbre between shades of bright and dark. He must also decide on the musical form, such as a string quartet or a symphony, or a concerto, with the soloist in dialogue with the orchestra.

According to a standard scheme, dance uses four elements in its vocabulary: bodily movement consisting of arcs and angles that are sharp or rounded, open or closed; energy which may be strong or light, dynamic or peaceful; space, where the dancers move in straight or curved lines, forward, backward, in diagonals; and time which dictates the pauses and leaps. Classical ballet has rigidly prescribed steps, and the ballerina must seem weightless, whereas modern dance allows improvisation and presses the dancer to the floor. In all cases, dance is considered living sculpture or poetry in motion. Literature, including poetry and plays, uses different elements of meaning, form, theme, setting, rhythm, and rhyme, simile and metaphor, assonance and alliteration. The connotation or emotional association of words is employed — the woman will 'faint,' not 'pass out,' and the term 'foot' is used not a woman's 'feet,' and symbolism is used — a lion for strength, a flickering candle for death. In literature, everyday language is disciplined and enhanced, used in a more restrained and imaginative way. And sculpture deals with materials, surface textures, forms and space, proportion, scale, and harmony. When sculptors use clay or metal, they build up their statues; with granite, wood, or marble they take away the extraneous parts, liberating the figure that lies within.

The good artist simply combines the elements of his medium into a successful composition. What we appreciate in all art is the pleasing arrangement of the parts. We may be lured by the likeness to something in the world, but what we value is the composition, with the figures or events as components in a design. A landscape painting is not good because it looks like the land but because of the relation between the earth and sky, that triangle of rocks against the round sun, the splash of green foliage against the blue of the lake. To appreciate art we must dismiss the resemblances to any known objects, and look for the abstract form that structures the whole.

Roger Fry writes,

> In proportion as art becomes purer, the number of people to whom it appeals gets less. It cuts out all the romantic overtones of life that are the usual bait by which men are induced to accept a work of art. It appeals only to the esthetic sensibilities, and that in most men is comparatively weak.

> For example, we might respond to the following picture because it resembles a (crude) human face:

But the formalist would say that, beneath the surface, we are appreciating the form, and when stripped of its representational qualities, the essence appears as abstract art.

In this view, to ask "What does that painting or dance mean?" is inappropriate. The work does not mean but is. It does not stand for something else but presents a reality in itself, an invention that the viewer can accept or reject. It does not represent something different to each person like a Rorschach test, or function like a mirror reflecting the world, but avoids meaning altogether in favor of a unique, pleasing design. It may not even mean what the creator says it means because artists are unreliable reporters, even of their own creations. As Salvador Dali remarked, "Artists can no more talk about art than vegetables can give a lecture on horticulture."

Haiku with its elegance and economy of expression exemplifies this theory:

> No sky
> no earth — but still
> snowflakes fall

Or the following poem by Emily Dickinson, although the form is atypical and reflects her withdrawal:

> I'm nobody! Who are you?
> Are you nobody too?
> Then there's a pair of us — don't tell!
> They'd advertise — you know!
> How dreary to be somebody!
> How public like a frog
> To tell one's name the livelong day
> To an admiring bog!

Significant form is a more sophisticated view of art, less obvious, maybe more profound. But at the end of the day we have to ask ourselves: Is it the form in a work that makes us respond and appreciate it?

The main criticism is that to judge a work of art in terms of its structure seems bloodless, sterile, and dispassionate. Geometry never moves us, and art that leaves us unmoved is hardly art. In analyzing a musical composition, for example, we may notice a rhythmic figure, or that it is a fugue with little motifs chasing each other, but although we may identify these elements afterwards, that is not what impacts us. The content seems to matter more than the form, and if we respond to the melody it is because it speaks directly to our emotions. That is, art seems more of an immediate, visceral reaction than a matter of elements identified by the intellect.

Also, the arrangement of formal elements matters much more in some arts than in others, and in certain styles of art. Literature certainly has form but it counts less than in architecture, and form is prominent in abstract painting but more implicit in representation. And since all art has form (a dab of paint has an outline), when is form significant? Even modern, atonal music with twelve tone rows cannot escape having a pattern. Does significant form consist of diversity or harmonious features, unity or deep complexity?

Formalism is a sophisticated theory, the critic's point of view. It shows a certain contempt for the average person's response. Experts profess to know the hidden reason for the appeal of great art, and How a work affects us is considered irrelevant.

But this approach seems precious, rarefied, and ingrown. If it is possible to differentiate between good and bad art, can we trust the connoisseur to make that determination because they are the best informed?

## Emotive Expression

The expression of emotion is still another theory of what makes good art good, and it treats art as the manifestation of sincere emotions in a moving way. According to Plato, it "waters the passions," and induces us to accept ideas we might otherwise question (which, to Plato, isn't a good thing). It does not try to understand the world but reacts to personal experience with an outburst of feeling. We see the artist's personality in the work, his impulses and effusiveness, not the order, decorum, or politeness of society. On this view, art is not an objective rendering of nature but an outer expression of our inner, emotional state.

Art should delight the senses not nourish the mind, otherwise it would be an essay, and its effect does not depend so much on context; rather, our emotions are immediately engaged. We find certain colors attractive — shades of blue or green, for instance, and respond to the texture of marble, wood, water, and skin. We like particular sounds such as the plaintive quality of stringed instruments, the flute, which produces a "white" noise like a boys' choir, or the general expressiveness of the human voice. Even the rhythm and sound of language can affect us — the English word 'memorable,' for instance, the Spanish 'golondrina,' or the French 'coquelicot.' In onomatopoeia — 'buzz,' 'gushing,' 'whisper,' 'rustling' — the words mimic the natural sounds. Nonsense poetry uses words without meaning, as in "The Jabberwocky" by Lewis Carroll: " 'Twas brillig and the slithy toves/ Did gyre and gimble in the wabe: / All mimsy were the borogoves,/ And the mome raths outgrabe."

Aestheticians speculate on whether our responses to qualities are universal or relative to the culture. Does red symbolize something strong to all people — terror, happiness, good luck; is it associated with fire, blood, the setting sun? Does black always mean tragedy and death? In the East, white is the color of mourning, but that may indicate a different attitude towards death. Do high notes represent hope, low ones, despair? Do we all like the tastes of sweet, sour, bitter, and salty, with the mix varying between cultures? In other words, does everyone respond to physical sensations in the same way, and is that which we appreciate in a work of art its emotional effect?

Images also have a strong impact in art, and not just of a visual kind. We can taste the salt-air in a vivid story of sailing ships; hear the gong in that painting of a Chinese procession; smell the flowers and feel the breeze in a description of the countryside. Very often, We also experience a bodily response to art. Our pulse pounds, our breath quickens, our skin prickles, and we tap our foot, clap our hands, sway and want to dance. In the presence of good art we also feel a sense of exaltation, a joy and enchantment. We are raised above our common life and realize what existence can be. And through the emotions of art, we come away with new insights. Perhaps all great art contains philosophic truths, imaginatively expressed.

Here is Matthew Arnold's celebrated poem "Dover Beach":

> The sea is calm tonight.
> The tide is full, the moon lies fair
> Upon the straits; on the French coast the light
> Gleams and is gone; the cliffs of England stand;
> Glimmering and vast, out in the tranquil bay.
> Come to the window, sweet is the night-air!
> Only, from the long line of spray
> Where the sea meets the moon-blanched land,
> Listen! you hear the grating roar
> Of pebbles which the waves draw back, and fling,
> At their return, up the high strand,
> Begin, and cease, and then again begin,

With tremulous cadence slow, and bring
The eternal note of sadness in...
The Sea of Faith
Was once, too, at the full, and round earth's shore
Lay like the folds of a bright girdle furled.
But now I only hear
Its melancholy, long, withdrawing roar,
Retreating to the breath
Of the night-wind, down the vast edges drear
And naked shingles of the world.

Emotion does seem a critical part of art, the way roundness is essential to a circle. And emotions can be expressed not just by representation but by an abstract work with clashing colors; in all cases, the perceiver is affected because of the feeling evoked. Unlike clock time, music presents the engendering and relaxing of tension.

But one question that arises is, "Whose emotions are relevant?" It could be that of the artist, and what impresses us is his passion, intensity, maybe his obsession. That is, we might be admiring the person behind the work, and since the 19th century there is the romantic view of the artist in his garret, who lives unconventionally and even cuts off his ear in a frenzy of emotion. He creates his art in a trance-like state or at white-hot temperatures, and believes in emotion poured out on canvas, not recollected in tranquility. Conventional morality does not apply to him because he lives a life of freedom, obedient only to his Muse. Even Plato refers to the artist as "inspired and possessed," and Shakespeare groups together the lunatic, the lover, and the poet.

But if the emotion of the artist is what we mean, then we are not judging the work itself but the person behind the work. Furthermore, awful people can create wonderful art, just as virtuous people can produce inane art. Beethoven, for example, seems to have been a short-tempered, suspicious, miserable person, but he managed to write nine symphonies that are among the finest ever composed. Even the state of mind of good people can be different from their creation, and the personality of the artist adds nothing to our understanding of the art.

Perhaps it is the emotions generated in the audience that matter most. Here the emphasis is not on the source but on the effect — the fear, desire, grief, hope, sadness, joy that the art communicates. Labels sometimes suggest the feeling that the art is intended to convey: "Flowering Garden," the "Pathétique," "Whistler's Mother," the "Emperor" concerto. In any case, if people's passions are aroused at listening to or viewing a work of art, then it has achieved its purpose. Indifference is an index of failure; stimulation means success.

However, that would mean that whatever stirs our emotions, or appeals to the largest number of people is good art. No distinction would be made between entertainment and art, pleasure and appreciation; public taste would be authoritative. Propagandistic posters, such as those in Socialist Realism, would be art, along with sacred music, and bad art would be good if it were popular. There can be a potency to cheap music. The works of art in museums are not those enjoyed by the majority of people, and the ability to appreciate good art might have to be acquired, the result of education. Some societies, in fact, have distrusted art altogether. Goering famously said, "When I hear the word 'culture,' I reach for my gun."

Perhaps art must stimulate the emotions of the critic, but critics are notoriously unemotional. Maybe they are moved at a deeper level, or control their feelings so as not to contaminate their judgment.

Is it the emotion contained in the work itself that counts? But an inanimate object cannot have emotions. There are no sentiments in canvases, scores, wood, or even words. They are non-living and exist as means for the artist to make a statement or to share his feelings with an audience.

Who, then, must experience strong emotion for a work of art to be judged good? Because this is unspecified, the theory of art as emotion may not be the last word.

Perhaps there is wisdom in the theory of art offered by Friedrich Nietzsche, the 19th century German philosopher. In *The Birth of Tragedy* Nietzsche describes two forces identified with the Greek gods Apollo and Dionysus: the Apollonian, which represents structure and reason, and the Dionysian, which stands for unrestrained passion, fueled by the thought of death. If the Apollonian predominates, then the art calcifies like a skeletal structure; and if the Dionysian is overwhelming, the passions cannot coalesce into a whole; as Marianne Moore said, it would be like playing tennis with the net down. Both are necessary forces that must be kept in equilibrium or a dynamic tension, for without limits we cannot build upward. This holds true in art, religion, and in civilization as a whole.

To Nietzsche, the genius of Aeschylus and Sophocles was to write plays that balanced the two. Oedipus commits patricide and incest, but the horrors are held within the framework of inevitability. And perhaps this is the secret of good art: an ideal blend of formalism and emotivism, with representation appearing cheap by comparison.

The ball is now in your court, and you must play it as you see fit — but always according to what is reasonable.

# CHAPTER 9. BUSINESS IS BUSINESS: DO CAPITALISTS HAVE A SOCIAL RESPONSIBILITY?

In 2008 the United States experienced a financial crisis, precipitated by the bursting of the housing bubble. This had repercussions for markets across the world, from Europe to Asia and beyond. High-risk mortgages, with insufficient guarantees and low down payments, had been sold by banks and bundled into securities held by global financial institutions. The big funds ignored the risks, looking for a high rate of return on their investments. They assumed, without good reason, that real estate would continually increase in value. This was also the assumption of mortgage lenders at banks who pushed through weak applications, driven by pressure to sell mortgages.

When the price of real estate dropped precipitously, so that the value of a house was lower than that of the mortgage, those homeowners had little incentive to continue making payments. In 2008 alone, 3.1 million people defaulted, walking away from their properties; that is 1 in every 54 households. "For sale" signs sprouted like trees in the suburbs. In a domino effect, the financial institutions that held these "toxic assets" in their portfolios began to fail, and since the world's financial system is interconnected, economies across the globe were seriously affected. The "great recession" resulted — the worst financial crisis since the 1929 depression.

Technically, a recession is defined as two quarters of negative economic growth. More colloquially, a recession is when your neighbor loses his job; a depression is when you lose yours! In the 2008 recession unemployment officially reached 12.5%; in 2006 it had been 4.1%. Between 2007 and 2008, Americans lost over one quarter of their net worth, the value of their property dropped 29%, and their total home equity declined from $13 trillion to $8.8 trillion. What's more, their retirement assets dropped 22%, savings were reduced by $1.2 trillion, and they lost $1.3 trillion in pensions. Altogether, the total came to $8.3 trillion.

During this period, the five largest investment banks either went bankrupt (Lehman Brothers, the largest bankruptcy in history), were taken over by other companies (Bear Sterns and Merrill Lynch), or were bailed out by the U.S. government (AIG, Goldman Sachs, and Morgan Stanley). Two automobile manufacturers, General Motors and Chrysler, were also bailed out, while the government-sponsored enterprises of Fannie Mae and Freddie Mac were placed in receivership.

Much of the activity to save the economy involved the federal government intervening in the markets. In 2008 President Bush pumped $168 billion into the economy in the Troubled Asset Relief Program (TARP), and in 2009 President Obama infused another $787 billion through the American Recovery and Reinvestment Act. This stimulus package included $75 billion for struggling homeowners. The purpose of such governmental actions was to rescue Wall Street, halt the recession, and stabilize the markets, as well as to maintain financial confidence across the globe.

There was a great deal of controversy over these bailouts, especially of the financial institutions that caused the recession. The government argued that we needed to put out the fire in our neighbor's house, even if he was responsible for it; otherwise, the whole neighborhood could go up. But aside from bailouts for specific companies, such as Goldman Sachs and General Motors, people questioned whether the government should interfere at all in the free market.

Classical economics, which originated with Adam Smith in *The Wealth of Nations*, wanted markets to operate unimpeded, in a laissez-fair model. The economy can maintain its own equilibrium, Smith argued, through market forces. Self-interest guides society more effectively than community concerns, and government intervention will only disrupt the flow of goods and services. If a company cannot compete successfully, then it must fall by the wayside, making room for more efficient firms. Marx labeled this classical model "vulgar political economy," but Adam Smith reasoned that risk entails loss, and he trusted the "invisible hand" to guide the economy.

On the other hand, the followers of John Maynard Keynes favored government regulation of the economy for the greater good. Private sector decisions sometimes led to undesirable outcomes for society overall, and this necessitated an active response by the public sector. Keynesians applauded the steps taken by the federal government, especially decisions on monetary policy by the federal bank.

This debate is still being played at both ends of the political spectrum, sometimes in intemperate and vitriolic ways, and mainly on the ideological level rather than by empirical data. Higher mathematics and econometric models do not seem to have helped very much, despite their sophistication. For failing to predict the recession, the reputation of economics as a science was blighted — even as the "dreary science."

## The Causes of the Near Meltdown

Both the causes and the cures of the recession are hotly debated, and the problems may be easier to identify than to solve. Some of the chief explanations are the following:

1. According to Nobel Laureate Paul Krugman, "Regulation did not keep up with the system." Or as Ben Bernanke, the head of the Federal Reserve Bank, stated, "Financial innovation + inadequate regulation = a recipe for disaster." There was a regulatory failure in the law as well as inadequate policing of the players in the market. This was the conclusion of the Financial Crisis Inquiry Commission in its 2011 report: "Mortgage fraud flourished in an environment of collapsing lending standards and lax regulations." This in turn was the result of deregulation under President Reagan and the repeal of the Glass-Steagall Act, which had separated commercial banks and investment banks.

Throughout the years, the business community has steadily lobbied Congress to reduce regulations. And whenever market reform is proposed, an army of lobbyists descend upon Washington to defend the autonomy of corporations.[1]

2. Some analysts fault Alan Greenspan, then Chairman of the Federal Reserve Bank which exercised considerable power over the economy. Greenspan kept interest rates unusually low, which created a heady, bullish climate for investors. Financial institutions and stockholders thrived, and both banks and consumers were encouraged to purchase real estate. This produced a credit bubble that was destined to burst.

As a free market economist, Greenspan was taken by surprise. In 2006 he stated "the worst may be over for housing," and afterwards he told Congress that the downturn violated everything he had assumed about economics. His excuse was that it was "a perfect storm," an event that happens once in a hundred years.

Greenspan and the Securities and Exchange Commission also testified to Congress that the failure was due to allowing the investment banks to be self-regulating.[2]

---

[1] Cassidy, John. How Markets Fail. NY: Farrar, Straus, and Giroux, 2009.
[2] Labaton, Stephen. "SEC Concedes Oversight Flaws." New York Times, 9/27/08

3. A third explanation is that the credit rating agencies, principally Moody's and Standard and Poor's, acted improperly due to a conflict of interest. They underestimated the risk of mortgage backed securities, and gave a higher rating to securities than was warranted. These inaccurate credit ratings were due to the fact that the agencies were paid by investment banks — the very banks that sold securities to investors. This created "misjudgments" by the credit rating agencies, and a lack of transparency about the risks that were undertaken by banks. Afterwards, there were calls for protection against the collusion of these institutions.[1]

4. Another major factor was predatory lending practices by banks. Lenders gave home mortgages to people whose repayment capacity was extremely doubtful, so called "toxic" mortgages.[2] The borrower's low assets, poor employment record, and low credit score should have warned them off. Of course, according to "caveat emptor," or let the buyer beware, customers should not have taken on debt they could not afford. They should have shopped more carefully, scrutinized the conditions, and read the fine print. But as in most business transactions, the responsibility is shared between buyer and seller. For their part, The lenders should not have encouraged borrowers to take on more debt than they could afford. This is especially true of the elderly, the uneducated, and minorities who were vulnerable to enticements of variable rate mortgages. If important information is put in fine print, the intention is to fool the customer. Taking advantage of innocence, gullibility and ignorance is not ethical behavior.

Simply put, these "subprime" mortgages were issued without sufficient security by loan officers and lending institutions that were in the grip of a feeding frenzy. When the borrower could not pay, foreclosure and repossession occurred, stripping the homeowner of equity in his property. In 2011 one federal investigation concluded "Lenders made loans that they knew borrowers could not pay and that could cause massive losses to investors in mortgage securities." By one estimate, abusive practices and outright fraud was responsible for the loss of $112 billion between 2007 and 2009.

One ironic aspect of mortgage defaults was "credit default swaps." Here the seller of a mortgage, CD, or other instrument agrees to compensate the buyer in the event of a default. This is meant to provide safety for the buyer. However the down side was that security firms encouraged high-risk lending because, in case of default, they would profit. If they lost, they won, gaining financially either way.

5. A more intangible cause was the atmosphere of "irrational exuberance" in the business world. In the 1990s and well into 2000, a great deal of

---

[1] United States Congress Senate Committee. *Predatory Lending.* Dec. 31, 2010.
[2] Reinhart, Carmen and Rogoff, Kenneth. *This Time Is Different.* Princeton: Princeton University Press, 2009.

money was made by corporations and in the stock market. This optimistic spirit made traders and executives take excessive risks, counting on an economy that would continue to grow; it was an unconscious but powerful assumption.

As outlined above, C.E.O.s and top executives took home enormous salaries and bonuses, and bought mega-houses. Corporations had a "too-big-to-fail" attitude,[1] and American economic power in the world could not be challenged. Even prime time ministers preached a gospel of wealth. People such as Sandy Weill, Ivan Boesky, Michael Milken, Bernard Madoff, and Jack Welch rode the crest of this wave.

In this culture, the recession caught business flat-footed. The burden of mortgage based securities was enormous, and businesses as well as individuals were over-exposed and over-extended.

Another element in the equation is the U.S. trade deficit and national debt. The numbers are certainly alarming. According to the U.S. Census, the 2014 trade deficit was $51.8 billion annually, which is down from 4800 billion in 2008. Our national debt reached $15.7 trillion in 2012, 50% of which is owned by foreign nations, especially Japan and China. The high figure is the result of numerous factors: the Bush tax cuts, the Iran/Iraq War ($1.3 trillion), the recent drug benefits and health care entitlements ($1.1 trillion), bailouts ($200 billion), Obama's economic stimulus plan ($800 billion), and lower tax revenues because of a poorer economy.

However, as mind-boggling as the figures are, economists disagree over the role played by the trade deficit and the national debt in creating the recession or in inhibiting the growth of the economy. Many argue that the trade imbalance is not at all related, and that at this stage, fiscal expansion is necessary, even at the expense of increasing our debt.

Various other explanations have been offered for the economy collapsing like a house of cards. These include high oil prices, excessive credit, a service economy, overconsumption, hedge funds, competition from China, and other issues in the global economy. Even stupidity, stubbornness, shortsightedness, incompetence, and willful blindness have been mentioned as partial causes.[2] In recent years this list has included the financial problems in Europe, specifically Greece, Italy, Spain, and Ireland. Keynes referred to "animal spirits" affecting business, such as confidence, uncertainty, and pessimism, while Marx talked about the inherent instability of capitalism; to Marxists, boom and bust are normal features of a capitalist economy.

---

[1] Sorkin, Andrew Ross. *Too Big to Fail*. NY: Penguin, 2009.
[2] Fox, Justin. *The Myth of the Rational Market*. NY: Harper Collins, 2009.

## The Dark Side of Capitalism

None of the above elements can be wholly excluded; all were contributing factors: Lax federal regulations, the classical economics of the Fed', the collusion of credit rating agencies, predatory lending practices, and the feeding frenzy of the market. But is there a fundamental reason for the great recession?

Logicians differentiate between necessary conditions and sufficient ones. For instance, a necessary condition for salt would be sodium, because you cannot get salt without it. A sufficient condition for salt would be both sodium and chloride in equal parts. So a necessary condition is a required element, without which something cannot occur, while a sufficient condition compels something to happen. What, then, was the sufficient condition for the recession?

Some critics identify the basic problem as greed. As Ronald Walters put it, "Corporate greed is the subtext of the entire economic crisis."

Greed is one of the seven deadly sins, and like lust and gluttony, it is a sin of excess. In greed, a person wants more than he needs or deserves. He desires more than his fair share, and what he wants above all is wealth. Greed can take the form of an excessive need for love or knowledge or fame, but its object is usually material possessions, along with status and power. It is "covetousness or avarice for base gains." In Dante's *Purgatory*, the greedy were bound and laid face down on the ground for having concentrated too much on earthly things.

But as Arthur Schopenhauer remarked, to be motivated by greed is like drinking sea water; the more the person drinks, the thirstier he gets. There is an overwhelming desire to have more; the wealth that is accumulated is never enough. The person continually tries to reach the horizon, but the horizon line moves as he does. And although greed is self-defeating in this way, it has been elevated almost to a virtue in recent years.[1]

In the film "Wall Street," Gordon Gekko says, "Greed, for lack of a better word, is good. Greed is right, greed works. Greed clarifies, cuts through, and captures the essence of the evolutionary spirit." This speech is taken from Ivan Boesky's commencement address to the School of Business Administration at the University of California Berkeley in 1986, and it captures some of that mentality. It is the attitude that was at the root of America's financial problems and that precipitated our economic recession.

In a deeper sense, material wealth is not the motivation. Vacation homes, yachts, prestigious schools, luxury cars, and so forth may only be symbols, the way a cigar is not so much a pleasure as the outward sign of success,. The

---

[1] Naylor, R. T. *Crass Struggle: Greed, Glitz, and Gluttony.* Montreal: McGill-Queens University Press, 2011.

greedy person wants an enlargement of his being as a glutton wants food, or the domineering person wants to absorbs others into himself, to become more. It is the need to establish one's superiority, to have greater power over life.

Capitalism assumes that people are motivated by self-interest, but that need not mean selfishness or greed. Self-interest implies an incentive of personal gain, whereas selfishness implies advancing yourself at someone else's expense.

As we have discussed, selfishness is often thought to be endemic to the human species, an inherent "depravity" associated with original sin. The word has a negative connotation, and selfish acts are shameful acts. Self-interest is a more benign concept, but even so, it may not be the whole of human nature. There seem to be numerous instances in society of altruism and selflessness. A common example is the main breadwinner of the family (usually the husband) who will share his earnings with his wife and children, taking very little for himself. Non-profit organizations, philanthropists, social workers, doctors in a third world clinics, 9/11 firefighters and so forth seem sincerely willing to help people in need. And although they may feel good about themselves as a result of their actions, it is doubtful that their intention in acting was to feel good. They appear to be honestly generous. Adam Smith, in *The wealth of Nations*, treats self-interest as the driving force of capitalism; nevertheless, he says "There are evidently some principles in [man's] nature, which interest him in the fortune of others, and render their happiness necessary to him, though he derive nothing from it, except the pleasure of seeing it."

Greed seems to include selfishness because the greedy person is willing to step on others to get ahead. We speak of "blind greed" that, myopically, does not see other people's rights, needs, or distress, and never has enough. The avaricious person is hard-shelled, putting personal gain above all other considerations. Pure greed is perpetually dissatisfied, not wanting what it has, never having all it wants. It is an overwhelming desire to have more — even at others' expense; the bad side of the good life.

Imelda Marcos, the wife of the President of the Philippines, had thousands of pairs of shoes while Philippine children went barefoot.

Evidence of greed was apparent during the financial crisis. The top executives of Fortune 500 corporations awarded themselves multi-million dollar salaries, bonuses, and stock options after laying off thousands of employees. What's more, their compensation was not performance-based, in fact, several C.E.O.s had been responsible for the near collapse of their companies. Besides seven-figure salaries, the bonuses seemed obscene to the average American, showing uncontrolled ambition for more. Henry Paulson at Goldman Sachs received a bonus of $11 million; William Harrison at J.P. Morgan, $16 million; Sandy Weill at Citicorp, $27.5 million; and Jimmy Welch at Bear Sterns, $33.6 million. Bernie Madoff became enormously rich ($50 billion) with a pyramid investment scheme at the expense of charities and individuals who had trusted him. That is the very definition of greed. People lost their homes, investments, and life savings to someone who had more money than he could ever need.[1]

When executive compensations were made public, people were understandably angry and disaffected. Business was distrusted by the American people more than it had been in decades. Banks even hired security guards as protection against violence, and the Occupy Wall Street movement spread to a dozen cities. The protesters called for reform at the top, not reform of the Welfare system; and the poor resented being belittled or blamed for their poverty. The defense that was offered seemed lame rather than reassuring: that wealthy people create jobs. In actuality, the fortunes that were amassed were largely hoarded by the richest families and not plowed back into the economy.[2]

## A Fair Profit and Just Compensation

Is there such a thing as a fair profit as opposed to an excessive profit, or are businesses within their rights to charge customers as much as the traffic will bear? Are profit margins fair if they are set at the average in the industry? Do business leaders have an obligation to make as much money as they can for the company and its shareholders?? Are landlords only entitled to a fair rent, and farmers to a fair market price for their fruits, vegetables, milk, and livestock? If "fair profit" is a legitimate concept, how is it to be determined?

An advocate of the free market system would say that businesses should charge as much as people are willing to pay. The law of supply and demand will balance out the price. If the supply is low and the demand high, companies can charge more; if the demand is low and the supply high, then companies must lower their prices. The amount of profit or the profit margin will depend upon fluctuations in the market.

Of course, taking advantage of people in a crisis is always unfair, for example, selling water at an exorbitant price after an earthquake or tsunami. And business relations must be free from fraud, misrepresentation, and predation, but if there is an honest exchange, then the profit is legitimate. But To the classical economist, even if one of the parties is hurt that could still be fair — provided the exchange is an open one. Each party has freely

---

[1]  Kothari, Vinay B. *Executive Greed*. NY: Palgrave Macmillan, 2010
[2] Madrick, Jeff. *The Age of Greed*. NY: Random House, 2011.

assumed that risk, and many business transactions are a "zero sum game." One person's victory is another's defeat, as in sports. The hope of winning had induced them to play, and in a competitive system, they knew the odds. Other business relations are of an "I'm OK, you're OK" type, a win-win scenario. If a neighbor has an excess of apples, the other an excess of tomatoes, an exchange will benefit them both. In such situations, there is minimal risk or chance of failure. Sometimes cooperation works better than competition.

Some economists have suggested that a fair profit should be tied to effort. Lazy companies like lazy people are not entitled to rewards; only the industrious organizations deserve their profits. At the individual level, this is the main objection to food stamps and welfare payments. Some of the recipients are lazy, and only those who work hard deserve the "goods" in life. A certain percentage of welfare recipients are ill or old, but others are able bodied and have no excuse. We should earn our money by preparation in school and perseverance on the job; only then are our earnings justified earnings. The same holds true for business. A fair profit is one that is achieved through the determination, skill, and effort of a company and its employees.[1]

Of course, we know that the world does not operate this way for the individual. Those who do strenuous labor in fields or factories do not have the highest salaries, otherwise coolies would be millionaires. Hard work does not always pay off. Intelligence, connections, and opportunities factor heavily into the lottery of success. Even luck plays a part, although as Thomas Jefferson said, "The harder I work, the more luck I seem to have."

But the question is whether the world should operate this way. Should a fair profit be determined by the amount of work involved?

The main problem with this theory is that it does not take into account the value of the item produced. As Leonard Reed points out, "If as much effort is used to make a mud pie as a mince pie, they are of equal worth."[2] That hardly seems the proper index.

What about the value of the product to the nation? Would a fair profit consist of earnings that are proportional to the good the product provided? Using this criterion, cigarette companies should make little or no profit because cigarettes cause serious illnesses; they are responsible for half a million deaths a year. Conversely, hospitals that help rather than harm people, treating the sick and injured, should receive a substantial profit. House builders would receive more, polluting industries less; producers of healthy foods more, manufacturers of junk foods less.

---

[1] This, incidentally, is the objection to gambling: any winnings are unearned income. The winner then consumes without having produced.
[2] Marketing with websites.com/fair_profit.html

If we rely on market forces, some of the companies that threaten our welfare the most are also the most prosperous. This is because capitalism, per se, offers no incentives to pursue the greater good. If helping society is profitable, then that is done, but the profit is the motive and the good is incidental. For instance, if it is cheaper to emit greenhouse gases that contribute to global warming, then manufacturers use that method of production, unless they are forced to stop. That is, it may be cost-effective to harm ecosystems. The same is true in the operation of oil rigs, the agribusiness, coal mining, and harvesting lumber trees.

The chief problem, of course, is that a governmental agency must be set up to allocate profits according to social worth. The economic freedom of classic capitalism to make as much profit as you can would come to an end. Americans are unwilling to surrender this freedom to a central government, even one that pegs rewards to public welfare.

Maybe the idea of a fair profit could be related to our discussion of greed. Perhaps a fair profit does not mean as much as you can get, and is not even connected to effort or social value. It may consist of profit that helps the company as well as the people, while an unfair profit harms other people in significant ways. The good of the company should be commensurate with the benefit to the society.

Profit need not depend on harming society at large, even if it is a zero sum game with competitors. Profit can be made ethically. To consider the effect on people does not mean going out of business but maybe making less profit than one would otherwise. And if one can only profit by harming society, then one should not be in business. To argue for the existence of a harmful company, perhaps because it contributes jobs for the nation's workforce, is like arguing for the mafia.

For example, suppose an American company can realize an enormous profit by paying low wages in a sweat shop in Viet Nam. The company might still make sufficient profits by paying the workers a decent wage and thereby invest in the nation's economy. The wage need not be at an American level but certainly above subsistence. And instead of taking from the host nation much more than it gives (which is the accusation against colonialism), the ratio could be changed so everyone affected would be better off. A rising tide raises all boats. Companies are not charitable institutions, and if there is no profit, they will go out of business. But they can exist comfortably with a fair profit — one consistent with the success of the company but also mindful of the welfare of its employees and the society.[1]

---

[1] Ferguson, Charles. *Predator Nation*. NY: Crown, 2012.

Profit and salaries are, of course, interconnected, and the same question of fairness arises. Is there is such a thing as just compensation, or should salaries be negotiated between employer and employee in a free market.

Here the government has intervened to protect the worker from both exploitation and discrimination. The Fair Labor Standards Act of 1938 covers minimum wages and overtime requirements, and the Equal Pay Act of 1963 focuses on sex-based discrimination, calling for equal pay for equal work. The Fair Pay Act of 2009 also prohibits discrimination in hiring, firing, promotions, or increments on the basis of sex, race, or national origin. It even mandates equal pay for equivalent work, comparing a secretary to a lab technician, a clerk to a maintenance worker, a social worker to a parole officer.

Is it wrong to impose such laws on business, specifying minimum wages or maximum hours, excluding children from the workforce, having health and safety standards, and environmental regulations?

Suppose that a woman is willing to accept a lower salary than a man. She is not the main breadwinner but supplements the family income and therefore requires less. The employer, for his part, wants to minimize costs and that includes expenditures for labor. If both parties agree on the terms of employment, freely and without coercion, shouldn't that agreement be allowed?

Suppose a mine worker takes a job at a dangerous mine for high pay. The mine owner knows the mine is unsafe, and he has made full disclosure of the chances of injury or death. Taking that into consideration, he has offered a substantial salary for the job. The worker is fully aware of the risks involved — the collapse of rotting timbers, black lung disease from poor ventilation — but is willing to play the odds for the sake of the money. Should the Mine Safety and Health Administration stop him from making that choice?

Such cases lie at the juncture of freedom and government regulation. Whenever there are laws governing conditions, salary, or workplace rules, that places a burden on business, and interferes with the freedom of the marketplace. It seems paternalistic, treating adults like children in need of protection. However, if there is a significant power differential between employer and employee, then the choices are not free and people need to be shielded from abuse. How much government regulation is needed while still allowing business to flourish, is an open question. But some legal protection is necessary as long as businesses do not police themselves.

In particular, a fair day's work for a fair day's pay, or vice versa, seems a principle worth upholding. Salary levels are supposedly determined by the nature of the job, the education required, the security of the position, the worker's experience, the financial capability of the organization, the cost of living, the pay scale in the industry, and so forth. Work that is predominantly mental in character, especially that which requires advanced knowledge, will generally pay more than unskilled labor. However, those criteria do not account for the tremendous gap between the salaries of top executives and blue-collar workers. Businesses should adjust the income of its personnel in accordance with fair standards of compensation. It would take an extraordinary day's work for a fair day's pay to be several thousand dollars.

We would not want complete government control of profits or wages, even though government regulation is sometimes justified. But business should so conduct itself that government intervention is unnecessary. The culture of companies should include fairness, to both employees and the public, and success should include benefit to the nation as well as financial gain. We cannot say "Business is business," for as a part of society, business is not exempt from social responsibility. A mentality of greed need not be a part of capitalism, and as we have seen, it can lead to a recession and great suffering.

The ball is now in your court, and you must play it as you see fit — but always according to what is reasonable

# Chapter 10. Persons As Matter In Motion: Is There a Ghost In the Machine?

'Self' is a strange word. We speak of myself, yourself, themselves; we say I am not feeling myself today, I am beside myself with worry. We refer to self-interest, self-deception, and self-centeredness; and of my better self, my former self, self-fulfilling and self-negating prophecies. (Self-love could be multiple personality disorder, and we hope that our love is reciprocated.) We hold conversations with ourselves, dialogues inside our heads as if there were two of us, and at times the self seems both subject and object: "I" can contemplate "me." What's more, we regard ourselves regarding ourselves regarding ourselves *ad infinitum*, and we are not sure at what level we reach our true self. For this reason Jean-Paul Sartre speaks of people as divided beings in search of wholeness. He asks, "What separates us?" and answers, "Nothing" — but it is an eternal nothing that will last as long as we have consciousness.

In short, speculation about the self means questioning our identity, wondering who we are as individuals. The Temple at Delphi bears the inscription, "Know Thyself"; and the *Tao Te Ching*, the classic Chinese text, says that "Enlightenment is knowing the self."

Generally we think of ourselves as the conscious source of all our actions, a complex, integrated entity that persists through time. We are the substance behind what we say and do, the things we think, perceive, and imagine, the knower more than the known. Our self is "immediately given" rather than being the conclusion of a syllogism or the object of sense experience. We exist at the center of our personal narrative, the central figure in the stories we tell, the main character in our autobiography.

Some philosophies deny the existence of the self altogether, dismissing selfhood as a grammatical fiction. Sentences need subjects, as when we say "It is four o'clock" or "It is raining." But there is no referent for the "*it*," we don't know *what* exactly is raining, and we can't identify any "I" behind action. That is, some philosophers reject the self as merely a name for activities, claiming there is no mysterious, colorless, noiseless, invisible entity behind the activities. Aristotle, for example, claims our body acts in various ways but is not moved by any internal agent. An axe can be defined in terms of its function to chop, and each human being exists to function rationally. There is no separately existent thing, a gremlin or homunculus, that occupies the body and directs our conduct. Behaviorists today agree, and want psychology defined, not as the study of the "mind" or mental states, which cannot be detected in the lab', but the study of behavior. We will never see a mind transplanted. A stimulus-response model is best, and the strongest stimulus always wins.

Mystical religion agrees that an internal self is a fiction, but its claim is based on different reasons. Mysticism sees no distinction between ourselves and the external world, subject and object. Meditation and even hallucinogenic drugs may help us realize this truth, and to relinquish the illusion of the "I". Just as in the drug experience, the boundaries vanish, and we understand ourselves to exist in everything.

Similarly, Indian religion, and Buddhism in particular, denies the reality of the self — the doctrine of *anatman* or no soul. To believe in a separate individuality is *maya* or illusion since everything is fundamentally One — the people around us, the natural world, and the universe itself. We are an ever-changing state of consciousness, flowing moments, without beginning or form or limits. What is inside and what is outside are the same; we are the rock, the tree, the sky. "*Tat tvam asi*," the Veda says: that art thou. Each person is part of the whole, and so long as we believe in this imaginary self we will suffer from personal desires. Our insatiable hungers will thrust us into life after life, in an endless series of reincarnations. However, if we free ourselves from the myth of self, attaining the awake state of enlightenment, then we will be poised to enter *Nirvana*. Then our sensations will be melted and fused, our bones liquefied, and we will be absorbed into the cosmos. The drop will join the eternal river of Being, the spark with the eternal conflagration, and we will merge with the All.

In the West we do not long for oblivion, even if our pain would cease. We do not want to blend into the void but to live forever with awareness. The thought of "dust unto dust," the body and the person disintegrating in a hollow of earth, is not reassuring. The loss of consciousness does not seem the ideal state. What's more, we do not believe that suffering characterizes life, that "living is loss," or that the self is an illusion. In fact, nothing seems more certain than that we ourselves exist

Nevertheless, feeling assured of our self and proving its reality are two different things; and when we try to analyze its nature, we find it a difficult job. The Scottish philosopher David Hume denies the reality of the self altogether. He declared "Our perceptions do not belong to anything...We are never intimately conscious of anything but a particular perception; man is a bundle or collection of different perceptions which succeed one another with an inconceivable rapidity and are in perpetual flux and movement." The problem with his analysis though, is that something must exist to be aware of those perceptions. If there are only a series of perceptions, what is it that receives those sensations?

One interesting aspect of the debate is whether we can know ourselves better than anyone else can know us, or whether the reverse is true. We sometimes claim privileged access to our inner self, the result of introspection on our personal identity. We have been present throughout our lives, monitoring our internal conversation. On this basis, transgender individuals claim to self-identify as male or female (e.g., Caitlin [Bruce] Jenner), and self-identify as a particular race (e.g., Rachel Dolezal). Other people can make a mistake about who we are but we have private insight into our nature; we can be trusted to know ourselves.

On the other hand, we sometimes feel too close to ourselves to judge our thoughts and behavior; we lack objectivity. We find scapegoats for our mistakes, rationalize our wrongdoings, and generally think more highly of ourselves than is warranted. Bronisław Malinowski, for example, showed that anthropologists can understand a tribe's customs and folkways better than the members of the tribe themselves, and Freud believed that a trained psychoanalyst has greater insight into a client's motivations than the client himself. Why we do things can be hidden from us, repressed beneath the elaborate fortifications of the ego?

Should we then rely on self-knowledge or defer to people close to us, or experts who have greater awareness such as therapists?

A central question in the debate is What exists continuously as our self? What is our ongoing self, the unbroken history that is us through time? What entitles us to use the same name from birth to death? Also, What does the self include, and what lies outside of it? What is us and what is not us? We wonder in particular about the relation between our bodies and ourselves. Is our physical body something essential or extraneous?

Oscar Wilde expressed the strangeness of the relation in terms of the soul:

Soul and body, body and soul — how mysterious they were! There was animalism in the soul, and the body had its moments of spirituality. The senses could refine, and the intellect could degrade. Who could say where the fleshy impulse ceased, or the physical impulse began? How shallow are the arbitrary definitions of ordinary psychologists! And yet how difficult to decide between the claims of the various schools. Was the soul a shadow seated in the house of sin? Or was the body really in the soul, as Giordano Bruno thought? The separation of spirit from matter was a mystery, and the Union of spirit and matter was a mystery also.

## The Self in Time and Space

The problem in defining the self in *time* has vexed thinkers for centuries. That which defines a person should remain constant throughout his existence. If an object kept changing from a tree to a cloud to a frog, we would not know what it is. In a similar way, whether we are referring to mind or body, some element must remain the same from birth to death; otherwise we are not the same person. But what is the common denominator, the golden thread of identity that makes a person the same, continuous self?

A comparison with a sailboat may help clarify the point: If we replace the halyards and tackle on the boat, the sails and boom, the tiller and rudder, the decking, cabin, and so forth, until nothing of the original boat remains, we could not call it the same sailboat. This problem is mentioned in Plutarch as "The Ship of Theseus." Or to use a simpler analogy, if we have an axe and change the head, then the handle, we cannot say it is the self-same axe. And as Thomas Hobbes pointed out, even if the process took place over a period of years, the handle replaced first, then the head some time later, the axe would be similar but not the same; the old axe could be placed on the rack next to the new one, and obviously the two are not one. Applying this principle to people, if someone changes in all respects, he or she could not be called the same person from the beginning to the end.

That seems the case with all human beings; nothing of either a mental or a physical nature remains constant throughout a person's life. Our bodies grow, mature, and decay, changing radically in shape and size. Our skin expands and grows slack; our hair thickens, then becomes sparse and changes color; our muscles gain in strength, then atrophy; our senses become more acute, then degenerate in old age. Even our skin cells are replaced every seven years as well as the RNA in our nerve cells, and although our organs perform the same function throughout our lives, they change in texture and composition. Our DNA stays the same but that does not separate one identical twin from another, much less clones. What's more, our DNA or RNA seem beside the point; they do not make us who we are.

Mutability also characterizes our mind, for every part can change, from thoughts to values to disposition. If we are brutalized, we can go from an optimistic outlook to bitter cynicism during our lifetime. All cynics are, in fact, former idealists. If we suffer from Alzheimer's disease, our memory and rationality can disintegrate into amnesia and senility. In addition, our values can shift, from liberalism in our youth to conservatism as we mature; traveling the road to old age, we turn left, then turns right. Our ideas are certainly different at six years of age and at sixty; our ambition and willpower can change from strong to weak; and our politics or religion can change during our lives. And although everyone's experience is unique, that does not tell us what it is that undergoes those unique experiences. What is the nature of the person who becomes progressively optimistic or cynical, clear thinking or confused, progressive or reactionary, dissatisfied or content?

The Greek philosopher Heraclitus typifies the view that everything is in flux, including ourselves. Mountains are worn down by wind, ice, and water; and rivers change their courses. Even the sun is losing power and in 5 billion years will erupt in an explosion that will encompass the earth. Nations change as do laws, buildings, communications, and so forth. Nothing remains constant; whirl is king, and we seek in vain for permanent things, even searching the heavens. Heraclitus is reputed to have said, "We cannot step twice in the same river," because the second time we step into the river, new water will have flowed down from the source; therefore, it is not the same river. A follower improved on the example, saying that "We cannot step once in the same river," because not only will the river have changed but we will have changed as well.

What, then, remains constant? Growth and decay seem part of the world's dynamism — as well as characterizing ourselves — so we have a difficult time identifying any fixed element that is *us* through time. When we look at our baby photographs we say, "That's me," but only because we have been told so. Without prompting, we would not see anything in the picture that indicates we are the same person today. Similarly, we cannot look down at an infant in the cradle and predict the kind of individual he will become. A person in old age bears little resemblance to the baby he once was.

Perhaps we are different people at different times, and as a corollary, we should not be held responsible for what our previous selves did. Neither should some future self be bound by a promise we make now. If we are not the same people from moment to moment, then there is no responsibility for past behavior, and we cannot make commitments for the person yet to come.

We are, then, like scattered beads rather than beads on a chain, much less the chain itself. In fact, we would be too random to be selves at all. The statute of limitations on crimes recognizes this fact and does not prosecute a person for what, in effect, someone else did. We have to make allowances for youthful aberrations and recognize that a different person exists today than the person who committed the crime.

A further problem has to do with the location of the self in *space*. What should be included as necessary to the self and what should be excluded as extraneous? What is fundamental, "that without which we would not be ourselves," and what lies outside the circle? How far out does our self extend, and how deeply do we have to descend within to find our basic self? What are our limits?

We generally do not identify with our physical property; what we own is not our self. But some things are highly personal, have sentimental value. For example, we might feel our house or land are a part of us, a favorite chair, tools worn from our labor, a musical instrument we play. Or we might have books or paintings that are meaningful to us, or as Thoreau remarked, "clothing that has conformed to our body from a lifetime of use." If these objects were lost in a flood or fire we would feel diminished by that much.

We might also identify with the people we love, so that their joys are our joys, their tragedies registering as our own. Fans identify with athletic teams in this way, taking personally their victories or defeats. Perhaps we are a part of everyone we meet, folding them into ourselves, and parents live on through their children, perpetuating themselves through their genes. Or perhaps we can enlarge the self to embrace the whole of humanity within our consciousness. John Donne expressed this idea best in his *Meditations*:

No man is an island,
Entire of itself,
Every man is a piece of the continent,
A part of the main.
If a clod be washed away by the sea,
Europe is the less.
As well as if a promontory were.
As well as if a manor of thy friend's
Or of thine own were:
Any man's death diminishes me,
Because I am involved in mankind,
And therefore never send to know for whom the bell tolls;
It tolls for thee.

Martin Luther King and Eugene Debbs said it more simply: If any man is in prison, then I am not free, and Christ said, "If ye do it unto the least of these, my brethren, ye do it unto me."

But above all we wonder about our relationship with our own body. Is it something we have or something we are? Do we occupy our body, and does it merely represent us to other people?

The scientific and the common sense view is to think of ourselves as a physical entity, existing in the same tangible form as any other object or animal, its existence verified by sense perception. We recognize ourselves in the mirror just as we identify other people on sight; we can be distinguished from others in a crowd by our appearance. In short, our bodies are our visible selves, and we look out at the world from our eyes.

But perhaps physical appearance does not constitute the self. In fact, the identity of the self may not consist of the body at all. If someone happens to lose a limb in a war, that person's self is not diminished; he remains the same person only without that limb. Similarly, people who have heart or liver transplants, prosthetic parts, or reconstructive surgery do not become someone else. If our hair is cut, we do not leave part of ourselves on the hairdresser's floor any more than breaking a tooth means that part of us has broken off. And if an athlete becomes handicapped as a result of an accident, or a pianist's fingers are gnarled by arthritis, they may act differently afterwards, not because of the physical event but because of the mental changes that result. They may become embittered or introspective or despondent, and this is what would make us say they are not the person they were. If there were not any internal changes, then regardless of their physical disabilities, they would be regarded as the same person.

This is reinforced by the fact that we say people have changed if they lose the ability to think, to imagine, to remember, or to love. A major mental event, such as severe major trauma could mean a loss of identity in a way that a losing limb would not.

Rene Descartes rejects the materialistic view of the self for similar reasons — although he does champion a mind/body dualism. He uses the example of wax to illustrate his point, wax being a common material at the time. At one point the wax may be sweet, hard, white, and cold, but the sweet odor could turn sour, the hardness become soft, the whiteness grayness, and the surface warm. Still, it remains wax, which shows an object is something other than its physical characteristics. The nature of the wax, like the self, is its inner essence, known by the understanding.

We can sympathize with this idea because to think of anyone as a body alone does not capture the person; it seems extraneous and superficial, almost beside the point. If we simply regarded each other as physical beings, then we would become commodities and could be treated as machines, bread-winners, sex objects, an ally or the enemy. Some psychologists say that women identify more with their bodies, while men tend to treat their bodies as a way of carrying their head around — unless they're involved in fitness or sports. But whatever our gender or role in life, we cannot think of ourselves purely in animal terms.

More deeply, the self seems internal, a mental or spiritual entity lying beneath our appearance and behavior. It is the non-material source of our actions, with the body as the mind's agent, the hardware to our software. On this view, the essential self is known through introspection, when we descend within and uncover our essential core. The body serves as a shell, the bus we drive, the machine we program; it is our brute form even though, as Yeats said, we are "chained to a dying animal." From this perspective, the essential person lies within, receiving impressions, storing memories, deliberating, willing, suffering, rejoicing. In short, the self can be identified as the mind, something non-material. In the Michelangelo painting, "The Creation of Adam"; man needed God's touch to animate his body.

However, certain problems also arise with this interpretation of the self. Our body may not lie at our core but it does seem a necessary component of ourselves; the image in the mirror does appear to reflect us at some level, and when we see another person, we seem to be seeing the person himself. Conversely, it is hard to imagine being a whole, unified self without a body. If our mind could be suspended in a vat, connected by tubes and wires to a life-support system, it would be hard to say that we are still there. So if the mind alone is present, that may not be enough to say that the self has continued in existence.

Certain parts of our body seem more intimate to ourselves than others. Our face in particular represents us, especially our eyes ("the windows of the soul"), but also our nose, our mouth, our expression. Dyeing our hair ("a woman's crowning glory") affects us more than cutting our fingernails; plastic surgery is done most often as a face-lift or to change the shape of our nose; and when we use our mouths to kiss, that is something intimate. Millions of dollars are spent annually by women on cosmetics — lipstick, mascara, foundation, eye shadow, and so forth, as well as on perfumes and hairdressers to enhance their appearance. Conversely, a scar on a person's face is more of an injury than one on his back. Clothing is an extension of ourselves, and according to the German poet Rainer Maria Rilke, we become the person suggested by our clothes. If we impersonate a teacher or an athlete or a soldier, we become the role we play, and we find it difficult stop playing the part, to take off the costume. We have all these selves hanging up in the closet, and we decide what image we want to project on a given day.

We assume different characters by the way we look, and our external facade affects how others respond to us. That in turn influences the person we are.

The well known short story "The Metamorphosis" by Franz Kafka explores the issue of mind and body through an elaborate fantasy. The main character, Gregor Samsa, awakens one morning to find that he has been transformed into a beetle. Obviously, Kafka does not mean this literally but symbolically, and the reader is left to interpret its significance. As a parable it can be understood on numerous levels, and the ambiguities are intentional, designed to induce reflection.

In one common interpretation, Gregor had been an insect all his life but now he has the appearance to match his identity. In his job as a salesman he had been a diligent provider, a methodical food gatherer, but he had never grown beyond this function to become a complete person. Perhaps Kafka is saying that it is not enough to look human; we should be human within as well. Gregor had not developed any of the qualities that are distinctive to a person, consequently his metamorphosis into a beetle is perfectly appropriate. Then at least his appearance would not deceive people.

Another interpretation is that Kafka is exploring the nature of the self, the external part and the internal part. In Gregor's thoughts and feelings he remains unchanged; the metamorphosis is entirely to his body. At the same time his transformation into a beetle limits the range of his actions, just as our bodies dictate what we can do. We are all imprisoned within bodies, subject to its demands for food, sex, shelter, and sleep. Perhaps Kafka is suggesting that our physical self cannot be entirely dismissed; to some extent, we are the person we appear to be.

Furthermore, Gregor's transformation could represent the disfigurement of our bodies in old age. In this sense, we all undergo a metamorphosis from birth to death, and in the end we become similar to a beetle-like creature. Our skin grows crusty, our voice becomes shrill, our hearing and eyesight degenerates, and our mouth becomes toothless. We must be careful getting out of bed in the morning because our bodies have grown stiff in the night and our thin arms and legs hardly support us. Our archaic language may be difficult for people to understand, although it makes perfect sense to us; and when we die it may be a relief to everyone because we have become an embarrassment, repulsive, rejected, unwanted.

Feminist theory is especially concerned with the way women's identities are built round their bodies and how their gender has been formed by society. Feminists often claim that men define women as inferior, second-class, or even non-persons, a defective man. As Simone de Beauvoir observed, "He is Subject, he is Absolute — she is the Other." Although our society is less patriarchal than most, women are still subordinated and demeaned by the privileged males who retain the social, economic, and political power. Women do not have equal status as persons, but are treated as commodities — sex objects, housekeepers, nurturers of children. In the workplace the supporting jobs are assigned to women — nurse, secretary, maid, grade school teacher, and in these roles they receive salaries that are one third less than that of men. If a woman takes her husband's name at marriage, then her identity is subsumed under his. And why should it be her father who gives her away.?

As women graduate from college at a higher rate than men, and become executives, professionals, and political office holders, they are being treated more and more as complete people, not as some man's daughter, girlfriend, or wife. Women themselves are beginning to respect their abilities more, and to think of themselves as independent, whole persons.

## The Philosophy of Mind

Just as we talk about the self in ordinary conversation, we also refer to the mind: "It slipped my mind," "She's strong minded," "Make up your mind," "I've changed my mind," "Out of sight, out of mind," "He's not in his right mind," and so forth. But is this just a convention or is there a thing that the word 'mind' stands for, a place where thoughts reside?

Philosophers refer to this issue as the problem of mind, and it has occupied thinkers since we first thought about ourselves. Describing the body is not difficult: we can see it, feel it, even hear it sneeze, cough, and talk and we can smell ourselves when we sweat. We are reminded of our bodies when we are sick or injured, make love, exercise our muscles, eliminate wastes, and so forth. Women are more embodied than men, and especially aware of their physical functions during their menstrual cycles, at childbirth, and when nursing babies. We all have size, weight, shape, color, extension, and motion.

But characterizing the mind requires more subtle thinking. It seems undeniable yet inexplicable, immediately known yet so amorphous that we cannot fully grasp it. The mind appears to have properties of consciousness, intention, desire, will, and emotion, but these elements cannot be detected by litmus paper or a spectrometer. Our skin feels the pin prick, but how is the pain experienced, and how can it be reduced through meditation where we recite a mantra, or by medication that blocks receptors? Christian Science treats pain as unreal, mere appearance. Only good is real and pain is at the imaginary end of the spectrum, just as cold does not exist, but only degrees of heat, and darkness does not exist, but only degrees of light. And how can amputees feel pain in phantom limbs? Furthermore, how do we know that someone else is suffering when emotions are private and might even be unreal? Hypochondriacs report being sick from assorted diseases but their pain is "a delusion of mind" and treated with a placebo; although that delusion can make a person physically sick. In early societies there are reports of people dying of dread if they know black magic is being practiced against him.

Generally the responses to the question of mind assume two forms: a dualistic or a monistic view. Dualism splits the person in two, conceiving of the mind and body as distinct entities, and selfhood might encompass both. Monism, from the Greek *monas*, maintains that the mind and body are one, and that our body houses our mind or that our mind contains our body to create a unified self. Physical states are really mental, and our bodies are projections of our mind.

The dualistic tradition began with Plato, whom we have encountered before in discussing human nature. In the *Phaedo* Plato argues that the "soul" (*nous*) is pre-existent and survives death. Unlike the body, it has no parts that can change, and therefore it is indivisible and cannot disintegrate. The mental and the physical are both modes of reality, but the soul is more real and imprisoned in the body. His view is similar to Shakespeare's phrase, to "shuffle off this mortal coil" at death, or Gerard Manly Hopkins' view of freeing ourselves from this "mean house, bone house." But Plato admits the physical world has at least a shadow reality; representative paintings are a shadow of a shadow.

However, Descartes, whom we also discussed, is usually taken as the principal source of dualism. The immaterial mind and the material body are radically different substances that somehow interact with each other. Basically, we are "a thing that thinks," but we have a physical part that is extended in space and time. To Descartes, the interaction takes place through the "pineal gland," the only part of the brain that is not duplicated.

Descartes did suggest that if he cut off his foot, his mind would not be affected, but if he were decapitated (which is the meaning of capital punishment), it would impact his mind. Some of our physical parts are more personal than others.

Another version of dualism is usually mentioned with a smile. The German philosopher Gottfried Leibniz maintained that both mind and body have "ontological status," that is, they are both real but they never interact. This is because two such radically different entities cannot possibly influence one another; there is the "physical realm of nature and the moral realm of grace." To account for the common notion that we control our body, he posited a "double-clock" theory. The mental and the physical run along parallel tracks in a pre-established harmony that was instituted by God. Leibniz's famous analogy is of two pendulums hanging from a beam, which swing in unison because God set them in perfect, synchronized motion. This means that we do not eat because we are hungry, but eating follows hunger in a corresponding track.

Despite Leibniz, the mind does appear to affect the body. When we're angry our cheeks flush and we feel an adrenalin rush; if we're nervous, our pulse races, our palms sweat; and there is psychosomatic sickness when we experience imaginary illness. There are even hysterical pregnancies. We want to eat that chocolate cake, and when do, we experience a sugar high, and sexual images can lead to physical arousal. Conversely, the body affects the mind. If we run a marathon and our body secretes endorphins, that will relieve stress and induce euphoria; an airline that plays soothing music on take-off, knows it will relax the passengers; and sometimes we do not laugh because we're happy, but are happy to be laughing.

Still, we have the problem of how mind and body can interact when they are such different entities. It is the same question in the philosophy of religion: if God is spirit and outside of time, how can he enter into time as the corporeal Christ, the word made flesh, and affect the physical world? Can there be a man-god?

A further question is "How can we separate body and mind when the one seems to merge with the other?" It is like trying to differentiate between the symptoms and the disease. Is a head cold the sneezing, coughing, fever, and headache, or the viral infection in the upper respiratory tract? Technically, cold remedies only treat the symptoms, but still when we take the medicine we feel the cold has been relieved. The cold is the virus (the way that people are their DNA), but it is also an external characteristics. We aren't sure where one leaves off and the other begins.

Monism takes the opposite view: that mind and body are the same substance. That can mean Physicalism (that all is material), or Idealism (that everything is mind).

Physicalism is the most common form of monism, a scientific view that reduces all supposedly mental events to occurrences in the brain. Love, for example, or anger or spite or depression, correspond to certain brain states. If we cannot now identify the exact place where love comes from, scientists will soon locate it. Phrenology was the first attempt to associate areas of the brain with physical functions, feeling the bumps on the outside of the skull. But today we are able to map cortical areas using neuro-imaging and electrodes. This is especially useful in brain injuries but also in studying memory, learning, ageing, and in carrying out brain operations. If a surgeon, treating a concussion, uses a suction pump to relieve pressure, he can remove years of piano lessons if he gets too close to the brain tissue.

In any case, the most prominent form of physicalism is the school of behaviorism in psychology. Trading on the research of J.B. Watson and B.F. Skinner, behaviorism rejects introspective evidence as well as the "anecdotal" studies of Sigmund Freud. The introspective reports of a person's interior life cannot be taken as accurate; they are incapable of being duplicated and do not allow predictions. In fact, they can be classified as "folk psychology" because there is no proof that our interior life is real at all. Scientific psychology should only focus on descriptions of observable, public behavior, and accounts of the psyche do not qualify. The mind, to use Gilbert Ryle's phrase, is a ghost in the machine.

In the field of social science, behaviorism has declined in importance since the second half of the 20th century, largely displaced by cognitive psychology. According to this theory, mental processes are central to the individual — in language acquisition and comprehension, attention, perception and memory, creativity and problem solving. Experiencing a headache does not seem a type of behavior but it can be studied mentally. This cognitive approach is used in several branches of psychology from educational to abnormal psychology, with excellent results. Aaron Beck, the father of this theory, treats clinical depression not so much through pharmacology as through therapy. The mind is restored to its primary place in psychology.

The physicalist version of monism seems to violate the common feeling that our mind is something other than our body. And from a philosophic standpoint, we cannot explain how mind could emerge from brain — a lump of gray and white matter filled with electrochemical impulses. The quality of our mental experience of happiness or pain seems radically different in quality from firing neurons, in fact quality itself suggests another modality. Perhaps our thinking is too primitive to comprehend how mind can be reduced to body, the way a horse cannot understand quantum physics, or maybe the mind occupies another sphere altogether and our common reaction can be trusted.

In keeping with this view, the Idealist interpretation of monism claims that mind and body are one, and that that one is mind. In philosophic terms, Idealism does not mean striving after perfection, but that the world, including the self, is mental in nature. Our knowledge is restricted to our mind, our mental picture, and we cannot assert the existence of material objects outside of us. Matter is an abstraction. As the scientist James Jeans writes, "The Universe begins to look more like a great thought than a great machine."

Many religious philosophies are Idealistic because they claim an underlying spiritual reality, and that the material world is a thought in the mind of God. "The Word became flesh and dwelt among us," but Christ was never of us. Now we see through a glass darkly but then face to face. Our earthly existence is a testing ground for the life to come, and if we survive the temptations of the body we will live everlastingly with the spirit of God.

It is easier to imagine that the body contains the soul than that the soul contains the body, but at the same time we think of ourselves as spiritual beings, closer to angels than machines. At a funeral this is why we feel the person is gone even though the body remains; the spirit that animated the person is no longer there.

As we have seen, defining the self is challenging for all philosophers, and it persists as a major intellectual issue. It is also a highly personal one. If we can complete the sentence, "I am nothing if I am not...," then we know who we are, what our personal identity consists of. What are the indispensable elements in your nature that make you yourself and no one else? What is it without which you would no longer be you?

The ball is now in your court, and you must play it as you see fit — but always according to what is reasonable.

# Chapter 11. Culture and Conduct: Are Values Relative, and Are We All Selfish?

Today's fashion is to believe that right and wrong are a matter of opinion. Just as in judging art, whatever a person believes to be valuable *is* valuable — to that person. No outside standard exists to evaluate anyone's moral views, so right and wrong, good and bad are relative judgments, correct only to the individual who is judging. Values differ between people and between cultures, reflecting a variety of perspectives and tastes, so we can only resolve disputes though compromise, appeal to the courts, or violence. There is no universal manual of conduct that everyone acknowledges to be correct.

## Cultural Relativism and Subjectivism

Cultural relativism is the name for this position — that values only reflect the standpoint of a particular group of people. On this theory, if I say that stealing is wrong, that merely means my society disapproves of stealing; It does not mean there is anything inherently wrong with stealing. Punishment is meted out only for getting caught, for violating the social rules and the law. Stealing, in fact, is sometimes considered a sign of cleverness, braver than begging. For spies it is required, a job qualification. And if the theft is done at a high level, by powerful people, they can get away scot free and be admired for being smart.

It is the society or dominant group that determines what is acceptable. Feminists will sometimes claim that our laws were enacted by men and show a distinct male bias. Because of this, women have been subordinated to men under the law. Blacks level the same charge against whites — discrimination by the majority. The attitude of white males is evident in laws against blacks in voting, owning property, and integrating schools, businesses, or sports. It is not just that the rules are made *by* white males; they are made *because* they are white males, and blacks are the victims of the dominant culture.

Subjectivism is a subset of relativism for it maintains that values only reflect the feelings or taste of the individual. From this perspective, if I say stealing is wrong, that merely means I dislike stealing and I wish you did too. Sometimes it is called the "boo–hurrah" theory: boo to stealing, hurrah for honesty. In other words, our sentiments and emotions lie behind our values; they are not objective or a function of the society. Different people respond in different ways, and we should not criticize anyone for wrongdoing; our values are a personal choice, and we have a right to our opinion. Different strokes for different folks. It all depends on where you sit, how you look at it.

Numerous examples can be found that seem to support relativism. In ancient, Inuit culture, for instance, the clan would force the very old under the ice in an act of euthanasia, while in Japan the old are honored and cared for, in accordance with their tradition. But both societies are right — to themselves. Among the Inuit, the old must be sacrificed if they cannot keep up with the hunting party; it is a matter of group survival. The Japanese need the old as repositories of the knowledge and skills of the culture; their loss would harm everyone.

In the same way, early man was cannibalistic, maybe by necessity, while modern man regards this as an abomination. Western societies enjoy eating beef while among Hindus in India it is repulsive. Insects are delicacies in some parts of the world, and disgusting food in others. In many developing countries children are forced to work, while in the developed world there are child labor laws. Slavery is customary in some places, outlawed in others. Bikinis are worn on the beach in France, while in Saudi Arabia a woman must be shrouded and can scarcely show her skin. Homosexuality is accepted in some nations and gay marriage is legal, while in others, homosexuality is treated as a capital crime. In still others, the death penalty is prohibited for any crime. In China blowing your nose in public is rude; "What do you do for a living?" is an impolite question in Holland; showing your teeth when you laugh is offensive in Japan; and being late is expected in Argentina and bad manners in Germany.

In the light of these diverse views, the relativist concludes that morality is a matter of geography. Judgments on polygamy, drugs, incest, war, abortion, racism, and so forth, vary enormously across the globe. Therefore, values are determined by the social attitudes of a culture. The joke is that in Italy 60% of men kiss their wives goodbye when they leave their houses; in the United States 60% of men kiss their houses goodbye when they leave their wives. It is a cultural difference.

Relativism probably owes its popularity to our present emphasis on tolerance. Today we value diversity and multiculturalism, respecting the practices of other nations, almost on a par with our own, and we hesitate to believe that America possesses the final truth. There is, of course, the doctrine of exceptionalism, the notion that our country is special and privileged in the world, but overriding that idea is a new openness to other traditions. We used to be a melting pot and now we are a tossed salad, more receptive to different ethnicities, sexual orientations, religious practices, music and literature. Spanish is our nation's second language, and Latino culture suffuses the nation.

Because of this receptivity toward other cultures, we have lost confidence in our singularity and are less righteous. The values of other societies might be equally correct, or rather, there may not be any correct values at all, only choices of various cultures and people. With greater awareness of the multiple ways of being in the world, maybe we have shed our arrogance, or perhaps we have lost our nerve. In any case, the temper of the times favors relativism.

Sociologists and psychologists tend to agree. *Patterns of Culture* by the anthropologist Ruth Benedict is a paradigm of the position of social science: that cultural differences account for the way people think and behave, including their notion of what is right and wrong.

To illustrate her thesis she described the customs and institutions of three radically different cultures: the Zuni Indians of the American Southwest, the Dobuans who live on Dobu Island off eastern New Guinea, and the Kwakiutl Indians of the northwestern region of the United States

The Zuni Indians are deeply religious — a sober, hard-working, peaceful people, deeply concerned with building a harmonious relationship between human beings, nature, and the gods. Their whole purpose is to achieve balance and unity between themselves and their natural environment. The Dobu culture, in contrast, prizes vigilance against evil forces that surround and threaten them. If people maintain an attitude of suspicion and defensiveness, and regard outsiders as enemies, then they are living properly. The Kwakiutl culture differs from that of both the Zuni and the Dobu by being highly competitive; personal success, achievement, status, and prestige are of paramount importance, not just reaching the heights but being able to look down on those beneath you.

Because of the great diversity in standards of conduct between these three cultures, Benedict concludes that there are no absolute moral principles accepted by all people but rather that each culture develops values relative to itself. And what is right in one culture can be foolish or shameful in another. A Dobuan male who acted aggressively would be respected by his culture as a strong man, but Zunis would disapprove of him and Kwakiutls might regard him with disdain. If an individual in the Kwakiutl culture should succeed in making himself important, this would be considered unseemly individualism by Zunis and thought childish by Dobuans. And the Zuni approach to life — the attitude of achieving tranquility, harmony, and peace — would be looked at as soft and puerile by the Dobuan and Kwakiutl.

Furthermore, if we step back and try to judge which society is best, we would only be reflecting our own culture's values. No verdict is impartial; no judgment pure and unbiased. We certainly cannot evaluate our own society because the principles we use for judging would not be objective but those instilled within us by our society itself.

The implication of the variety of ethical ideals seems to be that all values are relative to the culture. No ethical beliefs are universally held, and one value system is as legitimate as another. It is not that a pattern of culture *appears* valuable to each culture; in point of fact it *is* valuable. For the word "valuable" means nothing other than that which is socially accepted.

What's more, value systems change over time as a society adjusts to new conditions, responds to different needs. At one time arranged marriages were the norm, but now we marry for love (unless there's a pre-nuptial agreement); formerly armies raped and pillaged routinely as part of the spoils of war, but that is now condemned; pre-marital sex used to be a social taboo but now it is commonplace; and previously, dominant nations displaced native peoples such as the Aztecs, Aborigines, and Indians but that is no longer acceptable. The conclusion is that if values change, whether with respect to marriage, the conduct of war, sexual mores, the treatment of indigenous peoples, or whatever, then values are not eternal. Bibles, codes, and constitutions should be published in loose-leaf form.

## Objections to the Relativist Position

But before we get too happy about this, let's consider the argument. Can we really say that right and wrong are relative because of change and the diversity of views? Can we legitimately claim that values are invented not discovered? Do societies create moral principles such as thou shalt not kill, steal, or lie rather than recognizing their inherent importance? In making an ethical judgment that exploitation is wrong, that sex requires consent, or that freedom is better than slavery, are we just making an autobiographical comment, saying something about our tastes? If we state there should be equal protection under the law, are we only declaring that equality is right because of our society's preference?

We want to be open-minded and not condemn values because they are different than ours, but perhaps we need to draw the line somewhere. For example, it is not acceptable for women to be beaten or raped, even if it is part of a country's culture. Women deserve as much respect as men, having the same emotional life, thinking minds, and self-determination. Feminist groups criticize Eastern societies on these grounds, for subordinating women, not allowing them education, jobs, or freedom of movement. Similarly, genocide should be condemned wherever it occurs — against the Jews in Nazi Germany, the slaughter of Tutsis by Hutus in Rwanda, the Armenian massacre by the Ottoman government, or the "ethnic cleansing" of Muslims by Serbs in the former Yugoslavia. To try to exterminate an entire people is an atrocity and a war crime. In the same way, stealing property that belongs to someone else is morally wrong, especially if the person earned those goods honestly, through hard work. For a government to willfully take a person's land or livelihood falls into the same category; it is legal stealing. Some philosophers argue that the right of ownership is conferred through labor, and that the thief is appropriating part of a person's life.

How we package our bodies, the areas of skin we cover and reveal, seems trivial (although the burkha, for instance, seems to strongly enforce and symbolize confinement). Similarly, food choices, the age of consent, forms of marriage, manners and etiquette depend upon the society's customs; here, 'right' is simply a term of approval. But other judgments seem more significant and objective. We feel justified in condemning child prostitution, torture of prisoners, the kidnapping of boys as soldiers, clitoral circumcision, imprisonment without trial, human trafficking, forced labor in fields, mines, or sweat shops, and everything that preys on poverty, weakness, gullibility, and ignorance. Taking a human life is generally blameworthy, saving a life, praiseworthy, and there are other principles that have become truisms: we should keep our word, maintain our integrity, not deceive people, be faithful in marriage, be honest in our business dealings, care for our children, be loyal to our friends, be truthful, reliable, fair, trustworthy, kind, hard-working, grateful, compassionate, and so forth. In these cases behavior seems valued because it is right, not right because it is valued. To say otherwise, violates our deepest moral sense.

We want to be open and tolerant, but tolerance has its limits, just as we believe in freedom of religion but would not invite the Devil into an ecumenical conference, no matter how inclusive we want to be. And if we were tolerant toward intolerance, then tolerance would disappear.

The main line of defense for the relativist is to point to the multiplicity of moral systems and the changes through time. Across the world each society maintains that its standards are right and others wrong, therefore values are relative. But take an analogy with science: We do not assume that all theories are equally correct, because a society believes in them — including the stork theory of birth and denying global warming. And the findings of science have changed over the years, but we do not assume that Ptolemy was as right as Copernicus, that the sun used to revolve around the earth but now the earth orbits the sun. Rather, we assume that people's understanding can be clearer or dimmer, that we can be closer to or further away from the truth. We certainly do not say that because scientific theories change over time, that every scientist is only right to himself. Rather, we think there is a reality out there and that we are gradually gaining understanding.

In other words, what a society accepts does not become correct just because a society agrees with it. Instead, we test a society's beliefs against what is actually the case. And this holds true whether we are discussing what we value. The alcoholic may want alcohol, the drug addict may want drugs, but that does not make these things good for them, or for their families. In other words, what a person or a society values may not be valuable. Thinking does not make it so. If people hear voices, that does not always mean that someone is talking to them; they could be psychotic and the voices exist only in their heads.

The English philosopher John Start Mill makes this mistake in trying to justify his Utilitarian theory that happiness is the goal in living. In his view, we should seek the maximum happiness for society as a whole. Mill may be right, but not for the reasons he gives.

Mill argues that whatever is seen is visible, and whatever is heard is audible. In the same way, if something is desired, then it is desirable. Happiness is something we all desire, therefore.... But even though 'seen' implies 'visible,' and 'heard' implies 'audible,' something desired may not be desirable; in fact, it may not be worth desiring. Driving recklessly or under the influence is not a good idea, even if we think so at the time. We might even want to kill a person we hate, but we ought not to act on that impulse because it violates that person's rights.[1]

Another problem with relativism is that it ignores one of the primary rules of logic: it contradicts itself. For if the relativist argues that everything is relative, that must include the statement that everything is relative, in which case the claim is not true in any objective sense but only relatively true; that is, it is true to the relativist or his society. And if the relativist asserts that relativism is an objectively true doctrine, then it can't be true that everything is relative, because that doctrine at least is not. The only

---

[1] Mill does not say the reverse, that if something is visible it is seen. That would not be true because the dark side of the moon was always visible but it was not seen until a space probe flew by. Neither does he say that if something is audible that it is in fact heard; we know today that Big Bang was audible even though no one has ever heard it.

consistent position for the relativist is to say that, for my culture, relativism is correct, and to abandon any claim that relativism is really true.

And under the relativist thesis we could never say that a society is brutal, another more humane. It certainly seems that the Aztecs can be condemned for practicing human sacrifice, the Romans for their gladiatorial contests, the Nazis for their program to exterminate Jews, and ISIS for terrorist attacks that kill innocent civilians. Conversely, we could never praise the age of Pericles in Greece or the European Renaissance. We could never say there had been progress here, regress here, that advances had occurred in medicine, science, technology, politics, economics, psychology, the treatment of the old, the insane, the handicapped. The cynic will say we have acquired greater knowledge over the centuries but not moral enlightenment; we have merely changed and become more subtle in our cruelty. But that viewpoint seems too jaded. Genuine progress seems to have been made across time and between cultures, and that is only possible if people could imagine better possibilities than their own.

Above all, we cannot get our minds round to accepting that all judgments are relative when it comes to basic values. Preserving peace and protecting life seem right in themselves. Wanton killing, child abuse, sadism and rape, slavery, oppression, and so forth, the whole catalog of horrors, seem wrong and not just different. We may want to abolish guilt as a destructive emotion, but we ought to retain feelings of moral shame.

At the political level, the United Nations has issued a Universal Declaration of Human Rights, which captures some of the values prized by civilization. Eleanor Roosevelt chaired the U.N. committee that wrote the declaration, one of the key accomplishments of her political life, but all nations were signatories. The document, in abbreviated form, contains the following passages:

PREAMBLE:

Whereas the recognition of the inherent dignity and of the equal and inalienable rights of all members of the human family is the foundation of freedom, justice, and peace in the world,

Whereas disregard and contempt for human rights have resulted in barbarous acts which have outraged the conscience of mankind...

Whereas it is essential if man is not to be compelled to have recourse, as a last resort, to rebellion against tyranny and oppression, that human rights should be protected by the rule of law,

Now, Therefore THE GENERAL ASSEMBLY proclaims THIS UNIVERSAL DECLARATION OF HUMAN RIGHTS as a common standard of achievement for all peoples and all nations...

Article 1.

All human beings are born free and equal in dignity and rights. They are endowed with reason and conscience and should act toward one another in a spirit of brotherhood.

Article 2.

Everyone is entitled to all the rights and freedoms set forth in this Declaration, without distinctions of any kind, such as race, colour, sex, language, religion, political or other opinion, national or social origin, property, birth, or other status...

Article 3.

Everyone has the right to life, liberty and security of person.

Article 4.

No one shall be held in slavery or servitude; slavery and the slave trade shall be prohibited in all their forms.

Article 5.

No one shall be subjected to torture or to cruel, inhuman or degrading treatment or punishment.

Article 7.

All are equal before the law and are entitled without any discrimination to equal protection of the law.

Article 9.

No one shall be subject to arbitrary arrest, detention or exile.

Article 12.

No one shall be subjected to arbitrary interference with his privacy, family, home or correspondence, nor to attacks upon his honour and reputation.

Article 18.

(1) Everyone has a right to freedom of thought, conscience, and religion; this right includes freedom to change his religion or belief.

Other articles include the right to freedom of movement within and between countries, the right to marry freely and found a family, to own property, the right to education, peaceful assembly, participation in government, the right to work, rest and leisure, an adequate standard of living, and so forth. These principles are not thought to vary by culture, but are intended to apply to all people across the globe.

## Psychological Egoism

Although we may be convinced that we can identify values, that is not the same as saying that we freely act on them; and the doctrine of psychological egoism claims that our basic motivation is never to do what's right but only what's best for ourselves.

This theory has a long pedigree with numerous philosophers supporting it, claiming that we always act in terms of our self-interest. The altruist assumes that sometimes we act for the good of others, but to the psychological egoist, we invariably behave in ways that benefit ourselves — even if we know it is wrong. By definition, people only do what they want to do, and that means they pursue their own welfare.

To the psychological egoist, We often claim to others (or convince ourselves) that we are acting for noble, unselfish reasons, but upon analysis, our motive is always what is to our own advantage. Some psychological egoists state that we *always do* act in accordance with our self-interest, that it is a sound observation about human behavior, while others state we *must* act for our own good and cannot do otherwise; that is the nature of the beast. The latter, of course, is the stronger position, purporting to be an iron law of human nature, and for that reason we will never encounter a case of altruism.

Another important distinction is between self-interest and selfishness, and the psychological egoist only maintains the first. Self-interest refers to actions carried out for our personal benefit, whereas selfishness means benefitting oneself at someone else's expense. For example, it is in our self-interest to obey the law, but in general, other people do not suffer because of it. On the other hand, if a company's success depends on sweat-shops, that is selfish. In any case, the psychological egoist can maintain either or both: that people always do act out of self-interest, and that they are unable to do otherwise.

Most psychological egoists conflate their position with "the pleasure principle," that the cause of all behavior is to obtain pleasure and avoid pain. It may not be immediate enjoyment but it is enjoyment nonetheless. That is, we will sometimes postpone our pleasure in the hope of greater pleasure in the future, just as we will sometimes endure pain now for the pleasure we will receive then. We do not expect a good time when we visit the dentist, but we endure it in order to prevent greater pain if the problem were ignored.

But doesn't the masochist want pain rather than pleasure? The psychological egoist answers that Masochists do not seek pain but experience pain as their mode of pleasure; they find enjoyment in their suffering. (Some cynics treat self-sacrifice as a form of masochism, which takes away all moral merit.)

Whether immediate or deferred, our desire for our own welfare is what motivates us, usually in the form of pleasure-seeking. All philanthropy is disguised Narcissism; we want to deserve to love ourselves. This view probably began with the ancient Greek philosopher Epicurus who saw human behavior, whether in the infant or the adult, as driven by the desire for self-gratification. The baby cries because it wants a full stomach or to avoid being wet or cold, either satisfaction of its needs or the cessation of discomfort. At first the baby will cry as a reaction to distress, then to communicate what it wants, but never out of consideration for the parents. Babies are self-centered and want to feel satisfied and comfortable. To Epicurus, this characterizes all behavior.

Thomas Hobbes, whom we have encountered before, underlined this view:

> ...no man giveth but with the intention of good to himself, because gift is voluntary; and of all voluntary acts, the object is to every man his own good; of which, if men see they will be frustrated, there will be no beginning of benevolence or trust, nor consequently of mutual help.

The 19th-century English philosopher Jeremy Bentham is also a proponent of psychological egoism, as evidenced by this passage *The Principles of Morals and Legislation*:

> Nature has placed mankind under the governance of two sovereign masters, pain and pleasure. It is for these alone to point out what we ought to do as well as to determine what we shall do. On the one hand the standard of right and wrong, on the other the chain of causes and effects are fastened to their throne. They govern us in all we do, in all we say, in all we think...

Bentham is a major spokesman for "the greatest pleasure principle," recommending the pursuit of the greatest amount of happiness for the greatest number of people, but he bases this on hedonistic or psychological egoism. This is problematic, because if people must pursue pleasure, then it becomes meaningless to say that they should. It is as if he were advocating breathing when people have no option, this side of the grave.

The school of behaviorism in psychology also favors the standpoint of egoism, although it is generally opposed to innate tendencies. But in the reward and punishment model of operant conditioning, behavior is manipulated through pleasure and pain.

How does the psychological egoist explain away actions that are, by all appearances, wholly unselfish? Suppose a little girl is drowning, and a stranger swims out to save her. Isn't that prompted by concern for the little girl's safety? Such instances are reported regularly on the news, and they seem show generosity without thought of personal reward.

But the psychological egoist dismisses such cases, saying "The person was not brave or selfless because he received a great deal of publicity on social media. His picture appeared on the news, the girl's parents showed immense gratitude, and he was regarded as a hero by his neighbors. Furthermore, he could not have lived with himself if he hadn't responded to the girl's cry for help. In a number of ways he benefitted from that action."

But what about the man who gives $20 to a beggar, without anyone seeing him do it, and suppose no one ever finds out? Surely that is a purely charitable act. But the psychological egoist is not impressed. The man feels good about himself; his self-esteem is elevated because he is the kind of person who gives $20 to beggars, anonymously. The fact that no one knows about his generosity makes it even more virtuous. Besides, he comes away feeling superior to the beggar; he is able to give hand-outs, the beggar is grateful to get them. Giving is not only more blessed than receiving; it is more satisfying.

But what about the soldier who throws himself on a live grenade to save his friends in the fox hole? How can that be a selfish action? He is dead, after all, and cannot derive any pleasure from the act. The psychological egoist answers that because he died courageously, he left behind a glorious memory. His parents might receive a medal awarded posthumously, which they will display with pride. And the soldier himself would rather lead a short, heroic life than a dreary, unremarkable one, and that is what motivated him to make the sacrifice.

What about the firefighter who rushes through the flames to save the child who is trapped? He became a firefighter precisely for the glory of the job, as well as for the general gratitude of the public who admire firefighters even more than the police. Besides, he is looking for a promotion and a salary increase. The mother who scrubs floors so her son can go to college? She enjoys the admiration of her friends for her devotion, and she looks forward to the pride she will feel when he graduates. Mother Teresa, who lived in abject poverty ministering to the poorest of the poor in Calcutta? She hoped for eternal life in heaven, perhaps sainthood, and she received considerable recognition on earth, including the Nobel Peace Prize.

Everyone gives the impression of being noble and unselfish but, at bottom, people are only out for themselves. To the psychological egoist, altruism is a self-serving myth. Every alleged instance of altruism can be analyzed as having some form of personal reward — pride, control, fame. Social conditioning or habit alone can account for our feelings of sympathy, and out of self-interest we might induce us to avoid guilt. A person might even hope for reciprocal benefits; if I scratch your back, then you will feel obligated when I have an itch. One hand washes the other. It is an enlightened egoism, the appearance of kindness. At bottom, we only give in order to get.

Some even argue that, although we do things for others, we do it because we identify with them, and in that sense we are doing it for ourselves. Our empathy increases when we see ourselves in other people, and so does our generosity. Their interests become our interests, and help for them is help for us. In the experience of being in love, the line between people begins to fade. It has been called "transference," a projection of ourselves onto others. More recently, neuropsychology has uncovered "mirror neurons" — neurons that are activated when we are at one with another person. It is as if we were experiencing what they experience, participating in their lives. The German philosopher Friedrich Nietzsche expressed this view when he wrote, "The suffering of another person is felt as a threat to our own happiness and sense of safety, because it reveals our own vulnerability to misfortune, and thus by relieving it, one could also ameliorate those personal sentiments." Frances Hutcheson believes this is the basis of our love for our children: "Children are not only made of our bodies, but resemble us in body and mind; they are rational agents as we are, and we only love our own likeness in them."

The philosopher David Hume once wrote, "What interest can a fond mother have in view, who loses her health by assiduous attendance on her sick child, and afterwards languishes and dies of grief when freed, by its death, from the slavery of that attendance." Nietzsche's answer is that the child's suffering is the mother's suffering, and if the child is herself, then she is not showing devotion to any other human being.

To add fuel to his fire, the psychological egoist also points out that people quickly realize they are better off being cooperative rather than competitive. That collaboration is still self-serving. If the individual only acts for himself, then the group suffers a loss, which will affect the individual, and if the majority is injured, then so is the person; by definition, most people are part of the majority. We might have to defer our short-term gratification for long-term benefits, which are usually the same as that of the group. A retailer, for example, might make a fortune by selling water at a premium after an earthquake, but if he agrees to keep his prices the same, then he will benefit in the long run from a reputation for fairness and compassion.

This all sounds very convincing, that everyone acts or must act in their self-interest. But is psychological egoism a realistic view of everyone's behavior, or are they jaded and overly cynical? There are counter arguments that have been mounted by those who think that, at least some of the time, we can put others before ourselves. Some even argue that we are capable of sacrificing our lives for another person, for a nation, or an ideal, without any ulterior motive. And as we discussed earlier, there is a growing body of evidence that children are born with empathy — natural, unlearned empathy, and it seems odd to imagine that we know innately that concern for others will benefit ourselves.

## A Critique of Psychological Egoism

Most ethicists dispute the theory of psychological egoism, and they offer a number of reasons for dismissing it. One line of argument distinguishes between doing what we want to do, and doing what is best for ourselves. If we are in control of our actions, of course we do what we want to do, otherwise we wouldn't do it, but what we want to do could be to help other people. In other words, doing what we want to do need not mean doing what's best for ourselves. As the philosopher Bernard Williams remarked, "Desiring the satisfaction of one's desires" is not the same as "desiring one's own satisfaction." By failing to make this distinction, the psychological egoist assumes (erroneously) that we always act out of self-interest.

There is another respect in which we do not act for our own benefit. That is, people sometimes engage in self-destructive behavior. Millions of people still smoke cigarettes, knowing full well it causes lung cancer, heart disease, and stroke, and obesity poses a known health risk but people continue to overeat, contrary to their own welfare. Some women always go out with the wrong man, one who will treat them badly. Maybe they want to be punished for real or imagined wrongdoing, expiation for their sins or guilt; it could also be because of low self-esteem, feeling that they deserve no better. For whatever reason, they engage in actions that cause them harm rather than promoting their well being. Sometimes we do cut off our nose to spite our face.

The psychological egoist might also confused on the meaning of his doctrine. Is he saying that we always do what we *want*, or that we always do what is in our best interests? The two are not always the same. We might want the thrill of speed and travel in our car at 150 mph, but that might not be good for us. Or out of curiosity, we might want to inject ourselves with heroine, but that could cause a lifetime of problems.

Plato makes this distinction in *The Republic*, where Socrates debates Thrasymachus, who behaves "like a wild beast about to spring"; his name, in fact, means 'fierce fighter.' In the discussion on justice, Thrasymachus declares that rulers always function in their own interest, that "justice is the advantage of the stronger." Socrates counters this idea by saying that what the ruler might desire, may not be good for him, and what is to his advantage may be different than what he desires. He might want to steal some gold but that could lead to a bad end of imprisonment.

This goes back to our previous point that what we desire may not be desirable, even for ourselves, and it is unclear whether the psychological egoist claims that we seek what we want, or what is best for us. In his cynicism, he appears to endorse the first, which could be counter-productive.

But the principal mistake charged against the psychological egoist is that he takes the consequences of action for the intention or motive.

In the cases cited, the stranger who rescues the little girl from drowning could feel some satisfaction afterwards at having saved her life, but it is unlikely that he dashed into the water in order to feel that satisfaction. Neither was his motive the publicity he might receive, the gratitude of the child's parents, or the esteem of his neighbors, although he probably enjoyed receiving that recognition. Likewise, the man who gave the beggar $20 was probably pleased with himself and may even have felt superior to the beggar, but his initial impulse was probably to help out someone who was down on his luck. The soldier who falls on a live grenade did leave behind a glorious memory. His parents were probably proud of him because he died a hero, but it's unlikely that such thoughts crossed his mind when he sacrificed his life for his friends.

In the same way, the firefighter was praised, the mother who scrubbed floors was admired, and Mother Teresa might be canonized as a saint, but it is a stretch to say their behavior was prompted by the desire for this recognition. The more plausible conclusion is that these are admirable people who intended to help others, and the gratification they received as a consequence is irrelevant to the altruism that motivated their actions.

The waters become very muddy if there is recourse to "unconscious desires," the deeper self-interest behind our choices that we are unaware of. Such claims are difficult if not impossible to prove. In Freud's "talking cure" he even refers to patients dreaming in ways contrary to his diagnosis for the satisfaction of proving him wrong. That, of course, confirms his original diagnosis. As Shakespeare said, "Methinks the lady doth protest too much."

One question to keep in mind is, "Which side must prove its point?" If the altruist cannot find proof for his position, does that mean psychological egoism wins by default, or must the psychological egoist prove we are always motivated by self-interest. Whichever position is contrary to common sense must be proven.

The ball is now in your court, and you must play it as you see fit — but always according to what is reasonable.

# CHAPTER 12. ENJOYING LIFE OR HELPING OTHER PEOPLE: WHAT IS OUR REASON FOR LIVING?

Aristotle said we are more likely to hit the mark if we know the target. Translated to our reason for being, we are more likely to lead a worthwhile existence if we know what a worthwhile existence is and aim for it. Steering is better than drifting.

Various philosophers have offered suggestions as to what makes life worth living and what a wasted life might be, so we do not have to start from square one. We can consider the various definitions of a good life that have been proposed by various thinkers throughout philosophic history and evaluate their merits. Even if we come up with something original, we will have a background against which to measure it, and we will know the considerations that apply. As repeatedly stated, whatever we finally choose must not only be personally satisfying, but meet the standards of a sound, defensible goal.

## Wanting Enjoyment In Living

Let's begin with hedonism, which is probably the oldest, most common, and natural theory of a good life. Hedonism is the view that pleasure or happiness should be our purpose in life. Quite simply, we ought to enjoy ourselves while we are on earth, not lead a life of austerity, self-sacrifice, or dedication to some other life to come.

Pleasure usually refers to positive, physical sensations, the taste of delicious food, the joy of lovemaking, the warmth of sunshine, and the feel of fresh breezes on our skin. Happiness is more internal, a state of contentment and satisfaction, closer to well being or fulfillment. A relationship might make us happy, or success at our job, being useful and wanted, the rapport that comes from eating with friends. Ecstasy is a form of pleasure when it is sensuous, and as a religious experience, it yields happiness. Looking back at our life, we judge it as filled with pleasure or displeasure, we see it was a happy or an unhappy one, and maybe we cannot make that judgment until the end.

It was the Cyrenaics who originated the hedonist ethic. They were an early peoples living on the coast of Asia Minor in the 4th century BCE, part of the Hellenic world. Aristippus is the name of the principal figures in the movement, Aristippus senior and junior. They taught principally by example and by oral instruction, never writing a word, maybe because writing was not pleasurable to them. We know the Cyrenaics mainly through *The Lives of the Great Philosophers* by Diogenes Laertius, a historian who catalogued the thought of the ancients. Most of what we have learned about the early philosophers came from the filing cabinets Laertius filled. By the 3rd century BCE, the Cyrenaic movement was over, surviving only in a scattered way in later philosophic thought.

To the Cyrenaics, the intrinsic good in life is pleasure, the enjoyable sensations of the body. The *summum bonum*, or highest good, is to indulge ourselves in a vivid and intense array of pleasurable experiences. Sensuality should rule our lives, not the mind and certainly not the soul.

The Cyrenaics were not concerned with the future, with being prudent and premeditated, moderating our desires. It was more important to take advantage of pleasures that are available now, not hope for some long term enjoyment. *Carpe diem*, seize the day; don't count on pleasures that may never come. Posterity can take care of itself, and what might happen someday is only an empty wish, just as the past is like a dream. Only the present is real, and we should fill our moments with sweet sensations, heightened experiences, getting as many beats into the given time as possible.

All pain and sorrow must be avoided, even if they offer the prospect of some future bliss, because that could only be an empty hope. Life is nothing other than the pleasure you get out of it, so do not defer immediate experience for possible enjoyment that may never be realized. Although momentary pleasures are only pleasures of the moment, they are precious, the only treasures we will possess. Intellectuals sometimes feel betrayed at spending their lives with abstractions, which are a semblance of life, but sensualists seldom regret the days they spent in frank enjoyment. The Cyrenaics "burned with a hard, gem-like flame," in Walter Pater's phrase, and their intense pleasures have no equal. Direct sense-experience is unparalleled and constitutes the heart of life. It is what we recall in tranquility and at the time of our death.

Of course, we should have enough presence of mind to not run wild, flouting convention and the law, since that could lead to ostracism; outwardly we should be orthodox. And we should cultivate friends, not out of affection for our fellow man but for the pleasure of their company. Similarly, we should meet the social obligations of citizenship, otherwise society will punish us, and we should have no fear of the gods, not because they are benevolent but because that will make us anxious.

Nevertheless, the pleasures that we seek should be intense and brief: intense because all stimulation should be strong, and brief because there cannot be long, intense pleasures. Also, brevity allows a greater variety of pleasures, whereas a life of extended enjoyments is more limited and less diverse. No distinctions should be made as to the kind of pleasures we enjoy; lovemaking is as good as eating sweets, bathing as pleasurable as watching the Olympics. As long as an experience yields the same enjoyment, it is equally as good.

The Cyrenaics had an "eat, drink, and be merry" attitude toward life, an uninhibited hedonism with little patience for philosophic contemplation. Revelry, voluptuousness, and orgy were emblematic of their approach, self-indulgence of every kind, and drinking wine was the prime symbol; wine was both a pleasure and an outward sign of pleasure. They found enjoyment in excess, celebrated lust, and relished life with few moral scruples, sometimes without any conscience. Pleasures of the flesh were better than inner satisfaction, just as bodily pain was worse than mental anguish, which is why criminals were physically punished. They would agree with Oscar Wilde who said, "The only way to get rid of temptation is to yield to it. Resist it, and your soul grows sick with longing for the thing it has forbidden to itself." To the Cyrenaics, living should be rich and mindless, free and beautiful. If they lived in the present day they would want a life of lovemaking, rock music, fast cars, hard drugs, action films, heavy drinking, vacations in the sun. Their ideal future might be electrodes inserted into the pleasure centers of the brain.

The Persian poet Omar Khayyam expressed the Cyrenaic attitude, although he lived in another place and in a different era. He set temple and tavern in opposition, and has a melancholy outlook which separates him from the traditional hedonist; but as Victor Hugo said, "Melancholy is the happiness of being sad." In *The Rubaiyaat* he wrote,

VI
Come, fill the Cup, and in the fire of Spring
Your Winter-garment of Repentance fling:
The Bird of Time has but a little way
To flutter — and the Bird is on the Wing.

XII

A Book of Verses underneath the Bough,
A Jug of Wine, a Loaf of Bread — and Thou
Beside me singing in the Wilderness —
Oh, Wilderness were Paradise enow!

XXVII

Myself when young did eagerly frequent
Doctor and Saint, and heard great argument;
And this was all the Harvest that I reap'd —
Came out by the same door wherein I went.

LXIII

Oh, threats of Hell and Hopes of Paradise!
One thing at least is certain — This Life Flies;
One thing is certain and the rest is Lies;
The flower that once has blown for ever dies.

XCIX

Ah, Love! could you and I with Him conspire
To grasp this sorry Scheme of Things entire,
Would not we shatter it to bits — and then
Re-mould it nearer to the Heart's Desire!

XXIV

Let's make the most of what we yet may spend
Before we too into the Dust descend
   Dust into Dust, and under Dust to lie
      Sans Wine, sans Song, sans Singer, and —
      sans End.

In brief, the Cyrenaics extolled immediate, brief, and vivid pleasures. However, to many people the philosophy seemed too impulsive and short-sighted. If we decide in haste, we might repent at leisure. There is a story of a boy who was carrying a bag of gold, and because it was heavy, he threw it away. Why endure present pain for some elusive, anticipated pleasures that may never come?

For reasons like this, the Cyrenaics were displaced by the Epicureans who offered a more thoughtful hedonism, not sensuous but cerebral. Epicurus was the founder of the movement, an ancient Greek philosopher whose school was located between Plato's Academy and the Stoa or covered walkway, from which Stoicism got its name. Most of the instruction occurred in a garden — a garden with high, forbidding walls. The students sat at Epicurus' feet or followed him along the garden paths.

The walled garden is an appropriate symbol for the Epicurean philosophy because it was an enclave, or retreat where people could escape from the struggles and vicissitudes of the world and live undisturbed. Walls, of course, are ambiguous: they keep things in and keep things out, and which is their primary function is a matter of emphasis. The walled garden of Epicurus was clearly intended to keep the problems of the world at bay, at a comfortable remove.

There was something of the monk about Epicurus rather than the saint, for he did not dedicate himself to others but led a secluded life in the service of a philosophic ideal. His aim was to move the center of our being from body to mind, from excitement to quiescence, from activity to passivity, and from thrills to lasting contentment. He wanted to live life without pain or anxiety. Epicurus never married or had children, but devoted himself to his school where all were welcome, including women and slaves — provided they swore an oath to his ideals.

For a hedonist, his life was unusually ascetic and regulated, and he encouraged his followers to practice an equally austere and disciplined existence. Sumptuous food, intemperance, and riotous living were all condemned, and a basic diet of bread and water was thought sufficient, with a moderate amount of wine on feast days. A person's residence was to be modest and sparsely furnished, designed to satisfy basic needs, and the daily routine was reduced to essentials. The body too had to be cultivated, not for the refinement of feeling but to maintain the health of the organism; sickness must not disrupt our peace. But we should only exercise enough to keep our body from plaguing us.

In essence the Epicureans maintained that being in a state of tranquility is the ideal in living, specifically *ataraxia*, which means peace in the mind, and *aponia*, which is the absence of pain in the body. Our lives should be filled with modest desires and calm satisfactions, a life conducive to a state of equanimity, not physical enjoyment. The Epicureans wanted pleasantness not excitement, tenderness in place of passion; their goal was harmony, mellowness, and quiescence. This meant mental experience and the "static" enjoyment of not being in need. Happiness is freedom from suffering, a negative state in which we are protected from the pains of life.

To Epicurus, enjoyment is basically the absence of suffering. The good life consists in avoiding pain as far as possible, not seeking pleasures in any active way. If we can maintain ourselves in a neutral state, then we are in a good way.

The Cyrenaics were guilty of overindulgence and over-excitement, which made them oscillate between elation and depression, not mature enough to act sensibly. The Epicureans were more adult, confronting every desire with the question: "What shall I gain by gratifying this desire, and what shall I lose by suppressing it?" Acting spontaneously can be tragic, and moderation is best in all things. Intense pleasures tend to be followed by intense pains; the higher the wave, the deeper the trough. If we drink too much wine, we become drunk; if we lead a promiscuous life, we can contract a social disease; and if we are reckless in the Greek games, we run the risk of injury. To the Epicureans, we should be balanced and stable, not rash and impulsive, and then we will achieve a serene life. Even love ought not to be pursued too passionately; we should love wisely, not too well; and we should avoid prosperity, fine clothes and rich meals. "Luxurious food and drinks, in no way protects you from harm," Epicurus writes. "Wealth beyond what is natural, is no more use than an overflowing container. Real value is not generated by theaters, and baths, perfumes or ointments, but by philosophy."

Today, we think of an Epicurean as enjoying the good things in life, refinement and culture, dining in gourmet restaurants, being connoisseurs of whiskey and wine, but the original doctrine carried an almost opposite meaning. Epicurus urged a basic, simple existence. Enjoyment should be restrained and reasonable, never opulent or excessive. All of our desires should be easily fulfilled, or reduced to a minimum.

Friendship was an important value, not because it is good in itself or for the sake of the friend but for the self-gratification it would bring. We should always dine with others, Epicurus wrote, for "To feed without a friend is the life of a lion and a wolf." Without friends we feel vulnerable; with friends we have security. For this reason we should never betray friendships but cultivate trust, a *philia* or love to the point of being willing to die for a friend. "Of all the things which wisdom provides to make us entirely happy, the greatest is the possession of friendship."

As for the gods, they are immortal and eternal, but we should not ascribe any additional qualities to them. They function simply as ethical ideals, lolling on cushions on Mt. Olympus. Contrary to the orthodoxy of the time, the Epicureans thought the gods do not involve themselves in human affairs; they do not send "great evils to the wicked and great blessings to the righteous." In fact, Epicurus wondered about the goodness of the gods altogether, framing the problem of evil:

> Is God willing to prevent evil, but not able?
> Then he is not omnipotent.
> Is he able, but not willing?
> Then he is malevolent.
> Is he both able and willing?

Then whence cometh evil?
Is he neither able nor willing?
*Then why call him God?*

This is known as the "Epicurean paradox." It does not deny the existence of the gods, but raises questions about their limitations. The immortals exist in a state of benign indifference, models of transcendent peace. No help can be expected from above. A secular individuality is therefore best, tempered with the benefits of friendship. The gods should certainly not be feared because that would disturb our peace of mind, as will concern for the miseries of the world and anguish over death to come.

Some of the best known thoughts of the Epicureans concern their attitude toward death. Our fear of dying is founded on apprehension about the afterlife, but that anxiety should dissolve once we realize that death is the void, not an eternity of consciousness but annihilation. The bits of matter that make up ourselves and the world are "atoms" that collide, swerve, and become entangled. At death, those atoms disperses, so that we are no more. "Death need not concern us," Epicurus wrote, "because as long as we exist, death is not here. And when it does come, we no longer exist."

Of course, this Epicurean belief may not be reassuring. We dread the suffering of dying as much as the fact of death, and rather than fearing the torments of hell, what we dread is the thought of oblivion. "Man is mortal" is merely an abstraction; that we will die is an almost unimaginable, personal truth. And it is hard to dismiss this anxiety just because, as the Epicureans point out, it is wasted emotion, upsetting and unproductive.

Could the ethical ideal be a combination of the Cyrenaic and Epicurean philosophies? Perhaps, but combining them is hard. Could we have brief enjoyment of long duration, or feel an exciting tranquility? Could we alternate, and be Cyrenaic on weekends, Epicurean on weekdays, one way in summer, another in winter, or would that simply be an inconsistent life?

In general, the Epicureans offer a more mature formula for a good life than the Cyrenaics, one of self-possession and a rational tranquility. But it might be too careful, too deliberate and controlled. Are the Epicureans taking life too seriously, thinking it is no laughing matter? The Cyrenaics urge us to live spontaneously even if that means dying young, but at least they relish existence; the absence of stimulation, they say, is the condition of a corpse. They wanted to live before they died. The Epicureans, on the other hand, would rather prevent suffering than obtain pleasure, because pleasure is risky. But that attitude seems middle aged, middle brow, middle class. They shrink from conflict and withdraw from life rather than embracing it, taking the safe, prudent path of pleasantness. Is the purpose of life to avoid discomfort or to live as fully as we can?

So although it seems that Epicurean hedonism is an improvement over the Cyrenaic variety, it may not be all good. In essence, they are retreating from the world, turning inward and choosing a comfortable, guarded existence.

The Cyrenaics by contrast were vital, positive, adventurous, spirited. They wanted to take risks and affirm existence, saying yes rather than no to life. It is a young person's philosophy, stressing the pleasures of the body available now, fleeting but strong, and although that outlook may not be wise in an Epicurean sense, nevertheless it can offer a fuller life than careful, premeditated actions. To be reasonable in all of our decisions does not bring much joy, and the adultness of the Epicureans may be a truth that kills. Reacting with the immediacy of a child has its merits.

Edna St. Vincent Millay put the Cyrenaic's case succinctly:

> My candle burns at both ends
> It will not last the night;
> But ah, my foes, and oh, my friends —
> It gives a lovely light.

Aside from the question of which form of hedonism is superior, both forms can be criticized on moral grounds. That is, from an ethical standpoint, they are individualistic to the point where other people's welfare does not count. However, Some pleasures that entail other people's misery should be avoided. For example, *schadenfreude*, a satisfaction at someone else's misfortune. And we can enjoy ourselves badly as in a sadistic relationship, or finding pleasure in oppression, domination, exploitation, and exclusion.

Another criticism that applies to both the Cyrenaics and Epicureans is called "the hedonistic paradox." This is the irony that hedonism cannot be recommended. For it seems impossible to obtain happiness directly, but only as a by-product of the pursuit of some other goal. If we want people to enjoy life we should not tell them to seek enjoyment. For example, if people at a party are trying to have a good time, it will be a miserable party; by aiming to have fun, they are standing in their own way. It is like trying to fall asleep, which can keep us awake; we only fall asleep when we stop trying. In the same way, if we actively pursue happiness or pleasure we will never attain it; chasing happiness almost guarantees that we will be unhappy.

## Pursuing the Happiness of Mankind

Thus far we have been dealing with theories of hedonism that are self-centered — pleasure for the Cyrenaics, happiness for to the Epicureans, but in both cases, taking the individual as the point of reference. But hedonism can assume a universal form, that is, it can advocate enjoyment for society as a whole. The paradigm is Utilitarianism, the ethical principle that we should strive for "the greatest amount of happiness for the greatest number of people."

The most prominent Utilitarians were two 19th-century Englishmen: Jeremy Bentham, the originator of the movement, and John Stuart Mill, who promoted it most effectively. They both conflated pleasure and happiness into general enjoyment for all.

Bentham was a social reformer who wanted the "Principle of Utility" to be the criterion for individual action and for legislation; in that way there could be an increase in the total amount of happiness for society as a whole. He was also impressed with science that was emerging in his day, especially mathematics. To Bentham's mind, ethics had been much too vague and imprecise in the past but the time was ripe to introduce scientific rigor and exactitude into ethical thinking. So he devised what he called the *hedonic calculus, felicific calculus,* or *calculus of pleasures* — a scheme for scientifically measuring the amount of happiness that any action would yield. He tried to identify all the factors involved in pleasure and pain, and proposed a system for rating actions in terms of each factor. Then by doing the arithmetic, we could see which act had a higher total, that is, which would provide the-greatest-happiness-for-the-greatest-number.

In his hedonic calculus Bentham isolated seven factors or "marks." Intensity is important because we want our pleasures to be as strong as possible. Duration also matters — whether the enjoyment is extended or brief. Certainty or uncertainty is another mark, as is propinquity or re-moteness; the latter refers to whether a pleasure can be enjoyed immediately, which is superior to one we hope to enjoy at some future point.

Another factor, fecundity, refers to the tendency of a pleasure to be "followed by sensations of the *same* kind: That is, pleasures, if it be a pleasure: pains, if it be a pain." Here Bentham is counterbalancing the factor of intensity, for as intensity increases, fecundity decreases; the two vary inversely. Still another element in Bentham's list is purity, which he defined as the chance a pleasure or pain has "of *not* being followed by sensations of the *opposite* kind: that is, pains, if it be a pleasure: pleasures, if it be a pain." The final mark is extent, meaning the number of persons to whom the pleasure or pain extends. A pleasurable action that affects more people is better than one affecting fewer.

Having identified the relevant elements, Bentham used them as factors in his hedonic calculus. The seven marks would be applied to a given action, and the sum of "hedons" would be calculated, perhaps on a scale of, say, +5 to -5. The same process would be carried out with regard to pains. Then the one would be subtracted from the other to determine whether the act was highly pleasurable in general to the majority. If the result proved to be positive, then the act should be carried out, but if a negative result occurred, the act was largely painful and should not be performed.

Bentham's scheme possesses a certain practicality and efficiency, a useful handbook. Also, the attempt to put ethics on a scientific footing is commendable. However, we wonder whether pleasure can be numerically measured. Aristotle said we can only expect as much precision as the subject matter will allow, and enjoyment may not be amenable to mathematics. This becomes clear when we try to assign numbers of hedons to each factor. If an experience promises to last an hour should it be given a 4, 3, or 2 in duration? If an action promises immediate gratification, does that mean it is worth 3 or 5 in propinquity? With regard to a comparison of two actions, the problem is not so much deciding which action has a higher number of hedons but in knowing how much higher. An exact measurement of something as amorphous as pleasure may not be possible; and for the calculus to work, exactness is required. Ethics may not be quantifiable.

We also wonder about the ethical aspect of Bentham's theory. That is, by relying upon the maximization of pleasure as the criterion for conduct, we could endorse an immoral act that yields more pleasure over a moral act that yields less. This seems a serious flaw. An action can be both highly pleasurable and highly immoral. When we feel we should resist temptation, that tension is the reason for our struggle: although the experience will be pleasurable, we struggle with our conscience because we know it is wrong.

Even an action that yields pleasure to a great many people is not necessarily moral. For example, suppose the majority decides to destroy the minority, as in the case of the Holocaust. Even if the pleasure of the oppressors is greater than the pain of the victims, that still would not justify genocide. The implication is that the greatest happiness for the greatest number is not necessarily a moral criterion for actions.

Or suppose a man enters an Emergency Room because of a broken arm. If the doctors have read Bentham, they might decide to kill him and harvest his organs for the good of a number of patients. One patient might need a liver, another a kidney, and still others a pancreas, lungs, or a heart transplant. On Utilitarian grounds, it makes sense to sacrifice one person to save five. Nevertheless, it would be wrong to violate a person's right to life, even if that brings about the greater happiness. This is why most countries require the donor to be legally dead. In other words, a cost-benefit analysis can violate moral principles.

The problem may be illustrated further by the following story written by the Danish writer J. H. Wessel.

> A blacksmith killed a man in a fight and was in jail awaiting execution, but an eloquent spokesman for the citizens reasoned with

the judge: "Your wisdom, we know you are thinking of the welfare of this town, but this welfare depends on getting our blacksmith back. His death won't wake up the dead man, and we'll never find such a good blacksmith ever again."

The judge said, "But a life has been taken and must be paid for by a life..."

"We have in town an old and scrawny baker who'll go to the devil soon, and since we have two bakers, how about taking the older one? Then you still get a life for a life."

"Well," said the judge, "that is not a bad idea; I'll do what I can."

And he leafed through his law books but found nothing that said you can't execute a baker instead of a blacksmith, so he pronounced this sentence:

"We know that blacksmith Jens has no excuse for what he has done, sending Anders Petersen off to eternity, but since we have but one blacksmith in this town I would be crazy if I wanted him dead, but we do have two bakers of bread...so the older one must pay for the murder."

The old baker wept pitifully when they took him away.

In our contemporary society we want to operate with justice and fairness, not just in terms of favorable outcomes, but the Utilitarian could approve of terrorism and torture, slavery and grand larceny if many people were made happy by these actions. The end would justify the means. Utilitarianism, therefore, does not provide a proper standard of conduct.

A final criticism of Bentham's hedonism is that he only takes into account the *amount* of pleasure that an action promises to yield and is unconcerned with the *kind* of pleasure provided. By implication, Bentham would compare activities such as hearing a classical concert and wallowing in mud only with regard to the quantity of pleasure each activity produced; if the latter were more pleasurable, it should be chosen. Bentham even went so far as to state that "quantity of pleasure being equal, pushpin [pick-up-sticks] is as good as poetry." But surely pleasures should be differentiated in terms of higher and lower levels, and not judged solely in terms of amount. Qualitative distinctions between pleasures seem at least as significant as quantitative ones, and might be more important altogether.

Utilitarianism needed to be refined, and a correction was introduced by his compatriot and successor John Stuart Mill. According to Mill, hedonism had to take into account the qualitative aspect of pleasure if it was to become a doctrine dignified enough to be the goal of human life. In his book *Utilitarianism*, Mill wrote, "It is quite compatible with the principle of utility to recognize the fact, that some kinds of pleasure are more desirable and more valuable than others. It would be absurd that while, in estimating all other things, quality is considered as well as quantity, the estimation of pleasures should be supposed to depend on quantity alone." Mill is here acknowledging the need for utilitarianism to be uplifted.

Because of Bentham's failure to consider quality as well as quantity in his assessment of pleasures, and his treatment of animal pleasures as equal to those of human beings, his philosophy was referred to as "pig philosophy" by Thomas Carlyle. The pleasures of a pig and a person were not any different in value if they were the same in degree, and this implies that he would want people to lead the life of a pig, if the pig were happier.

But as Mill noted: "no intelligent being would consent to be a fool; no instructed person would be an ignoramus, no person of feeling and conscience would be selfish and base, even though they should be persuaded that the fool, the dunce, or the rascal is better satisfied with his lot than they are with theirs." Mill went on to say, "It is better to be a human being dissatisfied than a pig satisfied; better to be a Socrates dissatisfied than a fool satisfied." Utilitarianism needed to be elevated by qualitative considerations since the principle of the-greatest-happiness-for-the-greatest-number can produce an animalistic philosophy.

Upon analysis though, certain flaws appear that throw Mill's utilitarianism into question, and perhaps the whole of hedonism. That is, Mill's concern with qualitative experience inadvertently led him to deny the primary importance of pleasure itself. When Mill states that it is better to be a dissatisfied person than a satisfied pig, or a Socrates dissatisfied rather than a fool satisfied, he is saying that a certain quality of life is more valuable than enjoyment. A consistent hedonist would never approve of *dissatisfaction,* unless it led to greater pleasure in the long run, but Mill preferred a higher life to superficial pleasures. In this way, he was subordinating the hedonistic goal of enjoyment for a superior type of existence — that associated with the life of human beings.

The general point is that when Mill, or anyone else, attempts to refine hedonism by introducing qualitative distinctions, he places himself outside of hedonism altogether. That is, the quality that is used to differentiate between higher and lower pleasures becomes the basic goal, displacing pleasure as the criterion for a good life.

To many philosophers, experiencing pleasure does not seem sufficiently noble to qualify as the goal of human existence; it certainly does not raise us above animals. Pleasure or happiness may be a common and natural goal to seek but we might want a life that is finer.

## An Alternative Theory

At the opposite end of the spectrum from hedonism is an ideal proposed by Immanuel Kant, an 18th century, German thinker, celebrated in philosophy but relatively unknown outside the academy. Kant was a disciplined, formal figure, almost a Prussian stereotype, regular in his routine and precise in his writings; "neighbors would set their clocks by his daily walks." He was an uncompromising man with neither an eye for art nor an ear for music, a rigid bachelor who traveled little and lived inside his head. Nevertheless, he produced major philosophic works that have been highly influential in modern philosophy.

Kant's system of thought is usually juxtaposed against hedonism, even in its form of Utilitarianism, because it emphasizes duty and responsibility. Pleasure is the enemy, distracting us from our obligations. Judging from his biography, we might speculate that Kant followed his Lutheran upbringing which stressed strict obedience to principles.

"Nothing in the world ... can possibly be conceived which could be called good without qualification except a good will," Kant wrote at the beginning of his *Foundations of the Metaphysics of Morals*. He is asserting that the basis for evaluating conduct is not the consequences that follow from it but the will that lies behind it, that "good" does not stand for any end of action but only applies to the will of the agent. A person with high intentions, a noble nature, and a good will is praiseworthy regardless of whether his actions have a beneficial outcome, just as a correct decision is not one with a good result but one based on good reasons. Circumstances, chance, historical accidents and so forth may prevent the accomplishment of what a person wills, but that is irrelevant. The significant factor is whether the agent has moral motives, whether his heart is in the right place. If so, then praise is appropriate, and if not, then no praise should be given, regardless of whether the act happens to turn out well. A *mens rea* or evil mind overrides any positive results.

> A good will is good not because of what it performs or effects, not by its aptness for the attainment of some proposed end, but simply by virtue of the volition, that is, it is good in itself...Even if it should happen that, owing to a special disfavor of fortune, or the niggardly provision of a stepmotherly nature, this will should wholly lack power to accomplish its purpose, if with its greatest efforts it should yet achieve nothing, and there should remain only the good will ... then, like a jewel, it would shine by its own light, as a thing which has its whole value in itself.

> For the will to be good, however, Kant stipulated that it must not operate from inclination but out of a recognition of a moral obligation. For example, if we were moved to help a blind person across the street

out of a sudden rush of pity, that would not constitute a moral act, but if we offered our help because we realize our duty to help the blind, then the action takes on a moral character. Principles should guide action, not feelings.

Kant distrusted the emotions, regarding them as fickle and unreliable; we could not count on them for right behavior. The emotions could induce acts of generosity but they could also impel us to cruelty and destruction. Just because we feel certain emotions that is no justification to act on them, and this applies both to positive and negative impulses. On the other hand, if we recognize certain acts as morally binding upon us, then we have a sound basis for action.

Bur how is one to know where one's obligation or duty lies? Kant's answer is that if our act can be subsumed under some general principle of conduct, then we know that we are in the realm of the right. That is, if we can say that an action is an instance of some universal rule of behavior, we can feel confident in acting on it.

For example, suppose we are contemplating the rightness of stealing food rather than working for it. Maybe we are disgruntled about the unequal distribution of wealth and feel that blue collar workers get a small slice of the pie. We might even have Robin Hood tendencies and want to steal from the rich and give to the poor. In order to test the morality of that action, we must ask ourselves whether we would want such conduct to become common practice. Could we in good conscience recommend that everyone steal food instead of working for it? Obviously the action cannot be placed under an all encompassing principle, so it must be wrong.

Kant sometimes describes this standard of morality as respecting "the law" meaning the moral law. By this he meant operating with reference to rules of conduct in contrast to behavior that springs from emotions or is based on consequences; in other words, operating according to a rational, objective ethic.

> Duty is the necessity of an action executed from respect for law... Now as an act from duty wholly excludes the influence of inclination and therewith every object of the will, nothing remains which can determine the will objectively except the law, and nothing subjectively except pure respect for this practical law. This subjective element is the maxim that I ought to follow such a law even if it thwarts all my inclinations.

The most definitive formulation of Kant's views on duty and the core of his moral system are expressed in what he called the *categorical imperative*: We should act in such a way that the maxim (principle) for our actions could become a universal law. That is, in order for an action to qualify as moral we should be able to say that all people at all times and all places should do likewise.

It is a certain sign that we're doing something wrong if we make an exception for ourselves, saying that the action is generally unethical but we can do it anyway. A genuine rule of conduct has no exceptions, especially not personal allowances.

Kant gives various examples of the operation of the categorical imperative. Suppose we are considering borrowing some money, but in order to obtain the loan we must promise to repay it — which we do not intend to do. Should we make an insincere promise to repay a loan in order to obtain the money? What if we need the money for something important: our grandmother needs an operation, or a loan shark is threatening us? To decide this question we must apply the categorical imperative. Could we will that everyone should act accordingly, that whoever wants to borrow money is justified in making a false promise to return it? Obviously not, Kant said, for if everyone did this no one would ever lend money, which means that the conduct cannot be universalized and is not right. If everyone did it, it would become impossible to do.

Another example cited by Kant is truth-telling. We may be tempted at various times to tell a lie, perhaps to extricate ourselves from an embarrassing situation or to spare someone's feelings, but the acid test of the rightness of our behavior is whether it is universalizable. Can we will that everyone should lie? Apart from the undesirability of a world operating this way, Kant maintains that universal lying would be impossible because if everyone said the opposite of what they believed to be true, no one would ever be deceived. Universal lying, then, would be self-defeating, which means that lying is wrong.

Kant formulated the categorical imperative in another way that seems different from the concept of universalizability, although Kant regarded it as essentially the same. It is sometimes designated as the *Practical Imperative*. "Treat humanity," Kant writes, "whether in thine own person or in that of any other, always as an end and never as a means only."

He is here emphasizing respect for persons or, more specifically, rational beings, and stating that people should not be used merely as commodities, instruments, or objects. Notice that Kant says "as a means only," thereby acknowledging the fact that people must use each other as means to some extent, whether as employers, mothers, or doctors. But human relationships ought to be more than that. We should have regard for people as worthy of respect in and of themselves and, insofar as we can, treat them as the ends of action not as a way of achieving some end.

Kant therefore offers us a very pure, high-minded purpose for being: to meet our responsibilities to our fellow man. We should do what's right precisely because it is right, and not live a life of self-indulgence or even try to bring happiness to everyone. We have a duty to follow the moral law, and that should be our reason for being — respecting others and honoring our moral obligations.

But when we begin analyzing the Kantian position one of the problems that strikes us is the difficulty of finding any principle that is universal. This includes the seven classic virtues of prudence, fortitude, temperance, justice, faith, hope, and charity. For instance, the virtue of promise-keeping. It might be generally right to keep our word, but some promises should be broken. A wife has no obligation to stay with a husband who abuses her, even though she promised " 'til death do us part." Similarly, we do not have a duty to finish what we started, to stay the course, if we are heading in the wrong direction; for example, pursuing an unjust war. And we should not honor a promise to deliver a package when we realize it contains explosives and the owner is a terrorist.

In addition, two universalized principles can conflict, contradicting each other. Suppose, for instance, we maintain as part of our absolute principles that human life should be protected and that we should always tell the truth. Then one day a man with a smoking gun in his hand and a wild look in his eye asks us which way his wife went. In these circumstances we can either tell the truth and contribute indirectly to a murder, or protect a life by telling a lie. We cannot both tell the truth and protect life.

Furthermore, some principles might be moral even though they cannot be universalized. For example, self-sacrifice does seem commendable in various circumstances but it cannot be practiced by all people at all times. For if everyone were self-sacrificing, there would be no one left to accept the sacrifice. It would be an "after you Alphonse" dialogue for all eternity.

As numerous critics have pointed out, Kant's general mistake is in not distinguishing between qualifying a rule and making exceptions to it. For example, we might want to qualify promise-keeping by saying that "No one may break a promise unless a person's life would be endangered by keeping it." Lawyers must maintain the attorney-client privilege unless a third party is put at risk by keeping the confidence. Making exceptions, especially for ourselves, is in a different category.

Other questions arise with regard to Kant's formal approach to living. Would we rather live next to someone who follows the principle of neighborly love or one who is generous and kind by disposition?

A major weakness in Kant lies is ignoring the importance of beneficial consequences. In his concern to avoid the vices of this theory he throws out the baby with the bath water. To judge actions only in terms of their nature without regard to their results can make us callous to human suffering. He stated, for instance, that if a man were sentenced to be hanged today, the sentence should be carried out, even if we knew the world would end tomorrow; Justice should be done. But maybe we should cancel the execution if there were no earthly benefit to it. Kant's ethic sometimes seems like a cold-hearted moral machine that does not allow for wrong actions that produce a great deal of good. His stance toward life lacks subtlety, nuance, and grace

In the final analysis, however, Kant's ethical theory is intriguing and persuasive, perhaps because of its purity. Despite the flaws, it seems appropriate to say that an intrinsically right action should always be done. Kant wants us to lead a virtuous life, not a happy one, which seems severe but commendable.

Comparing hedonism and Kantianism is very difficult, the one appealing to our heart, the other to our head. And we can certainly relate to Joseph Butler's statement that "when we sit down in a cool hour we cannot justify any pursuit 'til we are convinced that it will be for our happiness, or at least not contrary to it." More movingly, Homer wrote "Dear to us ever is the banquet and the harp and changes of raiment and the warm bath and love and sleep." By contrast, Kant's theory seems like an icy wind, but he appeals to the honesty, self-discipline, and sacrifice that human life should contain.

In this short analysis of our purpose for living we might have discussed such ideals as self-realization, following nature, the glorification of God, the Stoic value of equanimity, using evolution as our model, being virtuous, and so forth. But that would take us beyond the scope of this book. That terrain must be explored on your own.

But the ball is now in your court, and you must play it as you see fit — but always according to what is reasonable.

# Chapter 13. The Just War: My Country, Right Or Wrong?

The United States has been involved in violence since its founding. In fact, the country was born in armed conflict — a revolution against England, the mother country that we judged to be oppressive toward its offspring. Our history includes over ten wars that have been fought for expansion of our territory, protection of our allies, and defense of our national interests.

Following the Revolutionary War we fought the second War of Independence or the War of 1812; the Mexican–American War in which we acquired Texas; the Civil War (or as the South terms it, the War Between the States) to preserve the union and abolish slavery; and the Spanish–American War in which Spain ceded Cuba, the Philippines, and Puerto Rico. We fought World War I, the Great War against the Central Powers; World War II which resulted in the defeat of the Third Reich and Imperial Japan; the Korean and Viet Nam Wars that were fought against communism, the Gulf War to protect Kuwait from invasion; and the ongoing Iraq and Afghanistan Wars.

We have also been involved in a series of smaller wars such as the Opium War, the Franco–American War, and the 1st and 2nd Barbary Coast Wars, as well as the Indian wars: the Black Hawk War, the Seminole War, the Navajo War, the Sioux War, and the Cheyenne War. The Drug War, in which we have been heavily involved, seems accurately labeled a real war; it has killed 20,000 people thus far, and the global War on Terror has taken the lives of 4 million Muslims. (In this country, jihadi terrorists are said to have killed over 5,500 Americans, including the devastation of 9/11. Most of our wars have been on foreign soil although, as Francis Fenelon remarked, "all wars are civil war because all men are brothers."

Beyond these, it becomes a matter of pedantic distinctions as to what constitutes a war. Do we count the Cold War, the war on poverty, the war between the sexes or the culture wars? All of these are wars in a metaphorical sense only, and indicate a concerted effort to deal with a situation.

America is certainly a beacon of democracy, justice, and freedom to the world, offering opportunity and a high standard of living for its citizens, but our past is filled with violence, both on the battlefield and in the streets. If we look at our internal violence today, the homicide rate is 5 per 100,000 population, compared to 3 for Canada, 2 for France, and 1 for Japan.[1] Organized crime, drug trafficking, gang culture, and firearms play a significant role in these statistics; guns, as we know, are readily available and easy to access. There are 15 youth homicides per day in the U.S., and a disproportionate number of perpetrators and victims are African Americans. In fact, murder is the leading cause of death among blacks ages 15 to 24. Sociologists remind us, of course, that poverty, ignorance, gender, and region are all significant factors along with race. Women are less likely to be victims of violence overall, but they are 6 times more likely to be injured by domestic violence. One startling statistic: the U.S. has 5% of the world's population but 25% of the world's prison population.

But let's not concentrate on crime but war which is technically defined as an intentional, widespread, armed conflict between opposing political entities. According to the distinction by Max Weber, it can involve nations whose peoples share a common language, ethnicity, and culture, or states that have governments and territory, or loosely bonded political groups.

We know that the projection of political power is not reason enough for declaring war. There is a distinction between power and authority, especially moral authority. Suppose a man is spanking a small boy, and when he is asked why he is doing that he replies, "Because I am bigger than he is and I can." That would not be adequate justification; might does not make right. But it might be acceptable if he answers "Because I am his father and he was shoplifting; he needs to learn a lesson." Whether or not we agree with corporal punishment, the man is establishing his right to act as he did.

Since St. Augustine and Hugo Grotius, and the definitive work *On War* by Carl von Clausewitz, the justification for war and the rules for the conduct of war and its aftermath has become a distinct field of study. Academics do not review the historical record to see what has been considered a just war but ask when is war truly just. They analyze the Geneva and Hague conventions for insights into the limits of war, realizing that legality does not determine morality; there can be unjust laws. Nations also have informal agreements as to how battles should be fought that reflect shared values as well as common

---

[1] See the US. Census Bureau statistics and the Uniform Crime Report.

sense. For example, countries hesitate to act in ways that could rebound against them, for example, torturing prisoners or using chemical, biological, or nuclear weapons. Similarly, we do not want an indefinite series of revenge attacks or assassinations which simply encourage retaliation. Pragmatic considerations can support the golden rule.

Some political theorists deny that ethics has any place in war. *Realpolitik* or political realism maintains that violent, mass conflict is a breakdown of civilized institutions, a reversion to barbarism. It has nothing to do with justice. As Francis Smedley famously said, "All's fair in love and war," and only a state's vital interests matter: power, security, and prosperity. Countries may use morality as camouflage, but they always pursue their own advantage in international affairs. What's more, they should do so because that is how the world actually operates. Any other thinking is naive.[1]

But that view may be overly cynical, leaning too heavily on Machiavelli and Hobbes, and there is a growing consensus about the ethics of war. We are now acknowledging that countries hold principles in common, some of which apply to the when and how of war. For instance, it is no longer considered honorable, as it once was, to slaughter the vanquished and take their wives and children as slaves.

This awareness is reflected in the Universal Declaration of Human Rights of the United Nations, and the International Criminal Court that prosecutes political leaders across the globe. Some offenses transcend national boundaries and are considered war crimes and genocide, crimes against humanity. Nazi leaders were tried in The Hague for atrocities following World War II, and the International Criminal Court recently issued summonses and indictments for dozens of officials from Africa to Eastern Europe to the Middle East.[2]

Unfortunately, the United States has a poor record of accepting the protocols of justice imposed by international bodies, partly because it infringes on our national sovereignty. For example, in discussing the issue of torture at Abu Ghraib and Guantanamo Bay, Attorney General Alberto Gonzales described the Geneva Convention as "quaint," and we have rejected the jurisdiction of the International Criminal Court. In 2002 John Bolton, Under Secretary of State, explained that he feared "our country's top political and military leaders" might be prosecuted. He was later appointed Ambassador to the U.N...

---

[1] For advocacy of this position see Morgenthau, Hans. *Politics Among Nations*. NY: McGraw Hill, 1993, and Kissinger, Henry. *Diplomacy*. NY: Simon and Schuster, 1994.

[2] Sikkink, Kathryn. *The Justice Cascade: How Human Rights Prosecutions Are Changing World Politics*. NY: W.W. Norton, 2011.

---

Opposed to making war is pacifism which, in its pure form, believes war is wrong wherever it occurs. There is always a better resolution to conflict than violence. Even if a country is occupied by a foreign power the people can resist in non-violent ways. They can refuse to cooperate, practice civil disobedience, go on strike, defy laws *en masse* and overwhelm the system. Eventually, the conscience of the invaders will force them to withdraw, as the British did in India in the 1940s when confronted by Gandhi's pacifism. Non-violence also worked for Martin Luther King in the 1960s against racism in the South (although both Gandhi and King were assassinated).

This pacifist vision strikes most people as naïve and unrealistic, or they regard it as demanding too much of a sacrifice; sometimes they accuse the pacifist of cowardice. The main charge is that it is Utopian, what John Rawls calls "an unworldly view." Some political groups such as the Nazis are too callous to be moved by non-resistance or the pain of their victims. They will murder those who oppose them, and the pacifist morality will only serve to oppress people. The effectiveness of pacifism always depends upon the humanity of the oppressor.

And by not using physical force, we may be encouraging evil by default. A bully may welcome a refusal to fight and not be taught by it. Besides, aren't pacifists only enjoying the benefits of their nation because others are fighting for them? They are parasites, "free-riders," and their security, freedom, and prosperity are due to the sacrifices of the military. Furthermore, the refusal to fight only rewards aggression and undermines a country's will to win.[1]

It seems that sometimes only armed resistance will work, and war might even be a moral necessity. Reason can dictate violence. Of course, those who fight then resemble the enemy, but that is brief while occupation by another country can last a long time.

Still, there is something honorable and admirable about pacifism. As JFK remarked, "War will exist until that distant day when the conscientious objector enjoys the same reputation and prestige that the warrior does today."

## What Makes the Just War Just?

Generally, the following distinction is made within just war theory: there is the *jus ad bellum*, the justification for going to war, and the *jus in bello*, legitimate conduct in war. Sometimes a third grouping is discussed, the *jus post bellum*, which has to do with a fair peace agreement — imposing

---

[1] For pro-pacifist positions see Teichman, J. *Pacifism and the Just War*. London: Blackwell, 1986, and Holmes, R. *On War and Morality*. Princeton: University Press, 1989. Holmes argues that war is clearly impermissible in a nuclear age.

reasonable conditions on the defeated nation. The first two are the most vital.[1]

The first category, *jus ad bellum*, has as its main principle that there be a *just cause*. That concept can cover a variety of cases, some legitimate, others disguised as legitimate. Self-defense against aggression seems a fair justification, which means primarily the physical violation of a country's territorial boundaries through invasion or occupation. In the U.S. we have a Department of Defense not a Department of War, because we assume that the military is purely protective, guarding our land and our people's way of life. Self-defense also applies to combating a trade embargo that chokes a country's economy, the wrongful imprisonment of its citizens, or an insult to national honor (although the last can be a slippery concept). If a plane is shot down or a ship is sunk, that can also justify a military response, although it might be too slight to provoke a war. The damage that is done must be certain, substantial, and lasting. On the other hand, going to war for territorial expansion would not be a just cause; neither would revenge, power, or hatred.

Today we wonder whether we are justified in violating a nation's sovereignty to track down terrorists, such as the raid in Pakistan to assassinate Osama bin Laden, and whether we should launch drone strikes against suspected terrorists without first determining their guilt in a court of law.

We also debate the propriety of pre-emptive strikes. If we believe an attack is imminent, should we strike first to gain the advantage? Those opposed to pre-emptive strikes argue that it is easily abused and could give *carte blanche* for any war. Hawkish leaders could always offer the excuse that an attack was anticipated. Also, a military buildup by a nation should not be treated as an imminent threat, any more than a man carrying a gun can be assumed to threaten our lives. Punishment should be tied to a crime actually committed. We do not imprison people whose profile shows them to be at high risk to be law-breaks. The pre-emptive invasion of Iraq has raised such questions because it is a departure from containment, which was our previous foreign policy.

War must also be a *last resort*. We must have exhausted all options for resolving the conflict peacefully, particularly diplomatic channels. Negotiations are at a standstill. The good offices of neutral countries have had no effect; neither have efforts by non-government agencies. Observers and peacekeepers have been expelled, and there is no hope of breaking the

---

[1]   See M. Walzer. *Just and Unjust Wars*. NY: Beacon Press, 1977, and Orend, Brian. *The Morality of War*. Peterborough: Broadview Press, 2006.

impasse. If we reach that point where there is no recourse through peaceful means, then and only then should a country resort to war.

In the Iraq War one lingering question was whether all options had been exhausted. The U.N. had observers in Iraq but their efforts had been thwarted, and the situation had persisted for six years. The U.S. therefore mounted a military offensive that was virtually a unilateral invasion. The fact that Saddam Hussein was a tyrant may not have been enough, since that could be a reason to invade of any number of countries.

A just war must also be declared by a *proper authority*. 'Proper,' of course, is the weasel word. An authority is proper when it consists of an established government or political entity that is justly and legally constituted. It cannot be despotic, corrupt, or incompetent but must have earned the allegiance of its people. In a democracy the government rules by the consent of the governed; it has legitimacy only if it protects the people's rights.

A proper authority should also have the power to give orders and enforce obedience. What's more, any war must be publicly declared; secret wars are unjust by definition. It is also assumed that authorities are sanctioned by some legitimate body. Suppose that in a baseball game a runner collides with a catcher at home plate, and a fan in the stands shouts, "Safe!" That decision carries no weight. But if the umpire says "Safe!", that counts because it has a proper authority behind it. In fact, one theory of legalism says that the runner is neither safe nor out until the umpire says so, just as a person is not guilty of a crime until convicted by a jury. (But couldn't a guilty person be acquitted?)

Wars must also be fought for the *right intention*, basically for the cause of justice rather than self-interest. Too often a country will pretend to fight aggression when, in fact, it is pursuing its national interests; rationalizing is always a temptation. But in order to fight a just war, a country must have genuinely good intentions.

Those who take a low, materialistic view of human nature say that wars are always financial in nature, but it seems that wars are fought for a variety of reasons: religious, political, ideological, social, ethical, and so forth. Business interests may always be a factor but they are not necessarily the basic reason why nations go to war. Sometimes, as in the case of World War II, the motives are relatively pure, and it is obvious who is on the side of the angel. At other times the situation is muddier, but economic benefits are not the only reason why wars are fought.

As a practical matter, there must also be a *reasonable chance of success*. That is a factor outside of morality altogether, but, it is argued, there is no point in fighting a hopeless fight. We must weigh the costs and benefits of engagements, and not waste our nation's youth and resources on a useless battle. A war might be overly expensive or too difficult to pursue as well as unwinnable. Our troops may be spread too thin, or have no stomach for a fight as in civil wars when soldiers are asked to kill their neighbors. Overall, if we have no chance of winning, then it makes little sense to declare war.

There is a counter view, of course, that says the impractical can still be justifiable. At various points in history nations have fought and won battles that seemed hopeless. The British resistance to Nazi Germany is a case in point, as Churchill's speech expressed: "We shall defend our island whatever the cost may be, we shall fight on the beaches, we shall fight on the landing grounds, and we shall fight in the fields and in the streets, we shall fight in the hills, we shall never surrender." Expecting to win was unreasonable, but the fight was still worthwhile for the preservation of the nation.

With a strong will a country could prevail, even when the odds are long, so the practical course of action may not always be the right course. And some people believe we should we do what is right even when it does no good.

The last of the criteria for a just war is *proportionality*: the means must be proportional to the desired end. In other words, the destructiveness of the war cannot outweigh the good we are trying to achieve. As the Catholic Church puts it, "the use of arms must not produce evils and disorders graver than the evils to be eliminated." At times we resort to the violence of war, but we want to minimize the destructiveness and maximize the good that is done, making sure the benefits are worth the cost.

Here the question arises as to whether the use of "weapons of mass destruction" is ever justified. Can there be enough good in any outcome to counterbalance the horror of chemical, biological, or nuclear weapons? The death toll in Japan from the atomic bombs that were dropped was 150,000 in Hiroshima and 75,000 in Nagasaki — almost a quarter of a million people, with an additional 25,000 casualties. In the aftermath, countless deaths and illnesses occurred from internal injuries and radiation. There were certainly benefits in the form of saving America lives that would have been lost in an invasion, but were they proportional benefits?

Oddly enough, American politicians were in favor of dropping the atomic bombs while the military thought it unnecessary. An offshore demonstration might have been enough, and we could have paused to allow time for surrender before dropping the second bomb.

In order for there to be a just war, all six criteria must be met, and together they form the sufficient conditions for declaring war.

The second category, *jus in bello*, or how wars should be fought, contains two main criteria: *discrimination and proportionality*.

In conducting wars fairly we are required to *discriminate* between combatants and non-combatants. Only the first are legitimate targets, otherwise we are fighting a war in a morally indefensible way. The enemy should not be attacked indiscriminately for the simple reason that not everyone is guilty. Civilians are innocent and should not be targeted; otherwise we have committed a war crime.

However, the line between civilians and the military can be hard to draw. Combatants do not have to wear uniforms; insurgents will blend into the population but still be proper targets. And spies are part of the war effort, as are those who supply or harbor the enemy, providing food, shelter, or comfort. In addition, civilian officials in charge of the war, those who give orders, and factory workers who furnish armaments, have thereby militarized themselves. The metaphor is that by stepping into the boxing ring, they know they could be hurt. But those who are truly civilians should be protected, and due care must be taken not to harm them. We cannot require absolute protection because that would prohibit war altogether; "collateral damage" is unavoidable, but it should be minimized.

In today's war on terror it can be difficult to distinguish combatants from non-combatants, but that does not justify indiscriminate killing, much less treating all Muslims as jihadi terrorists. In more barbaric wars, whole cities have been razed and crops burned, and in more recent wars, population centers have been bombed. For example, the rocket attacks on London, the fire-bombing of Dresden, and the raids on Berlin and Tokyo. But the rules of war have changed — for the better. It is not that morality depends upon the time and place but that we seem to have a clearer understanding of when killing is permissible. Today we separate civilians from soldiers, and we think it wrong to deliberately attack non-combatants. Military personnel are, in fact, brought up on charges if they intentionally kill civilians, even if commanded to do so. The Uniform Code of Military Justice requires military personnel to refuse to obey illegal orders, because killing should be distinguished from murder.[1]

Some theorists claim that if a people vote for war, or for leaders who promise war, then the entire population is responsible. This was argued in World War II when the German people voted for Hitler in a general election, knowing his program. Were we then justified in bombing German cities?

Collective responsibility is a knotty problem, as is the question of how many generations that lasts. Are present day Germans responsible for what their grandparents did? Must Germany live in the shadow of Auschwitz forever? Sometimes we hold a government accountable but not the people,

---

[1]   Anscombe, Elizabeth. "War and Murder" in *Ethics, Religion, and Politics.* Minnesota: University of Minnesota Press, 1981, and Nagel, T. "War and Massacre". *Philosophy and Public Affairs* !1971-72), 123-145.

separating the two. That occurs when the citizens did not make a free or informed decision. However, when there is a free choice, that may mean everyone is complicit in the war. Does that include infants and children, who can then be killed? More broadly, is there collective responsibility, as illustrated in Christianity where, because of Adam's Fall, all of humankind is born with original sin? Is it collective guilt if citizens identify with the group responsible for wrongdoing? Such questions call for deeper reflection.

In any case, we know there is no discrimination in missile strikes or shelling, much less in using bio-chemical agents or nuclear bombs. Land mines might soon be outlawed because they do not wound only soldiers. We have smart weapons that pinpoint targets but their accuracy is necessarily limited, and collateral damage is all but certain. For a "high value target," civilian casualties are sometimes judged acceptable.

*Proportionality* is the other criteria for the ethical conduct of war. It overlaps with some reasons for going to war, but here the concern is how wars should be fought. This standard requires that the military use only the amount of force that is necessary to achieve their objective. We want to limit the harm in battles, keeping the casualties and physical damage to a minimum, consistent with the goal of the campaign. Again, There should not be more evil in the means used than in the end produced.

We do not need a scorched earth policy, to kill the wounded, or take no prisoners. The enemy does not have to be pursued, because if he is retreating, he is no longer a threat. There is no need for retaliation much less forced labor, rape, looting, torture, or summary executions. The defeated army is still made up of human beings who deserve to be treated with some respect, and the victorious soldiers want to return home with a clear conscience. Aquinas talks about the virtues of mercy and charity that should prevent battles from becoming massacres.

In the recent invasion of Iraq the strategy was "shock and awe," that is, to use overwhelming force to end the war quickly. This is contrary to proportionality. A police officer who shoots a shoplifter can be charged with a crime. He used excessive force, more than the situation required. In recent years, blacks have charged police brutality in situations where they feel an unnecessary amount of force was used. In the case of the military the same principle applies. As we saw in World War I, even if poison gas would end a war sooner, that does not justify the use of poison gas.

The question of bio-chemical and nuclear weapons arises in this context, because using weapons of mass destruction could be an unethical way of conducting war. The fact that something would work does not automatically make it legitimate. As Mark Twain once noted, we could cure all human ills by taking the oxygen out of the air for ten minutes; in the same way, one remedy for migraine headaches is the guillotine. But obviously the cure is worse than the disease. Not only proportionality but discrimination makes nuclear war immoral by its very nature.

In addition to these rules of war, the Geneva Convention prohibits the destruction of medical centers, attacking ambulances or medical personnel, killing soldiers who surrender, and torturing or executing prisoners. Obviously, genocide is immoral as seen in the murder of 6 million Jews, and the Catholic Church has been criticized for remaining silent during the Holocaust.

## Terrorism

Terrorism is a major threat in the world today, universally condemned by the international community. Terrorism by definition is the unlawful use of violence against a civilian population, producing fear and intimidation in the furtherance of political, social, or religious objectives. More briefly, it is the indiscriminate use of violence against non-combatants for an ideological goal. Sometimes a state will sponsor terrorism but, more often, individual groups will instigate the attacks. In either case, the purpose is to draw attention to the terrorists' cause by the destruction of property and the death of innocents. Often high profile targets are chosen that symbolize the perceived oppression, as in 9/11 when the World Trade Center and the Pentagon were attacked.

But don't aerial bombardment, drones, and missiles also threaten civilians? Yes, but there is a critical difference, expressed by "the doctrine of double effect." According to this theory, intending to do harm is worse than foreseeing possible harm as a result of one's actions. Strategic bombing may be necessary, even though we know it could harm civilians, whereas terrorists deliberately target civilians.

One of the invidious effects of terrorism is that it places open democracies in a painful, no-win situation. If democratic governments try to maintain the freedoms of their society, they can be vulnerable; and if they curtail freedoms they undermine their own values. Putting democracies in this dilemma can be part of the terrorist's strategy.

Sometimes terrorists will defend themselves by saying that terrorism is an effective tactic for the weak. All legal alternatives have been tried and failed, so people must fight for their beliefs outside the law. Terrorism is the poor man's atomic bomb. But the answer to this is that we must work peacefully to change policies from within, not attack the system violently from outside. Another defense is to claim, "One man's terrorist is another man's freedom fighter." However, violent attacks on ordinary people in cities reduces the validity of the cause.

Kofi Annan, the Secretary General of the United Nations, summed up the grounds for the worldwide condemnation of Muslim extremists: "Any deliberate attack on innocent civilians, regardless of one's cause, is unacceptable and fits into the definition of terrorism."

## Humane Intervention

Another justification for war — one that has become prominent in recent years — is humane intervention. The notion has gained currency that nations have a "responsibility to protect" that goes beyond their own citizens. If the people of other nations are threatened by unwarranted aggression, then the world community has an obligation to respond. Although the sovereignty of countries should be respected, that right is forfeited if unjustified violence is perpetrated against the citizenry. The family of nations then has a responsibility to intervene, in accordance with the rules of war.[1]

This principle is parallel to criminal law where citizens are expected to protect other people from attack. Self-defense is a just excuse recognized by law, and so is the protection of a victim of assault. In fact, citizens have a responsibility to help in these situations, and to do nothing is reprehensible. Failing to act when you should can be wrong in itself, a sin of omission rather than commission, especially when the risk to yourself is minimal. If you could save a child from drowning by wading into three feet of water, it would be criminal not to do so. In the same way, if one country invades another for sheer imperialist motives, or a government brutally suppresses its people, then the world community has a duty to help.

On this basis the international community has responded with military force in Libya, Ivory Coast, Uganda, and Syria, in Serbia/Kosovo, Yugoslavia, and Kuwait (the Gulf War). In some cases it was the U.N. or N.A.T.O, that acted, and in others the U.S., virtually alone. Multinational interventions are better, but a unilateral response might be justified, particularly if the violence rises to the level of atrocity.

International law prohibits the violation of a state's sovereignty, but if human rights are violated, that could override the law. Maybe it is right to intervene in the affairs of another state if there are mass murders, genocide, or even widespread displacement. The U.N. and individual countries have tried to help the refugees that recently streamed into Europe from Africa. *The Responsibility to Protect* is the title of a 2001 report of the International

---

[1] A useful distinction can be drawn between humane intervention and the responsibility to protect. See Pattison, James. *Humanitarian Intervention and the Responsibility to Protect.* Oxford: Oxford University Press, 2010. Of course, intervention could mean a prolonged involvement, especially if there is regime change and nation building, and that must be recognized as part of the commitment.

Commission on Intervention and State Sovereignty, and that view is increasingly persuasive.

But there are serious criticisms as well. For example, Ann Orford argues that humanitarian intervention is a modern expression of Western colonialism. Northern countries are violating the borders of Southern ones, developed nations interfering in the internal affairs of developing ones, which is a familiar pattern. It reflects arrogance, a moral superiority, as well as being a way of controlling weaker nations.[1]

Henry Kissinger is also critical of the doctrine, charging that we have been hypocritical in applying that moral principle, only intervening in those cases that favor our national interests. We conducted a military campaign against Serbia while ignoring the genocide in Rwanda, among many examples.[2]

Noam Chomsky takes the same line, arguing that the responsibility to protect is a pretext for pursuing geopolitical goals. Selective enforcement is always morally suspicious, suggesting self-interest under the guise of altruism. To Chomsky, decisions on whom to protect and whom to abandon only reflect political advantage.[3]

Then there are the patriotic views of people like John Bolton (mentioned previously) of the American Enterprise Institute who dismiss any ethical considerations in matters of foreign policy. "All will agree," Bolton writes, "that there are situations of human suffering that deserve attention, but most are far removed from even the most expansive definition of national interests." The humanitarian crises in Sudan, Somalia, and Burma were certainly humanitarian tragedies but the U.S. had no vital interest there. In addition, there were no threats to the stability of the region, so there was no reason to become involved.

Skeptics have a point. There is the possibility of colonialism or cynical selectivity, and realism in politics excludes intervention for ethical reasons. Nevertheless, humanity might have an obligation to help those whose humanity is brutally violated.

To give a graphic illustration, in 1994 the Hutu dominated government in Rwanda attacked the rival Tutsis in a terrible ethnic massacre. The Hutu military were instructed to hunt down and kill "every journalist, every lawyer, every professor, every teacher, every civil servant, every priest, every doctor, every clerk." Over a three month period nearly 1 million Tutsis were shot,

---

[1] Orford, Ann. *Reading Humanitarian Intervention.* Cambridge: Cambridge University Press, 2003.
[2] Welsh, Jennifer. *Humanitarian Intervention and International Relations.* NY: Oxford University Press, 2004.
[3] Kissinger, Henry. *Does America Need a New Foreign Policy?* NY: Simon and Schuster, 2001. Chomsky, Noam. *A New Generation Draws the Line.* NY: Verso, 2001.

burned, starved, tortured, stabbed, or hacked to death.[1] In doing nothing, the global community seems blameworthy.

Perhaps a reasonable position would be for the countries of the world to acknowledge their moral responsibility to stop atrocities, and to accept that a just war includes humane intervention. However, before we violate a state's autonomy we must be sure our actions are necessary, that they are not a disguise for benefitting our country, and that there is broad agreement among nations. The fact that the world community supports the action provides some assurance that it is just.

The question of the just war, of when countries should fight and how, is extremely complex, but we should always look for moral justification before risking the death of vast numbers of people, especially the youth of a nation.

The ball is now in your court, and you must play it as you see fit — but always according to what is reasonable.

---

[1]  Malvern, Linda. *A People Betrayed*. London: Zed Books, 2000.

# Chapter 14. The Question of Immortality: Can We Live Forever?

All people, if they could, would continue to exist eternally. We sometimes qualify that yearning by saying, "Assuming we are healthy," or "Only if our family and friends did too." We might not want to live on if we were alone or sick, or a relic from another age, but all things being equal, we never want our lives to come to an end.

Birth is not a good omen for eternal life since it implies death by a type of symmetry. The oblivion before birth is matched by the oblivion after death. This is why Hindus think that all life continues endlessly: "That which is, will always be, that which is not, will never be." (They add that it's better never to have been [sic].) But in the West, despite our belief that life begins at a fixed point in time (perhaps at "ensoulment"), we long for immortality in the next world or even in this. We admit intellectually that man is mortal but our own extinction is almost inconceivable. We live as though we will live forever. Other people die, but we are not the type, although teenagers sometimes think they will die young because they can't imagine themselves old.

"We can no more look at death directly than at the sun" Rochefoucauld says, so we deny this truth, insulating ourselves from its reality. Or we use euphemisms as a defense mechanism: death in a hospital is "negative patient care outcome"; to NASA, the spacecraft with astronauts suffered a sequence failure; to the Salvation Army, the person was elected to glory. We speak of people's demise, breathing their last, meeting their maker, departing this life, passing, suffering cardiac arrest; there was a fatality, a loss of life, a lethal shooting. We give up the ghost, escape the prison house of the body, have a terminal episode, leave this vale of tears, or pass away. Dying is too real almost impolite. Like children, we fear going into the dark, and the religious dread the Day of Judgment. Above all, we cannot bear the thought of our conscious life ending.

The right to life is our highest value, murder our most heinous crime, and even though we say that heaven is better than earth, we want to postpone that bliss as long as possible. If we were offered a choice, we would prefer dying next year rather than this year. A woman who had "lost" her husband was asked where she thought he had gone. She replied, "I suppose he is enjoying everlasting glory, but let's not talk about unpleasant things."

Many faiths prohibit suicide, but there would not be a flood of suicides if the prohibition were lifted. Even those who believe in heaven would rather not die to get there. Except for Irish wakes, funerals are somber affairs, and though the cleric reassures the assembly that the dead person is in a better place, free from earthly troubles and living with God, somehow that is cold comfort. Death is far too real for us to imagine that one spiritual state is exchanged for another, too stark to conceive of shades of being. Overwhelmed by loss, we struggle with doubts, and resist crossing over to the land of the dead.

Determining when death occurs is problematic, because we're not sure how to define life. Viruses, for example, are not classified as living organisms because they cannot reproduce independently. We used to declare someone dead when they stopped breathing or when their heart stopped beating, but today we can use life-support equipment — pacemakers, heart–lung machines, artificial hearts, and artificial lungs. Therefore we now say that death occurs when the electrical activity of the brain ceases, or more simply, when someone will no longer regain awareness. If the electroencephalograph (EEG) registers a flat line for twenty-four hours, then the person is no longer alive. Legal death is brain death. We cannot use this definition for all life forms, since trees and insects are not conscious to begin with, and animal death simply leaves a creature insensate. But for human beings, life comes to a close with the permanent cessation of consciousness; then our lives are truly over.

Various ideas have been proposed as to the nature of life-after-death, as well as arguments attempting to prove the reality of an afterlife. Some are natural, others supernatural; some trade on biology while most take a spiritual form.

## Science As Salvation

From a scientific viewpoint, our lives need not end. No one dies of old age (senescence) but from some illness or injury, and in principle, all diseases are curable, all wounds can be treated and healed. It is simply a matter of finding the remedy, and medicine is continually making progress. One day, even the brain might be replaced by a sophisticated computer.

Why, then, do we have this mindset that life must end? People have always died but that does not mean they always must. Our bodies do break down, but we also have a history of cures for illnesses, a continual stream of medical breakthroughs.. And thanks to vaccinations, we have eliminated over a dozen diseases in this country, including diphtheria, polio, and smallpox. With stem cells, therapeutic cloning, transplanted organs, and artificial parts, it seems that the body can always be made whole again.

Must man have a fixed life span, perhaps "three score years and ten" (Psalms, 90:10) or "a hundred and twenty years" (Gen 6:3)? We often assume that death is inevitable, one of the few constants. However, nothing in nature must be as it is. In logic, if all fish have gills, and tuna are fish, then necessarily tuna have gills. But in the physical world, we cannot even be sure the sun will appear tomorrow. Nature does not contain any certainties, including man's mortality.

When we think of abolishing death today, we turn to science as our savior, just as we consider a good heart one filled with platelets and plasma, one that pumps blood at 60 to 100 beats per minute, not one filled with love. To have a good heart we should watch our diet and exercise regularly. Since the biological sciences have dramatically increased our life span, why not expand it indefinitely? If we could switch off the mechanisms of aging and death, and remedy all defects, then life would never have to come to an end. Of course, there would still be the threat of accidents, violent attacks, starvation, war, and suicide, but we could repair injuries as well as controlling the effects of sickness, disease, and physical degeneration. "Telomeres" at the tips of chromosomes, are our death clock. They exercise power over the ageing process, and research is now underway to adjust this mechanism. The goal is immortality.

In this connection, cryobiology has attracted a lot of attention — the science that investigates the effects of low temperatures on cells, tissues, and entire organisms. Thanks to cryobiology, we now preserve body parts for transplant, destroy tumors through cryosurgery, freeze-dry foods, and have cryo-banks with frozen sperm, eggs, and embryos. The specimens can be preserved almost indefinitely, frozen in liquid nitrogen the way we do with blood and breast milk. Infertile couples or singles who want to be parents routinely scan a book of embryos for the most desirable genes — the right gender, race, IQ, eye color, shade of hair, health, height, weight, and so forth. In storage centers and clinics, people select their ideal child, a process of "designer genes."

The companies that provide the service argue that choosing is certainly better than leaving matters to chance. Wouldn't everyone rather have an intelligent, attractive, healthy child than the opposite? People can even look for a face-match among the photographs of donors, or find a beautiful couple who are likely to reproduce beautiful children.

(Some organisms are immortal in their natural state. For example, one species of jellyfish (turnitopsis nutricula) replenishes its cells continually, alternating between old and young forms, and water bears (tardigradis) appear to continue indefinitely. Hydra do not undergo aging, and bacteria are immortal as a colony. Perhaps we could incorporate their strategies and attain an equivalent, immortal state.)

Frozen embryos are the present application of the sub-field of cryonics, the preservation of humans and mammals in hypothermic conditions. The intent is to revive them in the future, which gives people hope that, if they contract some fatal disease, they could be frozen then unfrozen when a cure is discovered. In this way death will be cheated. Some sci-fi scenarios have old people "body hop" into children, but with cryobiology you keep your own body. Just before death you could be put in a giant freezer, or launched into space (which has temperatures approaching absolute zero), then retrieved like satellites.

The main problem is reanimation, but some organisms can survive sub-freezing temperatures, be thawed and survive. A freezable frog can live for 6 weeks at temperatures of up to $-6°$. Some insects can survive at $79°$ below zero. Polar fish produce their own antifreeze proteins, and maintain themselves at $1°$ below their freezing point. Some tree branches can live at $30°$ to $40°$ below zero, undergoing a "vitrification" process, that is, turning into glass. Nematoid worms have been frozen and were reported in suspended animation for 4 years. Some mammals such as bats and the Alaskan squirrel are able to "supercool" their bodies below $32°$ and then restore their vital functions. There is similar evidence regarding turtles, clams, and oysters in northern climates.

For some years science has duplicated the feats of nature, for we can now freeze heart valves, blood vessels, and knee components for transplant. The heart and kidneys have been frozen for a short period of time, as have dog intestines, spleen, and lungs. Why not the whole, human organisms, which could then be restored to animate life?

However, in terms of the present state of our technology, that seems highly unlikely. Some companies offer this promise but there is little evidence that it can be done. According to cryobiologists, the process of freezing generally destroys tissues and causes disintegration, so restoring a large mammal to life may be impossible. People who have been found unconscious in icy water have been revived, but there seems to be a time limit. Certainly the freezing and thawing of the dead does not seem feasible, and for the present at least, brain death appears irreversible.

Another scientific approach to immortality is cloning — therapeutic cloning where damaged body parts are replaced or body functioning enhanced, and reproductive cloning where a new organism is grown from a cell.

In biology both are referred to as Somatic Cell Nuclear Transfer, and involve removing the nucleus of an egg and substituting the nucleus of the donor cell to be cloned. Embryonic stem cells are best, but every cell has the potential to develop into any body part or into an embryo. If the clone is intended for medical purposes, it is bathed in chemicals and stimulated with electricity for growth. If a reproduced organism is intended, then a surrogate mother is used for gestation. The cloned organism is genetically identical to the original, and in that sense, life is perpetuated; an exact biological copy lives on.

This asexual reproduction does occur naturally, in everything from fire ants to bananas to hammerhead sharks, so perhaps artificial cloning is feasible for humans. We could use cloning to supply organs for transplant without fear of rejected tissue since the genetic material is the same. We could reproduce livestock at a faster rate, feeding malnourished people across the globe, duplicate prize racehorses or bulls, save some of the 389 endangered species, and perhaps reconstitute extinct species; in fact, experiments are now taking place to re-create the woolly mammoth. If a child's kitten dies, leaving the child inconsolable, we can grow another one that looks and acts the same. This holds true if the child misses grandma... Thus far, we have cloned 18 species including mice, tadpoles, monkeys, and pigs, as well as cats, dogs, mules, and horses. Dolly the sheep was the first cloned animal, named for Dolly Parton because the cells were drawn from the mammary gland.

Human cloning is the most interesting and controversial area of cloning research: to enable us to duplicate ourselves so that we are projected into the future. It is especially useful for infertile couples who want to have children, for same-sex couples, and those who are afraid of passing on a defective gene. But any number of people may prefer non-sexual reproduction. In fact, it might violate our reproductive freedom for the government to dictate how children should be made. Even though we tell our kids to be themselves, we want them to resemble us, and in cloning we get a mirror image. Many people resist adoption because they want to reproduce their own genetic material, but in cloning our offspring is physically identical to us.

Opponents of cloning have presented various criticisms: we should not play God, cloned children will be ostracized, using embryonic stem cells means killing children, it is Narcissistic, the technology is unsafe, cloned humans will be used for spare parts, life expectancy of clones is less, and so forth. The U.S. has banned human cloning, mainly because of the health risks, but the government does allow meat from cloned sheep, cattle, and pigs to be on supermarket shelves — and without labeling it as cloned.

But does cloning people deliver immortality? No, because only the body is copied, and that is not the whole person. As previously discussed, we are a mix of heredity and environment, our genetic inheritance, social background, and experiences, plus the free decisions that we make. Cloned children will duplicate our physical identity but they will not be us. They will not even be the same person biologically, any more than identical twins are one individual.

Akin to therapeutic cloning is the creation of cyborgs. Here an artificial part is inserted into the body to maintain a continuous self in being. As in repairing a car, a new unit is installed, whether a carburetor or a heart, and the organic machine is able to function once again, sometimes better than before. The cyborg is part natural and part synthetic. Bones are combined with steel, flesh and blood with wires and circuits so that the person is partially transformed into a machine.

We already combine mechanical parts with our physical bodies, in fact, modern man is a cyborg. We now have hearing aids, teeth implants and contact lenses, plastic joints in our fingers, elbows, and knees, breast augmentation, collagen lips, and artificial arms, legs, and feet. Cyborgs can sometimes function better than natural bodies, as in the case of runners with curve-shaped, prosthetic feet that may provide the advantage of a spring.

Could we live forever, replacing broken bones, organs, and tissue with synthetic ones? Perhaps, but the question is how much of our bodies can be replaced with artificial parts before we are no longer the same person? When will it be a simulation of a human being, a reproduction of us?

If a miniaturized, supercomputer replaces our brain, would our humanness then disappear? Once we became virtual robots we would not be able to feel love, grief, regret, fear, or shame. We might live on, but "I" could become "it," and we might no longer be ourselves.

## A Spiritual Eternity

Most versions of immortality assume a spiritual form, and this is particularly true in Islam and Christianity, two world religions competing in the world today.

Islam is best understood in terms of The Five Pillars of Faith, all of which must be followed to win paradise. First is the *Shahada* or declaration of faith: "There is no god but God (and) Muhammad is the messenger of God." It is easy to remember and almost impossible to forget. Second is the *Salat*, the obligation to recite five prayers each day: before sunrise, at midday, after the sun has reached its highest point, an evening prayer and a night prayer. The worshiper must first wash as an act of purification, face in the direction of Mecca, and bow, stand, prostrate himself, and sit in a special posture.

*Zakat*, the third pillar, is charity, which is an obligation of all Muslims, but in accordance with their means. All things belong to Allah and alms-giving is holy, a duty to ease the hardship of others. Fourth, there must be ritual fasting during the month of *Ramadan*, mainly to express gratitude for the bounty of the earth. The faithful must abstain from eating or drinking from dawn to dusk. The final pillar is the *Hajj* or pilgrimage to the holy city of Mecca, which is obligatory once in a person's lifetime. The pilgrims dress in Ihram clothing consisting of two white sheets, and walk around the sacred *Kaaba* seven times, touching the Black Stone in the building.

The Quran contains very striking descriptions of the afterlife, the paradise for the faithful and the hell that awaits the sinner. *Jannah* or heaven is a place of blessings and delights, eternal pleasures, far removed from toil and sickness, sorrow and regret. The soul will exist in pure joy, receiving "all it could desire, all that the eyes could delight in." The faithful "will be adorned therein with bracelets of gold, and they will wear green garments of fine silk and brocade. They will recline therein on raised thrones" near flowing streams of water and purest milk; they will "eat and drink at ease," food that is succulent and wines that do not bring intoxication. The bricks will be silver, the mortar a fragrant musk, and the soil, saffron. It is a sensuous dwelling where men are given 72 *Houri* or virgins, and they can have intercourse whenever they wish. Women's satisfactions are unclear, but they will remain attractive forever. They will have modest eyes resembling pearls, full breasts, be white-skinned and eternally young; their youthful bloom will never fade. No person really know paradise; it is hidden from them as a reward for the faithful, but the joys are unimaginable.

*Johannam* or Hell is also vividly rendered, a place for unbelievers, hypocrites, and apostates, "the companions of the left hand."Here the unrighteous are punished by demons, scorpions, and snakes. Unearthly, roasting heat tortures them, "flames that crackle and roar," "fierce boiling waters," "scorching wind and black smoke," "roaring and boiling as if it would burst with rage." The wretched inhabitants have their skin scalded, then exchanged for new ones so they can be tortured afresh. They wear pitch for clothing, their faces are burned black, and iron hooks drag them back if they try to escape. The dimensions of this realm are unfathomable. "If a stone as big as seven pregnant camels was thrown from the edge of hell, it would fly straight through it for seventy years, and yet it would not reach the bottom." No one consigned to *Johannam* can ever leave, and the torment will never end.

Critics point out that this erotic heaven and demonic hell bears signs of the human imagination more than an insightful account of eternity. A desert people are likely to conceive of hell as extreme heat, "scorching fire and scalding water," and heaven would be a place of coolness, luscious drinks, fresh fruits, and sensuous delights. There are spiritual elements but they are overshadowed by physical pleasure and pain, especially by the descriptions of torture.

Christianity, the main religion of our country, certainly has eternal life as part of its creed. The criteria for immortality varies by denomination, but most specify faith in God the Father, in his son Jesus as the Christ, and acceptance of the Holy Ghost; there must be belief in the resurrection and the life to come, and we must practice the sacraments such as baptism, communion, and marriage. We should also lead a life of faith, prayer, compassion, and ritualistic observance. Some denominations stress works, others devotion, and some rely principally on the grace of God.

The Apostles' Creed is representative since it is the confession of faith used in the liturgy of the Roman Catholic Church, Lutheranism, and Anglicanism, as well as by Presbyterians, Methodists, and Congregationalists:

> I believe in God, the Father almighty,
>   creator of heaven and earth.
> I believe in Jesus Christ, God's only Son, our Lord,
>   who was conceived by the Holy Spirit,
>   born of the Virgin Mary,
>   suffered under Pontius Pilate,
>   was crucified, died, and was buried;
>   he descended into hell.
>   On the third day he rose again;
>   he ascended into heaven,
>   he is seated on the right hand of the Father,
>   and he will come to judge the living and the dead.
> I believe in the Holy Spirit,
>   the holy catholic Church,
>   the communion of saints,
>   the forgiveness of sins,
>   the resurrection of the body,
>   and the life everlasting.
> Amen.

This is the orthodoxy, and it includes death, resurrection, and ascent into heaven. It is open to all the faithful. The resurrection is specifically mentioned in the letters of St. Paul:

> Behold, I shew you a mystery; We shall not sleep, but we shall all be
> changed, in a moment, in the twinkling of an eye, at the last trump: for the
> trumpet shall sound, and the dead shall be raised incorruptible, and we shall
> be changed.
> O death, where is thy sting? O grave, where is thy victory?

At the Second Coming of Christ, every person will be judged "according to his deeds," and all those born again will live eternally in Christ's reflection, while sinners will be deprived of his glory forever. In Catholic teachings, there is also a realm called Purgatory where souls in an incomplete state of grace are purified before going to heaven. Limbo is where un-baptized infants reside, but it was abolished in 2007.

St. Thomas Aquinas, the chief theologian of the Catholic Church, maintained that the soul continues to exist after the disintegration of the body, until the two are reunited in a general resurrection. The soul has an "inclination" for the body, and when the two are joined again there will be "complete and full activity." But the soul is not dependent on the body and does not perish with it.

One specific argument used by Aquinas is that only corporeal things can be "corrupted," and since the soul is immaterial it is immune from decay. "God made man's soul of such a powerful nature, that from its fullness of beatitude, there redounds to the body a fullness of health, with the vigor of incorruption."

Life after death is thought to consist of either paradise or perdition. Heaven is described as a spiritual realm where those who believe in Christ will have fellowship with God:

> He will wipe every tear from their eyes. There will be no more death or
> mourning or crying or pain...There will be no more night...for the Lord God
> will give them light.

But unlike Islam, the Christian heaven is not sensuous; there is no suggestion of fine clothing or wine, and even the vestiges of hunger and thirst are absent. It is described as a spiritual place of eternal worship, praise, and adoration, and a fulfilling relationship with God. There is peace, blessings, honor, and glory, and the saved will contemplate the face of the Lord for all eternity.

Hell is described almost as graphically as in Islam, especially in Matthew. In most Christian versions hell contains intense heat, sulfur, and serpents, demons with pitchforks; it is a cavern filled with fire yet strangely dark. The biblical passages read: "I am tormented by flame" (Luke 16:24); "And the smoke of their torment ascendeth up forever and ever: and they have no rest day or night" (Rev. 14:11); "But the fearful and unbelieving...shall have their part in the lake that burneth with fire and brimstone" (Rev. 21:18); "And [God] shall cast them into a furnace of fire" (Matthew 13:42). There are torments of the body and of the soul, burning floors, outer darkness, bondage, thirst, worms, and beatings. A more liberal interpretation sees hell as a never-ending consciousness of one's sinfulness and, above all, eternal separation from God.

But according to most interpretations, life after death includes the body undergoing the physical torments of hell, and the purified soul which is the person's essence living in eternal bliss.

However, as stated at the beginning of this book, we aren't sure how to test certain claims, and this includes the existence of a soul. Litmus strips will not do; neither will microscopes or sociological surveys. And in the absence of proof, how do we know the soul is real and that gremlins, gnomes, sprites, trolls, and leprechauns are not, much less vampires and zombies? Perhaps it is imaginary like zero time or infinite temperature. And if we have a soul, does it survive the death of the body? Maybe the brain is real while mind or spirit is not, and the brain cannot persist when the body decays. If an electromagnetic field carries our consciousness, does that still exist without physical generation?

More important, the notion of hell-fire and brimstone, and devils torturing our body for all eternity, seems inconsistent with a loving God. As in the Muslim faith, there is no reprieve, no parole; the judgment is final and irreversible, which is at odds with forgiveness.

This is what troubled Dostoevsky as described in *The Brothers Karamazov*. In the novel, Ivan Karamazov presents accounts of children who are made to suffer by terrible people — one child locked in an outhouse overnight during a cold Russian winter, praying to dear, kind God for help, another torn to pieces by dogs before his mother's eyes. Dostoevsky asks what should be done to the perpetrators of such horrors. If they are given absolution as an all-forgiving God should do, then the universe has no justice, and if they are punished in hell, then there is no harmony or all-encompassing love. God must be both forgiving and just, but the two are incompatible. Therefore God is an impossibility, and Ivan, for one, will not worship him. He writes,

> Listen! If all must suffer to pay for the eternal harmony, what have children to do with it, tell me please? It's beyond all comprehension that they should suffer, and why they should pay for the harmony... I understand, of course, what an upheaval of the universe it will be, when everything in heaven and earth blends in one hymn of praise and everything that lives and has lived cries aloud: 'Thou art just, O Lord, for Thy ways are revealed.' When the mother embraces the fiend who threw her child to the dogs, and all three cry aloud with tears, 'Thou art just, O Lord!', but I don't want to cry aloud then.

While there is still time, I hasten to protect myself and so I renounce the higher harmony altogether. It's not worth the tears of that one tortured child who beats itself on the breast with its little fist and prays in its stinking outhouse, with its unexpiated tears to 'Dear, kind God'! It's not worth it, because those tears are unatoned for. They must be atoned for, or there can be no harmony. But how? How are you going to atone for them? Is it possible? By their being avenged? But what do I care for avenging them? What do I care for a hell for oppressors? What good can hell do, since those children have already been tortured? And what becomes of harmony if there is hell?

This problem calls into question the Christian image of life beyond the grave, not whether there should be a heaven but how to reconcile the existence of hell with God's absolute love and forgiveness.

A more humanistic idea is an immortality of influence. Instead of describing life-after-death in supernatural terms, some philosophers stress the effect that our lives have on others. Parents, for example, want to set a fine example and raise their families properly, influencing their children positively and perhaps succeeding generations. Teachers reassure themselves by thinking that one never knows where one's influence will end. Oftentimes, famous people will pay tribute to the teachers who first inspired them. Artists feel the same way. They intend to move those who view their paintings, hear their music, or read their poetry; otherwise they would create their work in the morning and burn it at night. Artists want to communicate their world view, hoping it will resonate with others, maybe even change their perspective. Art is meant to have an impact. The comparison usually made is to a stone thrown into a pond; the ripples spread outwards, never ending, although they may no longer be seen.

The "butterfly effect" in chaos theory also expresses this idea — the view that the flutter of a butterfly's wing in China can ultimately cause a hurricane in the Caribbean. Everything is connected through the web of space and time. This includes our effect on the lives of others.

Such reflections do provide consolation, but for most people their influence will not extend very far; and being remembered is a poor substitute for remembering ourselves. We want to remain who we are, and to retain our consciousness for all time.

### Would Life Have Meaning If It Ended At Death?

To some people's minds, life would be meaningless if we were snuffed out in the end. But why would more time give us a purpose? If we are put on earth for a reason, that would be unaffected by it ending, and if we create our own meaning, that would remain even if our life ended. Additional time does not confer significance to earlier time, and the fact that life ends does not render it pointless.

Perhaps our lives do not have any meaning, and the answer to the question "What is it all about?" is "Nothing at all." There may not be any reason for our individual lives or for life in general. Perhaps we invest life with meaning rather than discovering it in the stars. For example, we might want to realize our potentialities and interests, to serve something greater than ourselves, to leave the world a better place, to maximize enjoyment in living, to challenge oppression and liberate humanity, to create art, music, or literature, to help children to flourish, to protect the environment for future generations, to ensure just government, fair laws, and so forth. There are many ways to create meaning in life.

Death has been called the cure for life, but living is not a disease any more than it is a cross or a testing ground for the life to come, and we can find satisfactions in the time that we have. We share love with our family, friends, and fellow human beings, the fulfillment of work, the pleasure of leisure, the elemental connection with nature, the richness of learning and reflecting, the realization of our talents, the rewards of giving to others, and the sheer exhilaration of being alive on the planet. The philosopher William James remarked that whether life is worthwhile depends upon the liver, and that is largely true. As self-aware creatures we have enormous control over how we live and what we live for.

"I finally figured out the meaning of life," Dean Bokharis writes. "There's no such thing. And that's beautiful, because that means WE get to choose it ourselves...You are indeed the author of your destiny." Even if life has a period rather than a comma, it can still be meaningful.

Perhaps we cannot help wanting eternal life, aware that at some point we are no more, but this world might be enough. Maybe there is nothing more but we are something now, and we can spend our time as richly as possible. Our lives can still make sense and matter, even if we only have existence without any cosmic significance.

The ball is now in your court, and you must play it as you see fit — but always according to what is reasonable.

# AFTERWORD

After this immense mental journey, you might be sick of philosophic reasoning and vow never to become involved with philosophy again. But I'm afraid it's too late; you are already ruined. Even the decision not to philosophize is a philosophic decision, so your choice is either to think rationally or haphazardly. Obviously, we should choose to use logical reasoning, arriving at ideas that are informed by what the major philosophers have said. In short, we should develop a reasoned, knowledgeable perspective on life.

In studying philosophy, at least we are "released from the tyranny of petty things." The unexamined life is not worth living, Socrates said, and even though the examination may cast a shadow, we have greater self-respect at facing things as they are. Action is better than reaction, and a thoughtful existence seems consistent with human dignity.

## Note On the Author

In addition to the present work, Burton Porter is the author of twelve books in print form: *The Great Perhaps: God As A Question* (Rowman and Littlefield), *What the Tortoise Taught Us* (Rowman and Littlefield), *The Head and the Heart* (Humanities Books), *Philosophy Through Fiction and Film* (Prentice Hall), *The Voice of Reason* (Oxford University Press), *The Good Life* (Rowman and Littlefield, 5/ed), *Religion and Reason* (St. Martin's Press), *Philosophy Through Film* (Sloan Publications), *Personal Philosophy* (Harcourt Brace), *Reasons for Living* (Macmillan Publishing), *Philosophy, A Literary and Conceptual Approach* (Harcourt Brace), and *Deity and Morality* (Allen and Unwin, and Routledge).

He has also published five titles as eBooks: *The Moebius Strip, Lab Rats, Forbidden Knowledge, The Gadfly,* and *Black Swans and White Tigers,* plus numerous book reviews and papers.

Dr. Porter received his Bachelor's degree from the University of Maryland, and his Ph.D. from St. Andrews University, Scotland, which includes graduate study at Oxford University, England. He has been on the faculty of various institutions such as Russell Sage College, the University of Maryland (Europe), and Drexel University, and he has served as a Department Chair and Dean of Arts and Sciences. He taught at Mount Holyoke College as Visiting Professor of Philosophy, and he is presently on the faculty at Western New England University in Springfield, Massachusetts. Dr. Porter received the award of Outstanding Educator of America, and the Faculty Research Award from his institution.

He lives in Amherst, MA, with his wife Barbara, and indulges his interest in literature, music, and tennis. He has two children, Mark and Ana, and a stepdaughter, Sarah.

Printed in the United States
By Bookmasters